THE REAL ESTATE EDUCATION COMPANY

REAL ESTATE EXAM MANUAL

Fifth Edition

ESPECIALLY DESIGNED FOR

ETS

REAL ESTATE EXAMS

EXAM STRATEGIES

MATHEMATICS REVIEW

SAMPLE EXAMINATIONS

STUDY OUTLINES

DOUGLAS C. SMITH ■ JOHN T. GIBBONS

REAL ESTATE EDUCATION COMPANY
a division of Longman Financial Services Institute, Inc.

While a great deal of care has been taken to provide accurate and current information, the ideas, suggestions, general principles and conclusions presented in this book are subject to local, state and federal laws and regulations, court cases and any revisions of same. The reader is thus urged to consult legal counsel regarding any points of law—this publication should not be used as a substitute for competent legal advice.

© 1980, 1981, 1984, 1988, 1990 by Longman Group USA Inc.
Published by Real Estate Education Company/Chicago,
a division of Longman Financial Services Institute, Inc.

All rights reserved. The text of this publication, or any part thereof, may not be reproduced in any manner whatsoever without permission in writing from the publisher. Printed in the United States of America.

90 91 92   10 9 8 7 6 5 4 3 2 1

Library of Congress Cataloging-in-Publication Data

Smith, Douglas C., 1942-
    Real estate exam manual : especially designed for ETS real estate exams : exam strategies, mathematic review, sample examinations, study outlines / Douglas C. Smith, John T. Gibbons — 5th ed.
        p.   cm.
    ISBN 0-88462-894-9
    1. Real estate business—Examinations, questions, etc. 2. Real property—Examinations, questions, etc.   I. Gibbons, John T.
II. Real Estate Education Company.   III. Title.
HD1375.S42   1990   89-70249
333.33'076—dc20   CIP

Sponsoring editor: Margaret M. Maloney
Project editor: Ronald J. Liszkowski
Cover design: Renee Klyczek

Contents

Preface		v
Acknowledgments		vii
Introduction		ix
Chapter 1:	**Use of the Manual**	1
Chapter 2:	**Examination Strategies**	7
Chapter 3:	**A Strategy for Studying**	11
Chapter 4:	**Real Property and Laws Relating to Ownership**	17
	Review Checklist	17
	Outline of Concepts To Understand	18
	Diagnostic Test	25
Chapter 5:	**Valuation of Real Property**	31
	Review Checklist	31
	Outline of Concepts To Understand	32
	Diagnostic Test	34
Chapter 6:	**Financing of Real Estate**	37
	Review Checklist	37
	Outline of Concepts To Understand	38
	Diagnostic Test	43
Chapter 7:	**Transfer of Property Ownership**	47
	Review Checklist	47
	Outline of Concepts To Understand	48
	Diagnostic Test	51
Chapter 8:	**Real Estate Brokerage**	55
	Review Checklist	55
	Outline of Concepts To Understand	56
	Diagnostic Test	63

CONTENTS

Chapter 9:	**Specialty Areas**	**71**
	Review Checklist	71
	Outline of Concepts To Understand	72
	Diagnostic Test	74
Chapter 10:	**Real Estate Mathematics Review**	**77**
	Types of Math Questions	82
	Mathematics Review Test	83
Chapter 11:	**Sample Examinations**	**87**
	Sample Examination I	88
	Sample Examination II	102
	Sample Examination III	118
	Test Question Cross-Reference List	134
Chapter 12:	**Broker Examination**	**137**
	Broker Sample Examination	138
	Settlement Statement Worksheet	154
Glossary		**167**
About the Authors		**191**

Preface

The real estate industry has undergone significant changes in recent years with the development of brokerage franchises and relocation and national referral service systems. Consumer demand remains high because housing satisfies economic, social and psychological needs. As the industry becomes more complex, the public demands more informative and professional assistance in its real estate dealings. These additional demands necessitate increased standards for the real estate profession.

The growing emphasis on real estate education and professionalism is also seen in recent changes in state licensing examinations and educational requirements. States that formerly issued real estate licenses with no or minimal testing are now requiring prelicense and postlicense education. The trend toward annual or biennial education requirements for license renewal is another indication of increased concern with maintaining standards of knowledge. The testing process itself is undergoing revision. Many states that once developed and administered their own licensing examinations have contracted the testing procedure to professional testing companies. Because professional testing companies, such as the American College Testing (ACT), American Guidance Service (AGS) and the Educational Testing Service (ETS), test an individual's knowledge and skills of real estate principles and general practice in a thorough, reliable way, these services have also contributed to the development of the industry's professionalism.

We are pleased to present this study guide to the serious student. With it the student can prepare properly to complete a comprehensive examination of general real estate practices successfully, and embark on a challenging and rewarding career.

Acknowledgments

The authors wish to thank all of those who participated in the preparation of this text. First and foremost, thanks to Denise Trame of Edina, MN, and Arletta Smith, wife of the author, for their valuable support and encouragement in the development of the manuscript.

The authors would like to acknowledge the following reviewers of this fifth edition for their helpful suggestions: John C. Becker, Vice-President, Schlicher-Kratz Institute of Real Estate, Landsdale, PA; Robert L. Borkowicz, Chairman, Real Estate Department, Wright College, Chicago, IL; Terrence M. Zajac, DREI, Scottsdale, AZ.

Thanks must also go to the staff of Real Estate Education Company for their fine efforts in the development and production of this book.

Introduction

This syllabus provides a concise and thorough summary of the information that you need to study to pass the uniform portion of your state's real estate license examination. Because it organizes this material to coincide with the structure of the ETS exam, administered by the Educational Testing Service of Princeton, New Jersey, it maximizes your familiarity with the form and content of the exam. In addition, the text assists you to develop strategies for taking the examination and, through the use of several practice exams, the skills to complete it successfully.

The specific goals of this manual are to help you

- coordinate your study with the format and subject areas of the examination
- identify strengths and pinpoint weaknesses in your real estate knowledge
- develop a clear understanding of key concepts
- organize the facts that will be needed for recall, comprehension and application in the exam
- develop an awareness of the relationships between real estate principles and practices
- review fundamental real estate vocabulary
- develop a logical response technique for answering test questions
- build a positive mental attitude toward the examination

The uniqueness of the syllabus lies in its outline format. Long recognized by educators as an excellent study tool, this format allows you to concentrate on key concepts and to discern relationships among them. Thus, the most effective use of this manual is as a supplement to both classroom discussion and independent study of real estate theory and practice texts.

1
Use of the Manual

The aim of this manual is to prepare you to pass the real estate licensing examination compiled by the Educational Testing Service of Princeton, New Jersey. The guide addresses two primary aspects of test-taking: (1) the structure and format of the exam, and (2) the content of the exam. The organization of the guide follows these basic concerns. In addition to suggesting the most efficient use of this manual, Chapter 1 provides specific information about the ETS organization, testing procedures and the test itself. Chapter 2, Examination Strategies, suggests a strategy for optimizing test scores. Foremost emphasis in this guide, however, is on the content of the exam. Chapter 3, A Strategy for Studying, contains a five-part review section. Chapter 11, Sample Examinations, provides a valuable opportunity to measure all your test-taking abilities. Chapter 12, Broker Examination, contains an exam section and a settlement statement problem.

EXAMINATION INFORMATION AND BACKGROUND

ETS's Real Estate Licensing Examination is prepared by a committee of test development specialists, outstanding educators in real estate and representatives from half the licensing jurisdictions in the United States. This committee has devised both the state and uniform portions of both the broker and salesperson licensing exams. The most important step in building the ETS examination is preparing the blueprint for the exam. The committee members define in detail the test outline: what subject matter should be covered, how many questions should be devoted to each topic, what abilities should be tested and how difficult or easy the questions should be. Using the completed test specifications as a guide, ETS's item writers in the field submit a first draft of questions. These are reviewed and revised by other panels of experts for legal and factual accuracy. Their revision is then pretested on a representative group, and the scores are analyzed carefully to determine if the scores reflect the test specifications. Based on these findings, ETS assembles the final version of the test, which is again reviewed before its release for jurisdictional use. Even after a test is administered, it undergoes periodic reevaluation and updating.

Alternate forms of the salesperson and broker examinations are also compiled. To protect exam security, the questions and their presentation in each section differ from one alternate test to another. The system is fair to all examinees, because both examinations cover the same content and are equally difficult.

REAL ESTATE EXAM MANUAL

The broker and salesperson exams each contain 110 to 120 multiple-choice questions depending on the jurisdiction; the student may take up to 4-1/2 hours to complete each test. Each exam has two parts: the first is an 80-question test that measures your understanding of real estate practices and principles that are common to all the participating jurisdictions. The salesperson and broker discussions provide a breakdown of the five divisions of the uniform test and their relative importance in the exam. The second part of each exam (30 to 40 questions) is the state test; both the broker and salesperson state exams cover the same material. It deals particularly with real estate regulations and practices and state statutes that are unique to each jurisdiction. Questions in this exam may cover such topics as condominiums, subdivisions and administrative hearing procedures. More information on the content of this part of the exam can be obtained from your real estate commission.

All the questions on both the broker and salesperson examinations are multiple-choice, with four alternatives. Objective or multiple-choice questions are advantageous because they can test accurately several different levels of an applicant's knowledge in a limited amount of time, and can be scored quickly and inexpensively.

Each correct answer counts as one point; no credit is given for wrong answers, but neither are they penalized. This means, then, it will only benefit you to answer all the questions on the exam as best you can. The answer sheet should be free of all marks except filled-in ovals and identifying information; more than one answer to a question counts as a wrong answer. The example below illustrates the correct way to fill in an answer:

- How many alternatives does an ETS exam question have?

    (A) three   Sample Answer Spaces
    (B) four
    (C) five   A B C D
    (D) six

Some states use the Keyway® system, an electronic test-taking, scoring and reporting examination method. Students tested at these sites receive a test booklet and an electronic answer pad and complete a practice routine that allows them to become familiar with the system's basic operations before proceeding to the examination. Upon completing their exam, the students "lock-in" their answers in a two-step procedure and return the test booklet and answer pad to an ETS administrator who immediately scores the examination and gives the student a printout of test results. For information on states that have Keyway® testing sites, telephone ETS offices at (215) 750-8315.

You must pass both the uniform test and the state test. The required percentage of correct answers varies from one licensing commission to another; this information is available from your local jurisdiction. The ETS policy is to notify successful examinees simply that they passed. Applicants who fail either or both parts of the tests are provided with their score report. The score sheet gives the percentage of right answers on the state portion of the exam and a rating of "good," "fair," or "needs improvement" on each of the five divisions of the uniform test. At present, ETS does not allow an applicant to review his or her examination.

On the day of your real estate exam, take your admission letter, personal identification,

USE OF THE MANUAL

several No. 2 pencils, an eraser and a watch to the testing center. Many jurisdictions allow the use of calculators (if they are silent, battery-run and paperless) and slide rules, although you should be able to work the math problems without such aids. No other papers or aids should be brought to the test site.

Standard instructions and procedures are part of the written exam booklet and will probably be read to you by a test supervisor before you begin the exam. When you get your test booklet, read the directions completely. When you receive your answer sheet from the test supervisor, be sure to enter your identifying information on it properly. If you do not do this correctly, the report of your score could be delayed or lost completely.

A toll-free telephone service providing test information to examinees is available in twenty states by dialing (800) 544-3221. ETS operators are on duty Monday through Friday, 8:00 A.M. to 5:00 P.M., Eastern Standard Time; recorded messages may be left after 5:00 P.M. This service currently is not available to examinees in Alaska or Hawaii. Students in these states may request test information by calling an inquiry-line in Berkeley, California, at (415) 849-0950.

SALESPERSON EXAMINATION

Chapter 3's content outline exactly follows the organization of the six basic areas of ETS's uniform salesperson test:

1. Real property and laws relating to ownership (20%)
2. Valuation of real property (14%)
3. Financing of real estate (20%)
4. Transfer of property ownership (15%)
5. Real estate brokerage (25%)
6. Specialty areas (6%)

The salesperson section contains a series of brief examinations on the six areas listed above. These diagnostic tests will assist you to determine your particular strengths and weaknesses. In general, they will indicate which section of the examination needs additional review; in particular, they will identify the specific real estate concept, terminology and/or application that you do not comprehend fully. Each test is keyed to an outline of the information you need to know for that subsection. The concepts outlines are useful as a general review. In conjunction with the test, they can help you identify your problem topics quickly and accurately. The recommended procedure for using this section is to complete the test, and check your answers against the answer key provided at the end of the test in addition to the test question cross-reference list on pages 134–136. If your evaluation of the wrong answers indicates that you misunderstand the topic, review the topic in the concepts section. If necessary, consult other texts for additional clarification. If the mathematics is a problem, check the chapter in the salesperson section on basic real estate mathematics.

As a final check on your knowledge, read the study-and-review checklist. When you feel sufficiently prepared, turn to Chapter 11's three 80-question sample exams. These sample exams closely approximate an actual ETS exam in content and format. They offer an opportunity to test thoroughly your knowledge and test-taking skills. The Test Question Cross-Reference List will help you identify your problem topics based upon the results of your diagnostic tests and sample exams. As suggested above, you should

REAL ESTATE EXAM MANUAL

consider consulting real estate principle and practice texts if you missed a significant number of questions that relate to a specific topic.

ETS Test Specifications for Salespeople

In the uniform portion of the real estate licensing examination for salespeople, ETS has defined its testing priorities as follows:

Real Property and Laws Relating to Ownership comprise 20 percent of the test. Questions concern legal concepts of real property, rights of ownership, encumbrances and governmental power affecting property.

Valuation of Real Property (14 percent of the test) covers methods of estimating property value, factors that may influence value estimates and the appraisal process.

Financing of Real Estate (20 percent of the test) concerns sources of financing, forms of financing, methods of repayment, terms and conditions and lender requirements.

Transfer of Property Ownership (15 percent of the test) deals with issues of titles and settlement.

Real Estate Brokerage (25 percent of the test) covers agency relationships and responsibilities, listing of real property, negotiating real estate sales contracts and federal laws relating to fair practices.

Specialty Areas (6 percent of the test) concern knowledge of current tax laws affecting real estate ownership, ability to identify securities law situations, property management and lease agreements.

Throughout the uniform test, 20 percent of the questions involve arithmetic functions.

BROKER EXAMINATION

Like the salesperson exam, the broker test contains 110 to 120 questions (80 in the uniform test and 30 to 40 in the state test), and lasts up to 4-1/2 hours. In the guide, Chapter 12: Broker Examination contains a discussion of the broker exam. Chapter 3's diagnostic test, concepts outlines, math review and study checklist, and Chapter 11's sample exams also should be of considerable study value to the prospective broker in preparing for the exam.

ETS Test Specifications for Brokers

The uniform portion of the ETS broker examination contains questions in five general subject areas. Approximately 20 percent of the test consists of questions requiring arithmetic calculations. These questions are distributed throughout the test. The test topics are:

1. *Real Property and Laws Relating to Ownership* (23 percent of uniform test)
    a. *Ownership of Property:* You must know the components of real prop-

erty, how personal property differs from real property, methods of land description, interests in real property and forms of ownership.

    b. *Transfer of Title:* You should be familiar with various types of deeds and their clauses and warranties, wills, governmental or judicial actions and power of attorney.

    c. *Encumbrances:* You should understand the distinctions between easements, encroachments, liens, priority among liens, covenants, conditions and restrictions.

    d. *Public Power over Property:* You should be aware of the legal implications of public powers over real property as in the cases of eminent domain, escheat, property taxation, building codes, planning and zoning and hazard areas (e.g., flood, geologic, toxic waste).

2. *Valuation of Real Property* (13 percent of uniform test)

    a. *Appraisal:* You must be familiar with definition and report, the direct sales comparison approach, the income approach, the cost approach and reconciliation.

    b. *Competitive Analysis*

    c. *Influences of Value:* e.g., location, utility, economic trends and government policy.

3. *Federal Income Tax Laws Affecting Real Estate* (7 percent of uniform test)

    a. *Owner-Occupied Residential:* You should be familiar with legislation affecting mortgage interest, real property taxes, deferral/rollover and over-55 exemption.

    b. *Investment:* You should understand cash flow analysis before and after taxes and depreciation.

    c. *Other Tax Considerations:* You must be aware of refinancing, gain on sales, installment sales and exchanges.

4. *Financing of Real Estate* (20 percent of uniform test)

    a. *Sources of Financing:* You should be aware of the various sources and forms of financing including institutional, seller financing, existing financing and the secondary mortgage market.

    b. *Characteristics of Loans:* You should understand the characteristics of FHA, VA, FmHA, conventional and private loans, types of amortization and interest rates and nonrecourse financing.

    c. *Special Forms of Financing:* You should be familiar with various mortgage options including wraparounds, blanket, package, growing equity, bridge (swing), construction, home equity, and sales-leaseback.

    d. *Financing Instruments:* You should understand the characteristics of mortgages, notes, trust deeds and contracts for deed (land contracts).

    e. *Clauses in Financing Instruments:* You should be aware of such clauses in financing instruments including prepayment, release, alienation (due-on-sale), subordination, impounds (escrow), acceleration and default.

    f. *Foreclosure and Redemption:* You should be able to recognize the different types of foreclosure and understand the process of redemption and the redemption period.

    g. *Terms and Conditions:* You should be familiar with lender requirements including property insurance, escrow, underwriting criteria, and buyer qualifications. You should also understand loan origination costs such as appraisal fees, credit reports and points.

5. *Settlement* (12 percent of uniform test)

   a. *Evidence of Title:* You must understand the principles as well as the procedures involved in recordation, title search and opinion of title, title insurance (owner's and mortgagee's) and curing title defects (e.g., quiet title, quitclaim deed).

   b. *Reports:* You should be familiar with the general aspects of inspection reports (e.g., structural, pest, wells, septic, soil), survey reports and appraisal reports.

   c. *Settlement Procedures:* You must know the obligations of the settlement agent and how to prorate calculations. You should be familiar with settlement documents including deeds, bills of sale and settlement statements. You must also be familiar with the Real Estate Settlement Procedures Act (RESPA).

6. *Real Estate Practice* (25 percent of uniform test)

   a. *Agency Relationships and Responsibilities:* You must have a clear understanding of disclosure of agency and the relationships between the broker and the principal; the broker and the public; the salesperson and the broker; the salesperson and the broker's principal; the salesperson and the public; the salesperson as independent contractor or employee; and the broker or salesperson as principal. You must also be aware of the ethical responsibilities of brokers and salespersons.

   b. *Listing of Real Property:* You should be familiar with the characteristics of types of listing agreements, brokerage fees, building codes, zoning laws, and use permits. You also must be aware of data collection, both physical data (e.g., legal description, lot size, dimensions of structure, appurtenances, personal property, utilities, type of construction) as well as such data as assessed value, taxes, special assessments, existing financing, other liens and encumbrances. Other topics of importance include compliance with fair housing laws, ownership of record, homeowner's association bylaws and fees, right of first refusal and termination of listings.

   c. *Real Estate Sales Contracts:* You should be familiar with the elements of a real estate contract (e.g., essential elements, adequate description, need for writing, signatures, capacity of parties), notice of acceptance, rejection, revocation, rescission, transmittal of offers and counteroffers, contract contingencies, options, earnest money deposits and what personal property is included in the sale. You also must be aware of financing considerations, assignment and contract enforcement.

   d. *Other Federal Laws:* You must be aware of current fair housing laws, the Truth-in-Lending Act (Regulation Z), the Bulk Sales Act and the Tax Reform Act of 1986.

   e. *Specialty Areas:* You must be familiar with issues such as property management (services, agreements, leases), common interest properties (e.g., cooperative, time-share, condominium) and securities laws affecting real estate investments.

2
Examination Strategies

The Educational Testing Service real estate license examinations are achievement tests that candidates must pass before they can work as salespeople or brokers in their states. An achievement test measures an individual's proficiency in a given field. The ultimate objective of the license exam is to maintain the standards of the industry and to protect the public from persons not qualified to practice real estate sales and brokerage. The exam, therefore, tests the knowledge applicants have gathered through license preparation courses and individual study, and their ability to use that knowledge in real estate applications.

GUIDELINES FOR PREPARING FOR THE EXAM

Mental and Physical Preparation

Multiple-choice tests demand a special type of mental preparation. While studying, you should try to memorize facts; emphasize details and study definitions, terms and formulas. Many questions will also require you to apply your knowledge to novel situations. Concentrate on real estate principles. As you study, try to *apply the principles and facts* to real-life situations.

Another excellent method of preparing for an exam is to *take similar tests* prior to the actual exam. You can gain important percentage points simply by being an experienced test-taker. The more similar the practice test is in content and format to the actual exam, the more you will benefit. This is the strategy behind the presentation of the diagnostic tests, salesperson practice exam, sample exams and broker exam in this manual. Taking the sample tests under actual test conditions (see Chapter 1 for details) will improve both your knowledge of the subject and your psychological readiness.

It is only logical that you will earn a better score by being in top physical and mental shape on the day of the test. It is a good idea to review your notes within the 48 hours before the exam; it is *not* wise to stay up all night in a panic-stricken effort to cram. Get your normal amount of rest the night before the exam. Eat normally, but do not have a heavy meal before going to the test.

Your *attitude* is at least as important as your metabolic state. You should be prepared, determined and positive. A small amount of anxiety is natural and can even help you do

REAL ESTATE EXAM MANUAL

your best, but too much anxiety is a handicap. Try to stay calm before and during the exam–don't worry about results at this point. Panic is irrational and self-defeating. It will only decrease your score. Again, build your confidence by finding out ahead of time how to get to the test location and by arriving a few minutes early. Bring all the appropriate materials. Find a seat in the front of the room if possible, so you can hear the instructions. Identify the test supervisors in case you have a question.

Following Directions

One of the major causes of incorrect answers is carelessness. Listen attentively to the test supervisor's instructions. Try not to let your anxiety to start the test make you miss the general rules.

Remember that the scorer only registers pencil and cannot tell the difference between a stray mark and an intended answer. An answer will not be counted unless the pencil mark is fairly dark and in the correct place. Keep your responses within the oval, but entirely fill that space. Do not write your answers on scratch paper and then transfer them all at one time to the answer sheet. This procedure invites errors and wastes valuable test-taking time.

Read all written directions carefully, then *follow* them exactly. A worked-out sample problem is usually provided. Even if you think you are familiar with that type of problem, *never* skip the instructions. Place the answer sheet to the right of the exam booklet if you are right-handed; to the left if left-handed. When you actually begin to take the exam, read carefully, not quickly. Be sure to understand each question *completely* before answering.

Another major cause of test errors is simply failure to *think*. Many tests measure judgment and reasoning as well as factual knowledge. Always try to choose the *best* answer to a question; more than one alternative may be partially correct. Don't look for trick questions; choose the most logical answer to the premise of each question. Words used in the questions will have their standard meanings unless they are special real estate terms. It sometimes helps to *rephrase* a question if you are not sure of the answer. For example, you may suspect that (D) is true in the following item:

- In holding a deposit on an offer, which of the following would be the best place to put the money, provided you had no instructions to the contrary?

    (A) In your office safe
    (B) In a neutral depository in the buyer's name
    (C) In your checking account
    (D) In a neutral depository

By rephrasing mentally, "The best place to put a deposit on an offer would be in a neutral depository," you can clarify your thoughts about that alternative. Be careful, though, not to change the meaning of the question when rephrasing it.

EXAMINATION STRATEGIES

Pacing

Work through the exam at a comfortable rate. You are allowed up to 4-1/2 hours to finish the 110- to 120-question exam; however, you should work as rapidly as you can without sacrificing accuracy. Budget your time before beginning the exam. Keep a watch handy–plan on having more than half the questions answered before half of your exam time has elapsed.

You may want to take a short break halfway through the exam. If you are ahead of schedule, you can afford to look up from your paper, take several deep breaths, stretch your legs, relax in your seat and rest for a minute or two. This breaks physical and mental tension and helps prevent mistakes.

As you work through the exam, answer the easy questions first–they are worth the same number of points as the hard ones, and they will build your confidence. Mark difficult items and time-consuming calculation problems on your scratch paper and return to them later. You may find clues in later questions; or, if time runs out, you'll have all the sure points. Don't give hurried answers just because you are intimidated by the number of questions. Most objective items are not very time-consuming. Do not become discouraged if the exam seems difficult. No one is expected to get a perfect score.

Exam Strategy

Many people study diligently and simply show up at the examination site without having given any thought to a strategy for taking the test. To maintain your confidence, poise and positive mental attitude, it is suggested that you enter the examination with a game plan as to how to take the test.

We suggest that you develop your own strategy for completing the test. An example for an exam strategy follows:

Start with the state examination. It is the shorter test; the sample state exam is 30 questions. Read each question once to determine the particular subject matter the question pertains to, and carefully underline key words. You should read the question a second time, concentrating on determining the correct response. If you are not certain of the correct answer, eliminate obvious incorrect responses. If you are still not certain of the single best answer, circle the question number in the test booklet and move on to the next question. The entire state exam should be completed in this fashion, even if, hypothetically, you may have answered only six of the 30 questions. Your strategy should next be to move to the uniform exam, again answering the questions you know and skipping the questions you are uncertain about. By doing this, you divide the test into two parts: (1) the part you know, which you can answer quickly and efficiently and remove from further consideration, and (2) the part you don't know, which you have managed to isolate, and now have the remainder of your test time to devote your attention to.

If math is your strength, you should next complete the math. After completing the math (on a mental high), your strategy is to go back to the state portion and once again make a pass through the exam, until both tests have been completed. Multiple-choice items often test not only your knowledge of a specific point, but also your ability to relate other information to the point. Many important topics have more than one question allotted to them. The correct answer to one question can often be found in some portion of another, so jot down the numbers of questions you think contain clues. This will help you in rechecking answers or answering questions you skipped.

If math is not your strength, do not let yourself be intimidated by the calculation problems. A good approach to math questions is to estimate the answer before actually working the problem. Figure neatly and carefully–this reduces error; then compare your answer with your original estimate. If they are very different, you may have misplaced a decimal or used the wrong equation. If you cannot tell from the problem what equation to use, make up a simple, similar problem and determine the equation from that. If you cannot solve a problem, or if you obtain an answer that is not one of the options, check to see if you used all the figures given in your calculations. If you cannot solve a math problem in the usual way, you can sometimes find the correct solution by working backward from the given answers. Math problems often use varying units that must be converted. You may have to change income per month to income per year before applying a formula, or you may have to convert square feet to acres before proceeding with a calculation. Watch for this pitfall. If you really have no idea how to solve a math problem and must guess blindly, eliminate the two most extreme numerical answers and mark one of the remaining choices. This is not always correct, but the odds favor this tactic.

After completing every question on the exam, proofread your answer sheet. Make sure that your answers are next to the correct numbers, that you didn't misread any of the questions and that you marked the answer you intended for each item. Don't change an answer unless you are sure the new one is correct. Studies show that an examinee's first response usually is correct and that changes will decrease the score. By using extra time to correct any careless mistakes, you may boost your score significantly.

By developing an exam strategy similar to this, *you* will be in command of the exam rather than the exam in command of you.

3
A Strategy for Studying

The salesperson section contains six divisions corresponding to the testing areas on the ETS exam: Contracts, Real Property and Laws Relating to Ownership, Valuation of Real Property, Financing of Real Estate, Transfer of Property Ownership, Real Estate Brokerage, Specialty Areas and Math. Each of these content areas is preceded by a brief diagnostic test and answer key, and a list of items you should be familiar with or should review. It is recommended that you take the test and analyze your results before reviewing the content outline. If your progress score suggests that you need improvement, use the test results to establish your priority areas for study. In addition, review your test answers with the key on pages 135–136.

Keep in mind that the outline format of the concepts is primarily designed to organize your real estate knowledge in a concise fashion. If you are having difficulty with a particular topic, it is recommended that you consult real estate practice and theory texts for a comprehensive explanation of the topic. *Modern Real Estate Practice*, published by Real Estate Education Company, provides a solid core of information.

HOW TO USE THE PROGRESS SCORE

After completing and correcting the diagnostic test, count the number of questions missed and enter the number in the box under "Your Score." Then subtract each question incorrectly answered from the total possible points. Finally, analyze your results by finding where your score of correct answers falls in the "Range" column; the rating corresponding to your score describes your progress.

For example:

FINANCING OF REAL ESTATE
Progress Score

Rating	Percentage	Range	Your Score	
EXCELLENT	96% to 100%	20	Financing	20
GOOD	86% to 95%	18–19	Total wrong	– 2
FAIR	76% to 85%	16–17	Total right	18
MARGINAL	70% to 75%	14–15		
NEED IMPROVEMENT	69% or less	13 or less		

If your score on the diagnostic test is rated as "Excellent" or "Good," this demonstrates that this area is one of your strengths. A rating of "Fair," "Marginal" or "Need Improvement" suggests that this is an area that you need to concentrate on.

DEVELOPING A STRATEGY FOR STUDYING

After you have pinpointed the areas that need particular study, you can begin studying the material outlined in the "Concepts to Understand" section. To increase the effectiveness of your study time we suggest that you follow these three easy rules.

Organize your study time. Educators suggest that regular short study periods are better than lengthy cram sessions. In addition, you should study when you are at your best mentally and physically, e.g., early in the morning. The following chart will assist you in organizing your study time in relation to the specific areas on the examination.

ORGANIZE YOUR STUDY TIME
Scheduled Hours for Study

	Mon.	Tues.	Wed.	Thurs.	Fri.	Sat.	Sun.	Total Hours
Uniform Exam								
Real Property								
Valuation								
Financing								
Ownership								
Brokerage								
Specialty Areas								
State Exam								
Real Estate License Law								
Rules and Regulations								
Special State Considerations								

Study alone. It is important that you realize that you can't simply read the text in preparing to successfully complete the exam. You must arrive at a thorough understanding of the subject matter. This can be achieved easily by regularly asking yourself questions regarding what you just read after the completion of a paragraph. It is a good practice to outline the thoughts of the paragraph in your own words and then compare them to the study guide. A third method is to note comparisons and contrasts, or develop relationships between items. In other words, create mental images that will assist you to recall difficult concepts.

Regularly review materials studied. This, in many cases, can be accomplished by the use of a study partner to assist you in reviewing your knowledge of vocabulary words, concepts and relationships. This can also be achieved through taking regular exams on the subject matter. The following is a study-and-review checklist to use as you prepare for each of the testing areas on the ETS exam.

STUDY-AND-REVIEW CHECKLIST

UNIFORM EXAM

Real Property and Laws Relating to Ownership

- ☐ Legal concepts
  - ☐ Components of real property
  - ☐ Components of personal property
  - ☐ Types of legal descriptions of land
- ☐ Real estate ownership
  - ☐ Estates in land: freehold and nonfreehold
  - ☐ Types of legal life estates
  - ☐ Methods of taking ownership: Voluntary alienation (gift and sale); and Involuntary alienation (foreclosure and condemnation)
  - ☐ How ownership is held
- ☐ Other interests affecting ownership
  - ☐ Encumbrance: liens; easements; license; covenants; and restrictions
  - ☐ Taxes: (assessments)
- ☐ Government control affecting real estate
  - ☐ Police power
  - ☐ Private power

Valuation of Real Property

- ☐ The three methods of estimating property value
  - ☐ Market data approach
  - ☐ Cost approach
  - ☐ Income approach
- ☐ Factors influencing value
  - ☐ Characteristics of value
- ☐ Types of value
- ☐ Types of depreciation
- ☐ Improvements and economic trends
- ☐ The appraisal process

Financing of Real Estate

- ☐ Sources of financing
  - ☐ Institutional sources
  - ☐ Secondary money market
  - ☐ Assumptions
  - ☐ Seller financing
- ☐ Forms of mortgage financing
  - ☐ Deed of trust
  - ☐ Mortgage
  - ☐ Installment sale
  - ☐ Purchase-money mortgage
  - ☐ Insured/guaranteed loan
  - ☐ Special types of mortgages
  - ☐ Priority of mortgages
- ☐ Methods of repayment
  - ☐ Types of amortization
- ☐ Fixed rate
- ☐ Adjustable rate
- ☐ Payment calculations
- ☐ Special terms and conditions
  - ☐ Parties to a mortgage
  - ☐ Mortgage instruments
  - ☐ Foreclosure and redemption
  - ☐ Mortgage theories
  - ☐ Terms
- ☐ Lender requirements
  - ☐ Underwriting procedures
  - ☐ Underwriting criteria
  - ☐ Loan application
  - ☐ Origination costs

Transfer of Property Ownership

- ☐ The legal transfer
  - ☐ How ownership is held
  - ☐ Proof of title (ownership)
  - ☐ Documents conveying ownership
  - ☐ Types of deeds
  - ☐ Recording deeds and passing title
- ☐ The financial transfer
  - ☐ Real Estate Settlement Procedures Act (RESPA)
  - ☐ The settlement statement
  - ☐ Mortgage theories
  - ☐ The recording process

A STRATEGY FOR STUDYING

Real Estate Brokerage

- ☐ Agency relationship and responsibilities
  - ☐ Law of agency
  - ☐ Responsibilities of broker and sales associates
  - ☐ Ethical considerations
  - ☐ Agency disclosure
  - ☐ Other disclosures
  - ☐ Fiduciary obligations
- ☐ Listing of real property
  - ☐ The parties to the contracts
  - ☐ Listing agreements
- ☐ Types of contracts
- ☐ Contract classifications
- ☐ Negotiating real estate sale contracts
  - ☐ Essential elements
  - ☐ Earnest money
  - ☐ Purchase agreement
  - ☐ Acceptance and delivery
  - ☐ Legal effects
  - ☐ Forfeiture
  - ☐ Regulation Z
  - ☐ Fair housing law

Specialty Areas

- ☐ Tax laws
- ☐ Securities laws
- ☐ Property management
- ☐ Lease agreements

Real Estate Math

- ☐ Percents, fractions and decimals
- ☐ Commissions
- ☐ Area and volume
- ☐ Interest
- ☐ Points
- ☐ Taxes
- ☐ Transfer tax
- ☐ Depreciation
- ☐ Prorations
- ☐ Closing statements (broker only)

STATE EXAM

- ☐ State statutes, license laws
- ☐ State rules and regulations
- ☐ Responsibilities of broker and salesperson

- ☐ State considerations regarding:
    - ☐ The listing agreement
    - ☐ The purchase agreement
    - ☐ The closing
    - ☐ Title and method of transfer
    - ☐ Deeds, contract for deed, land contract, trust
    - ☐ Descriptions of land
    - ☐ Mortgages, financing and usury
    - ☐ Landlord-tenant relationship and leases
    - ☐ Zoning, taxes and control of land use
    - ☐ Fair housing laws and discrimination
    - ☐ How ownership is held
    - ☐ Interests in real estate
    - ☐ Condominiums
    - ☐ Other particular state matters

4
Real Property and Laws Relating to Ownership

REVIEW CHECKLIST

To complete a real estate transaction as a broker or salesperson you must understand how to describe the property you are selling. You must be able to differentiate between real property and personal property, know the rights to ownership and be aware of special restrictions and controls on the use of each particular interest. Furthermore, you will be required to have an understanding of the methods of transferring ownership. In Section Four of the examination you will be tested on the following items:

Real Property and Laws Relating to Ownership (20 percent of the test)
- Legal concepts of real property
- Rights of ownership
- Encumbrances
- Governmental power affecting property

Recognition and Recall

- ☐ 1. Fixture vs. real estate
- ☐ 2. Real property vs. personal property
- ☐ 3. Covenant vs. deed restriction
- ☐ 4. Trust deed vs. warranty deed
- ☐ 5. Dedication vs. eminent domain
- ☐ 6. Metes and bounds vs. rectangular survey
- ☐ 7. Townhouse vs. time-sharing
- ☐ 8. Freehold vs. leasehold estates
- ☐ 9. Ownership in severalty vs. co-ownership
- ☐ 10. Tenancy in common vs. joint tenancy
- ☐ 11. Tenancy by the entirety vs. community property
- ☐ 12. Fee simple vs. determinable fee
- ☐ 13. Estate for years vs. period to period
- ☐ 14. Tenancy at will vs. tenancy at sufferance
- ☐ 15. Life estate vs. legal life estate

REAL ESTATE EXAM MANUAL

- ☐ 16. Encumbrance vs. lien
- ☐ 17. Easement by prescription vs. easement by necessity
- ☐ 18. Deed restriction vs. encroachment
- ☐ 19. Eminent domain vs. adverse possession
- ☐ 20. Escheat vs. intestate
- ☐ 21. Gift vs. descent
- ☐ 22. Accrued vs. prepaid
- ☐ 23. Proration vs. amortization
- ☐ 24. Statutory (360-day) vs. per annum (365-day)

Comprehension

- ☐ 1. The two classifications of property
- ☐ 2. The private control of land

You must understand:

- ☐ 1. An estate is legally the use, possession, control and disposition of land and includes any freehold or leasehold interest.
- ☐ 2. Estates can be classified by quality and duration of interest.
- ☐ 3. The difference between freehold and nonfreehold (leasehold) estates
- ☐ 4. The differences among fee simple, determinable fee and life estates
- ☐ 5. The classification and distinctions between ownership in severalty and co-ownership

OUTLINE OF CONCEPTS TO UNDERSTAND

I. THE CHARACTERISTICS OF REAL AND PERSONAL PROPERTY–all property may be divided into two classifications: (1) Real property and (2) Personal property.

   A. *Real property* refers to the ownership of the land and improvements attached to the land. (Deed)
   B. *Personal property* is anything which is not real property. (Movable, temporary–Bill of Sale)
   C. *Fixture* is personal property that has been attached to land and is conveyed as real property.
   D. *Real Estate* is the right to own or use real property. In addition, both real and personal property can be divided into two practical and logical distinctions:

   1. Things
   2. Relationships

   E. *Real Property*

   1. Corporeal (things)–house, land and fixtures
   2. Incorporeal (relationships)–easements and licensee

   F. *Personal Property**

---

*Note about personal property. Changing the character of an item can also change the classification. For example, a tree is real property. If it is cut down and made into lumber it is personal property. However, if the lumber is used in a home it would again be real property.

REAL PROPERTY AND LAWS RELATING TO OWNERSHIP

1. Tangible (things)–auto, bed, table, washer, dryer
2. Intangible (relationships)–royalties, trademark

II. REAL PROPERTY LAWS

   A. Legal descriptions–Types of legal descriptions of land:
      1. Metes and bounds
         a. From a point of beginning, measurement proceeds around the perimeter of the parcel. The description uses feet and degrees.
         b. Monuments, or fixed objects, are used to define the boundaries of a property. If a discrepancy exists, the actual distance between monuments takes precedence over the quoted lineal feet.
         c. The measurement must return to the point of beginning. (P.O.B.)
      2. Rectangular (Government) survey
         a. Measurements are based on principal meridians (lines running north-south) and base lines (lines running east-west).
         b. East and west of the principal meridian, lines six miles apart divide the land into strips called ranges.
         c. North and south of the base line, parallel lines six miles apart divide land into strips called tiers.
         d. These two sets of lines form a grid that divides property into townships. A township is described by appropriate tiers and ranges, e.g., T3N R2E.
         e. A township is 36 square miles (6 × 6 miles).
         f. There are 36 sections in a township; each one is a square mile. Sections are numbered, beginning with No. 1 in the northeast corner; winding west and east, section No. 36 ends in the southeast corner. Each section contains 640 acres. An acre contains 160 square rods. An acre also contains 43,560 sq. feet.
         g. The description may pinpoint locations by referring to quarters and halves within a section, e.g., SW¼ of NE¼.
      3. Subdivision plats
         a. A subdivision is divided into blocks and lots, e.g., Lots 7 & 8 Block 4 of Hartley subdivision.
         b. Because all states use this method, a description of such property must include the county and state, to distinguish it from the same description in another area.
         c. Areas within a subdivision may be resubdivided.
   B. A street address is not a legal description.

III. RIGHTS OF OWNERSHIP: INTERESTS IN REAL ESTATE

   A. All interests in real estate are subject to certain governmental powers, including police power, eminent domain, escheat and taxation. (Acronym "P.E.E.T.")
   B. Estates in land–The degree, quality, nature and extent of interest an individual has in real property. There are two types of estates in land:
      1. Freehold estates
         a. Fee simple estate–This is the best interest in real estate recognized by law; it represents the most complete ownership.

1) It includes all rights incident to property.
2) It endures forever and is inheritable.

b. Determinable fee or conditional fee–Similar to fee simple, this interest, however, is limited by a condition on the estate. Party may hold the estate only as long as some specified act or condition does or does not occur. Key words are "as long as." An example is: in deed, one party grants property to a second party as long as it is used as a church.

c. Life estate–This differs from fee simple and determinable fee in that the estate cannot be passed on to the estate holder's heirs. An example is: in deed, one party grants property to a second party for life, thereafter to a third party.

1) Normally, a life estate is granted for the life of the holder of the estate; if dependent upon the life of another, it is called pur autre vie.
2) Rights and duties of the life tenant during that tenant's life

   a) Life tenant may receive income from the property.
   b) Life tenant may sell, lease or mortgage the life interest.
   c) Life tenant may pay real estate taxes on property.

3) Limitations of the life tenant's rights–The tenant may not damage the property nor harm the rights of the grantor or third party, who will later hold property.
4) Reversion–At the termination of the life estate, the property reverts to the grantor or the grantor's heirs.
5) Remainder–At the termination of the life estate, the property passes to a third party; the third party is referred to as a remainderman.

2. Leasehold estates (nonfreehold estates)

   a. Types of leasehold estates:

   1) Estate for years–The lease is in effect until a specified expiration date. The length of the lease may span from less than one year to many years. No notice of termination is required.
   2) Period to period–No specific expiration date is set, although the length of the period (e.g., month to month) is agreed upon by both parties. As long as the lease is not terminated, it automatically renews at end of each period. Notice of termination equal to the lease period is required to end the lease.
   3) Tenancy at will–This tenancy occurs with the consent of the landlord and runs for an indefinite period of time; for example, a tenant may be allowed to occupy a building until it is demolished. The death of either party or minimum notice required by law terminates this type of tenancy.
   4) Tenancy at sufferance–The tenant continues to occupy a property after his or her rights are terminated, without the consent of the landlord. An example is unauthorized holdover after a lease expires.

3. Types of legal life estates:

a. Dower–This represents the widow's rights in the real estate owned by her deceased spouse. Depending on the circumstances and state laws, this is one-half or one-third interest in the property. Curtesy–Curtesy represents the widower's rights in the real estate owned by his deceased spouse. In some states the term dower is used for either widow's or widower's interest.

1) If both marriage partners join in a written transaction to sell property, dower and curtesy rights in that property are automatically released.
2) Many states have eliminated both curtesy and dower rights through enactment of the laws of descent and distribution. The concepts of dower and curtesy have been replaced by statutory share–A wife or husband receives a specific portion of property or percentage of the sale amount.

b. Homestead–A tract of land that enjoys protection from certain debts

1) The land must be occupied as the principal residence.
2) The head of the family must own or lease the property.
3) In most states, a single person cannot homestead.
4) Protection is from general unsecured debts, not debts creating specific liens.
5) If a homestead must be sold to satisfy debts, a certain amount of the proceeds is typically given to the family.
6) Homestead rights are usually released in favor of the lender in modern mortgage instruments.

4. Adverse possession

a. A person takes possession of and uses property belonging to another. Possession must be open, notorious, hostile and uninterrupted for a state-specified length of time, e.g., 20 years.
b. Under state law, the person who satisfies the requirements of adverse possession takes ownership, and the original owner loses rights to the property.

C. Other forms of ownership

1. Condominiums

a. An individual owns a unit in fee and an undivided percentage interest in the common elements.
b. Taxes, mortgages and assessments are liens against individual interests only. There is no separate tax statement for common areas.
c. Individuals may free their interests from lien on work to common areas by paying off their percentage share.
d. Interest in common elements cannot be separated from interest in the apartment.
e. An individual may not partition condominium property.
f. Creation of a condominium generally requires:

1) Public offering statement–This protects the public by disclosing pertinent facts about a unit.
2) Condominium declaration–Commonly referred to as the

master deed, it describes individual units and details the formation of a homeowners' association plus rules and regulations.
3) Condominium plan–This describes the individual units and the common areas.
4) Bylaws–These contain provisions for administration and management by the homeowners' association.
5) Operating budget–This document projects revenues and expenses.
6) Management agreement–This authorizes the maintenance of common areas.
7) Purchase agreement–This is the sales contract used in the sale of each unit. The declaration and bylaws should be consulted.
8) Unit deed–A legal instrument, this conveys ownership of a unit.
9) Rental agreement–The rental contract is used in the rental of individual units. The declaration and bylaws should be consulted.
10) Unit tax duplicate and insurance policy.

g. Creation can be accomplished by the conversion of an existing building or construction of a new building.

2. Cooperatives

a. Land and building are owned by a corporation.
b. Purchasers hold stock in the corporation, and receive a proprietary lease for an apartment unit.
c. Mortgage, taxes, liens and legal responsibility lie with the entire parcel. This is an important difference from condominiums.

3. Ownership by a corporation–Stockholders are not liable for the debts of the corporation.
4. Ownership by general partnership–Partners are liable for the debts of the partnership.
5. Ownership by limited partnership–Limited partners are not liable for the debts of the partnership; general partners are.
6. Ownership by Real Estate Investment Trust–REITs are similar to mutual funds. Shares are sold to investors.
7. Real estate syndication–a group of two or more investors or a joint venture in the form of a corporation or partnership to own real estate.

IV. OTHER INTERESTS AND ITEMS AFFECTING REAL ESTATE

A. Items that affect marketability of title

1. Encumbrance–A claim or liability that attaches to the land, held by one who is not the fee owner. Types of encumbrances are liens, affecting the title and physical encumbrances, affecting the use of the land.

a. Liens–Charges against the property, as security for debt. The property may still be conveyed, but it is a risk for the buyer. Priority is usually determined by the order in which liens attach; earlier ones have priority.

    1) Specific liens–Liens on specific property

        a) Real estate taxes, including general taxes and special assessments, have priority over all other liens.
        b) Mortgages
        c) Mechanics' liens–These are claims of workers and suppliers of materials against the property they helped improve. In most cases, workers must give notice and/or file a claim to obtain a lien. In some states, a subcontractor can obtain a lien even if the property owner has paid the contractor.

    2) General liens–These liens apply to all the debtor's property, e.g., judgments or court decrees awarding money to the successful party in a lawsuit.

  b. Encumbrances affecting the physical use of the land

    1) Easement–The right to use property for specific purposes.

        a) Easement in gross–This pertains to an entity's personal right to use property. Person receiving easement does not own adjoining property.
        b) Easement appurtenant–The easement runs with the land. Adjacent properties of this easement are the dominant tenement (the tract of land benefiting from the easement) and the servient tenement (the tract over which the easement runs).
        c) Easement by necessity–This is created when there exists no other access to land. Usually arises in the sale of nonaccessible land.
        d) Easement by prescription–This is created through continual use for a certain period of time (prescriptive period). The use must be continual, visible and without approval. A private road may become a public street in this manner.

    2) Creation of easements may occur by express grant, by reserving in deed, by implication or by long-time usage.

2. License–An individual has the privilege to enter land for a specific purpose. This differs from easement in that it may be terminated by the licensor. Examples of license are parking a car in a neighbor's driveway and presenting a theater ticket to gain admittance to a play.
3. Encroachment–A building or other structure extends onto a neighbor's property, i.e., trees, fences and driveways, etc.

B. Water rights–Owners along waterways have the right to use the water as long as they do not interrupt the flow or pollute it.

  1. Riparian rights–Rights of the owner along a river or stream.

a. Along navigable waters, owners possess land to the water's edge; the state owns submerged land and filled land.
b. Along nonnavigable waters, owners possess land to the center of the stream.
c. Only land, not water, is owned.
2. Littoral rights–Rights of owners along an ocean or large lake. Owners possess land to the high-water mark.
3. Accretion–Physical addition to the land by natural forces.
4. Erosion–Physical loss of land due to natural forces.
5. Alluvion–The increase of soil on a shore or bank of a river.
6. Prior appropriation–The right to use water is controlled by the state. An individual who wishes to use the water must indicate need and generally beneficial usage.

V. GOVERNMENTAL POWERS–CONTROL OF LAND USE–Police power of states enables them to adopt regulations to protect the public health and welfare.
   A. Police powers include:
      1. Zoning
         a. Ordinances generally restrict the use of areas or regulate physical improvements. Ordinance restrictions may extend to such matters as density, building size and height.
         b. Zoning regulations classify land use as residential, commercial, industrial or multiple use.
         c. Nonconforming use–The use that existed prior to the zoning restriction. The use is allowed to continue even though it does not meet zoning requirements.
         d. Variance–In situations where complying with an ordinance would cause hardship, a person may ask to be excused from complying.
      2. Building codes
      3. Subdivision regulations–grading, sewers, etc.
      4. Environmental protection legislation
      5. Occupancy permits
   B. Private land use control–Deed and declaration restrictions. For example, a dwelling must conform to the dimensions specified in the deed; often used to restrict the buyer's use of a property.

VI. REAL ESTATE TAXES–These taxes take priority over all other liens against a property.
   A. Ad valorem tax–Taxes are collectively levied on real estate by several governmental agencies and municipalities. The amount of tax is based on the value of the property.
      1. Assessment–Real estate is assessed for tax purposes by county or township assessors.
      2. Equalization–This factor corrects general inequities in statewide tax assessments.
      3. Determination of tax rate
         a. The taxing jurisdiction defines its needs and develops its budget.
         b. The assessed values of all properties within the local jurisdiction are computed.

c. The appropriate tax rate is determined by dividing the total assessed values into the budget deficit.
d. The tax rate is generally expressed in mills. One mill is 1/1000th of a dollar, or $.001.

4. The tax bill is calculated by applying the tax rate to the assessed valuation of the property. Thus, a home valued for tax purposes at $30,000 multiplied by a tax rate of $3 per hundred would generate a tax bill of $900.

B. Special assessments are special taxes levied on real estate that require property owners to pay for improvements that directly benefit the real estate they own, e.g., the installation of a sidewalk.

VII. OTHER TERMS TO REMEMBER
A. Datum–An imaginary line from which heights are measured.
B. Benchmark–The reference point used to measure elevation.
C. Government lot–An undersized or fractional section.
D. Air lot–A space over a given parcel of land.
E. Escheat–The state takes property upon the owner's death if no will exists and no heirs can be found.
F. Eminent domain–This empowers government authorities to condemn and take the property.
    1. The taking must be for the public benefit, e.g., to build a freeway.
    2. The taking authority must pay just compensation to the owner.
    3. Due process must be followed.
G. Trust deed–An instrument used in many states to create a mortgage lien to a trustee as security for a loan.
H. Dedication–An interest in real property may be given to a state or municipality to be used for public purposes, i.e., property given to the city for a park.
I. Townhouse–A dwelling unit normally having two floors, with the living area and kitchen on the base floor and the bedrooms located on the second floor. Townhouses are very popular in cluster housing and often employ the use of party walls and shared common grounds.
J. Time-sharing–The owner of a time share has the rights to exclusive use of the property for a specified time frame.
K. Private land controls–Owner's restriction of land use (Covenant or Deed).
L. Covenant–A written document that can be a promise to do something.
M. Deed restriction–A provision in a deed that allows the control over future use of the property.

DIAGNOSTIC TEST

1. What are the rights of a surviving wife in the real estate owned by a deceased spouse during their marriage?

   (A) Curtesy
   (B) Dower
   (C) Homestead
   (D) Escheat

2. All of the following are true statements about condominiums EXCEPT:

   (A) A declaration must be filed before any units may be sold.
   (B) Each unit owner has a fractional undivided interest in the common areas and facilities.
   (C) Each owner receives a separate tax statement.
   (D) Each owner has a proprietary lease with the association covering his or her unit.

3. Sam Poulos is in possession of property under a tenancy at will. Which of the following is true?

   (A) Poulos has not received the consent of the landlord to possess the property.
   (B) The tenancy will terminate if Poulos dies.
   (C) The tenancy was created by the death of the owner.
   (D) The tenancy has a definite termination date.

4. Horace Plant owns a lot and gives his neighbor, Martha Channel, the right to use Plant's driveway to reach Channel's garage. What is Channel's interest or right called?

   (A) A lease
   (B) An easement
   (C) An encroachment
   (D) A prescriptive right

5. All of the following are examples of a specific lien EXCEPT:

   (A) real estate taxes.
   (B) a judgment.
   (C) a mortgage.
   (D) mechanics' liens.

6. Victor Laskowski receives possession of property under a deed that states that he shall own the property as long as the present building standing on the property is not torn down. The type of estate Laskowski holds is which of the following?

   (A) Life estate
   (B) Nondestructible estate
   (C) Fee simple estate
   (D) Determinable fee estate

7. Which of the following best describes a legal life estate?

   (A) A homestead estate
   (B) An estate conveyed by one party to a second party for the second party's life
   (C) An estate created by a will
   (D) An estate conveyed to a second party subject to a condition

8. What are the rights of the owner of property located along the banks of a stream or river?

   (A) Littoral rights
   (B) Hereditaments
   (C) Riparian rights
   (D) Avulsions

9. When land is to be condemned or taken under the power of eminent domain, which of the following must apply?

   (A) The taking must be for a public purpose.
   (B) Statutory dedication executed
   (C) Adverse possession action
   (D) Constructive notice

REAL PROPERTY AND LAWS RELATING TO OWNERSHIP

10. Kevin Grunder owns a parcel of property. Peter Lawlor takes possession of the land after obtaining Grunder's permission. Lawlor's possession continues for 15 years. Thereafter Lawlor attempts to get title to the property. Will Lawlor succeed?

   (A) Lawlor will be successful because he possessed the property for 15 straight years.
   (B) Lawlor will be successful because he satisfied all the requirements of eminent domain.
   (C) Lawlor will be unsuccessful because he cannot obtain title to abstract property through possession for the prescriptive period.
   (D) Lawlor will be unsuccessful because not all the requirements of adverse possession have been satisfied.

11. A section contains:

   (A) 36 townships.
   (B) 160 government lots.
   (C) 160 acres.
   (D) 640 acres.

12. What is the method of describing property by degrees, feet and monuments known as?

   (A) The angular system
   (B) The metes-and-bounds description
   (C) The government survey system
   (D) The rectangular system

13. Recently an ordinance was passed stating that no sign placed upon a building may extend more than three feet above the highest point of the roof. Thomas O'Connor wants to place a revolving sign nine feet high on the roof of his store. In order to legally do this, O'Connor must get:

   (A) a residual.
   (B) a variance.
   (C) a nonconforming use permit.
   (D) an aerial clearance.

14. What is the proper description of the shaded area?

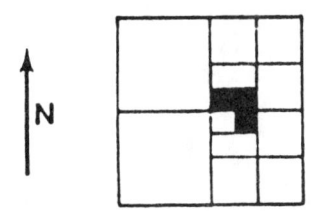

   (A) SW¼ of the SE¼ of the NE¼ and the N½ of the SE¼ of the SW¼
   (B) N½ of the NE¼ of the SW¼ and the SW¼ of the NW¼
   (C) SW¼ of the SE¼ of the NW¼ and the N½ of the NE¼ of the SW¼
   (D) S½ of the SW¼ of the NE¼ and the NE¼ of the NW¼ of the SE¼

15. A real estate tax lien takes priority over which of the following?

   (A) An encroachment
   (B) An encumbrance
   (C) A mortgage lien
   (D) A deed restriction

16. How many acres is in a description reading "The NW¼ of the SE¼ and the S½ of the SW¼ of the NE¼ of Section 4"?

   (A) 40 acres
   (B) 50 acres
   (C) 60 acres
   (D) 80 acres

17. Ranges are strips of land 6 miles wide and:
    (A) running east and west.
    (B) running north and south.
    (C) counted north and south of the base line.
    (D) of constant width.

18. What do the police powers of governmental authority include?
    (A) Foreclosure
    (B) Defeasance
    (C) Building codes and zoning regulations
    (D) Alienation

REAL PROPERTY AND LAWS RELATING TO OWNERSHIP

ANSWER KEY

Question	Answer	Type of Question	Topic Area	Outline Reference	Page
1.	(B)	Recognition Recall–Definition	Dower	III.B.3.a.	19
2.	(D)	Recognition Recall–Definition	Condominiums	III.C.1.	20
3.	(B)	Comprehension–Application	Tenancy at will	III.B.2.a.	20
4.	(B)	Comprehension–Application	Easements	IV.A.1.b.	23
5.	(B)	Recognition Recall–Definition	Liens	IV.A.1.a.	22
6.	(D)	Comprehension–Application	Freehold estates	III.B.1.	19
7.	(A)	Recognition Recall–Definition	Life estates	III.B.1.c.	20
8.	(C)	Recognition Recall–Definition	Riparian rights	IV.B.1.	23
9.	(A)	Comprehension–Application	Eminent domain	VII.F.	25
10.	(D)	Comprehension–Application	Adverse possession	III.B.4.	21
11.	(D)	Comprehension–Application	Township	II.A.2.d.	19
12.	(B)	Recognition Recall–Definition	Metes and bounds	II.A.1.	19
13.	(B)	Comprehension–Application	Zoning variance	V.A.1.d.	24
14.	(D)	Comprehension–Application	Rectangular survey	II.A.2.	19
15.	(C)	Recognition Recall–Definition	Tax lien priority	IV.A.1.a.1.a.	23
16.	(C)	Comprehension–Application	Acres of land	II.A.2.F.	19
17.	(B)	Comprehension–Application	Ranges	II.A.2.G.	19
18.	(C)	Recognition Recall–Definition	Police power	V.A.	24

REAL PROPERTY AND LAWS RELATING TO OWNERSHIP

Progress Score

Rating	Percentage	Range	Your Score
EXCELLENT	96% to 100%	18	Ownership 18
GOOD	86% to 95%	16–17	Total wrong – ___
FAIR	76% to 85%	14–15	Total right ___
MARGINAL	70% to 75%	12–13	
NEED IMPROVEMENT	69% or less	11 or less	

A.) *Important*: See the Test Question Cross-Reference List on page 000; circle all the questions you missed on the Ownership Diagnostic Section.

B.) How many questions did you miss in each area?

 1. Recognition Recall–Definitions _____
 2. Comprehension–Application _____

5
Valuation of Real Property

REVIEW CHECKLIST

The daily activities of a real estate agent require a thorough understanding of the principles of real estate appraising. One of the key questions asked by the consumer is "What is the value of the real estate?" Consequently, the real estate valuation portion of the ETS exam will test your knowledge in these areas. This part of the examination comprises 14 percent of the questions and covers the following topic areas:

- The methods of estimating property value
- The factors that influence value
- The appraisal process

Recognition and Recall

You should be able to distinguish between:

- ☐ 1. Utility vs. scarcity
- ☐ 2. Demand vs. transferability
- ☐ 3. Market value vs. assessed value
- ☐ 4. Market price vs. market value
- ☐ 5. Market data approach vs. cost approach
- ☐ 6. Income approach vs. cost approach
- ☐ 7. Capitalization rate vs. gross rent multiplier
- ☐ 8. The principles of supply and demand
- ☐ 9. Assessed value vs. insured value; market value vs. book value
- ☐ 10. Net operating income vs. gross income
- ☐ 11. Function vs. the purpose of an appraisal
- ☐ 12. Depreciation vs. the economic life

Comprehension

You must understand:

- ☐ 1. The differences among market data, cost and income approaches in determining value

REAL ESTATE EXAM MANUAL

☐ 2. The basic function and process of appraising
☐ 3. Computation of the capitalization rate, given all necessary data
☐ 4. The differences among physical deterioration, functional obsolescence and locational obsolescence
☐ 5. The differences between replacement costs and reproduction costs
☐ 6. The concept of highest and best use
☐ 7. The principles affecting value
☐ 8. The physical, economic, social and political factors that influence value
☐ 9. The appraisal process
☐ 10. The four basic elements of value
☐ 11. The definition of value
☐ 12. What an appraisal is

OUTLINE OF CONCEPTS TO UNDERSTAND

I. THE THREE APPROACHES TO VALUE

A. Market data approach (primarily single family)–An estimate of value is obtained by comparing the subject property with recently sold, comparable properties.

B. Cost approach (primarily commercial and industrial property)–An estimate of value is ascertained by determining what it would cost to replace or reproduce the structure. After replacement cost is determined, depreciation of present structure is deducted to arrive at value. Depreciation can be one of the following types:

1. Physical deterioration (curable)–Repairs when made are economically feasible.
2. Physical deterioration (incurable)–Repairs are not cost-justified.
3. Functional obsolescence (curable)–Features of the structure are no longer desired by purchasers, but are replaceable.
4. Functional obsolescence (incurable)–Undesirable physical or design features are not easily replaceable.
5. Locational obsolescence (incurable)–An example is proximity to a polluting factory or deteriorating neighborhood.

C. Income approach (primarily income-producing property)–The value is determined by analyzing the present worth of a future income stream.

1. The formula for computation is:

$$\frac{\text{net operating income}}{\text{capitalization rate}} = \text{value}$$

2. Gross rent multiplier–A method of arriving at a rough estimate of the value of income-producing residential properties primarily purchased for income, such as single-family homes. The formula is:

$$\text{monthly rental income} \times \text{gross rent multiplier} = \text{sale price}$$

II. THE CONCEPT OF VALUE

A. An appraisal is an estimate or opinion of value.
B. Characteristics that comprise value are:

1. Demand
2. Utility
3. Scarcity
4. Transferability
5. Anticipation
6. Highest and best use

C. Types of value–Real estate may have different values at the same time, e.g., market value, assessed value, mortgage value and depreciated value.
D. Market value vs. market price

1. Market value is an estimate of probable price on the date of appraisal.
2. Market price is what the property actually sells for.

III. THE ELEMENTS OF VALUE

A. Utility
B. Scarcity
C. Demand
D. Transferability

IV. FORCES INFLUENCING VALUE

A. Physical
B. Economic
C. Social
D. Political

V. ECONOMIC PRINCIPLES AFFECTING VALUE

A. Supply
B. Demand
C. Progression
D. Regression
E. Conformity
F. Change
G. Substitution
H. Diminishing returns

VI. AN APPRAISAL

A. Purpose: to determine the type of value
B. Function: to determine the specific value

VII. THE APPRAISAL PROCESS

A. Define the problem
B. Preliminary survey
C. Collect data
D. Data classification
E. Data analysis
F. Complete market data approach
G. Complete cost approach; complete income approach
H. Reconciliation–A step in the appraisal process where the appraiser compares the estimates from the market, cost and income approaches to arrive at a final estimate
I. Final estimate of value

DIAGNOSTIC TEST

1. In the cost approach, an appraiser makes use of which of the following?

    (A) Sales prices of similar properties
    (B) The owner's original cost of construction
    (C) An estimate of the building's replacement cost
    (D) The property's depreciated value for income tax purposes

2. Which of the following processes is used in the income approach to value?

    (A) Equalization (C) Amortization
    (B) Capitalization (D) Depreciation

3. In estimating the value of commercial property, what is the appraiser's most important consideration?

    (A) Its reproduction cost (C) Its gross rent multiplier
    (B) Its net income (D) Its gross income

4. To appraise a single-family residential home, a professional appraiser uses which of the following?

    (A) The market data approach (C) The gross rent multiplier
    (B) The income approach (D) The Certificate of Real Estate Value

5. What is an appraisal?

    (A) An estimate of value (C) The projected value
    (B) The market price (D) The net value

6. Which of the following provide(s) an estimate of value based on the cost approach?

    (A) Market price (C) Comparables
    (B) Replacement cost (D) Net operating income

7. The economic principles that affect the value of real estate include which of the following?

    (A) Reserves for replacement (C) Highest and best use
    (B) Operating expense ratio (D) Holding period

VALUATION OF REAL PROPERTY

ANSWER KEY

Question	Answer	Type of Question	Topic Area	Outline Reference	Page
1.	(C)	Recognition Recall–Definition	Cost approach	I.B.	32
2.	(B)	Recognition Recall–Definition	Capitalization approach	I.C.1.	32
3.	(B)	Comprehension–Application	Income approach	I.C.	32
4.	(A)	Comprehension–Application	Market data	I.A.	32
5.	(A)	Recognition Recall–Definition	Appraisal	II.A.	32
6.	(B)	Recognition Recall–Definition	Cost approach	I.B.	32
7.	(C)	Recognition Recall–Definition	Principles of value	II.B.6.	32

VALUATION OF REAL PROPERTY

Progress Score

Rating	Percentage	Range	Your Score
EXCELLENT	96% to 100%	7	Valuation
GOOD	86% to 95%	5–6	Total wrong ___
FAIR	76% to 85%	4–5	Total right ___
MARGINAL	70% to 75%	2–3	
NEED IMPROVEMENT	69% or less	1	

A.) *Important*: See the Test Question Cross-Reference List on page 135; circle all the questions you missed on the Valuation Diagnostic Section.

B.) How many questions did you miss in each area?

   1. Recognition Recall–Definition _____
   2. Comprehension–Application _____

35

6
Financing of Real Estate

REVIEW CHECKLIST

The second section of the ETS Examination is structured to test the candidate's proficiency in the area of real estate finance. The ultimate objective of this section is to test your knowledge of the purpose of the legal documents, the mortgage and mortgage note and the nature and the sources of mortgage credit. The finance section will cover these topics:

Financing (20 percent of the test)
- Financial instruments
- Means of financing

Remember, the exam tests your ability to perform on the learning levels of recognition and recall, comprehension and application. You should be prepared to review the following areas:

Recognition and Recall

You should know details of:

1. Mortgage documents:
   - ☐ a. Provisions of the mortgage
   - ☐ b. Provisions of the note
   - ☐ c. Types of mortgages
   - ☐ d. Methods of foreclosure
   - ☐ e. Types of redemption
   - ☐ f. First mortgage vs. second mortgage
   - ☐ g. Mortgagor vs. mortgagee
   - ☐ h. Note vs. mortgage
   - ☐ i. Lien theory vs. title theory

2. Sources of mortgage credit:
   - ☐ a. The money market

REAL ESTATE EXAM MANUAL

    ☐   b.   Conventional loan vs. insured conventional
    ☐   c.   FHA vs. VA mortgages
    ☐   d.   Purchase-money mortgage vs. blanket mortgage
    ☐   e.   Package mortgage vs. open-end mortgage
    ☐   f.   Wraparound vs. straight mortgages
    ☐   g.   Term mortgage vs. amortization mortgage
    ☐   h.   Default vs. foreclosure
    ☐   i.   Regulation Z vs. RESPA
    ☐   j.   Purchase-money mortgage vs. contract for deed
    ☐   k.   Assignment vs. novation
    ☐   l.   Alienation vs. due-on-sale

Comprehension

You must understand:

☐ 1. The differences between a mortgage and a note
☐ 2. The differences between judicial and nonjudicial foreclosure and equitable and statutory redemption
☐ 3. Buyer qualifying ratios
☐ 4. Loan application and origination costs
☐ 5. The methods of seller financing

OUTLINE OF CONCEPTS TO UNDERSTAND

I. SOURCES OF MORTGAGE FUNDS

    A. Primary mortgage market

        1. Savings and loan associations
        2. Mortgage banking companies
        3. Mortgage brokers
        4. Mutual savings banks
        5. Commercial banks
        6. Life insurance companies
        7. Pension funds
        8. Private parties
        9. Credit unions

    B. Secondary mortgage market

        1. Many first mortgages are sold by lenders to the secondary market.
        2. Principal agencies operating in the secondary market include:

            a. Fannie Mae, the Federal National Mortgage Association, originally a federal agency; it became private in 1968.
            b. Ginnie Mae, the Government National Mortgage Association, set up originally under HUD to administer special assistance programs.
            c. Freddie Mac, the Federal Home Loan Mortgage Corporation, created in 1970 as a subsidiary of the Federal Home Loan Bank System. Freddie Mac does not guarantee payment of mortgages.

        3. The secondary market purchases mortgages with funds obtained from investors.

FINANCING OF REAL ESTATE

II. FORMS OF FINANCING
   A. First mortgage–This is the most common type of mortgage, applicable to one piece of property. First mortgage lien usually has priority claim.
   B. Second, third mortgages, etc.–These are similar to first mortgage, except rights are subject to first (and prior) mortgages.
   C. Purchase-money mortgage
       1. Mortgage is given by buyer to seller.
       2. Title passes, in contrast to contract for deed.
   D. Blanket mortgage
       1. Covers more than one piece of property.
       2. Issued to finance developments or an individual's multiple properties.
       3. Allows partial releases; that is, small parcels of the property are released from lien as the loan is paid.
   E. Package mortgage–Covers real estate, fixtures such as appliances and personal property.
   F. Open-end mortgage
       1. Term applies not only to present loan, but also to future advances from lender to borrower, up to original amount of mortgage.
       2. When making future advances, the lender must check for intervening creditors who could have prior rights to payment.
   G. Wraparound mortgage
       1. This form generally is used in refinancing.
       2. A new mortgage is placed against property that encompasses original mortgage and any additional amounts loaned.
       3. Original mortgage remains in existence.
       4. New mortgage is subordinate or subject to original mortgage.
   H. Seller financing
       1. Purchase-money mortgage–A note secured by a mortgage or deed of trust given by a buyer, as mortgagor, to a seller, as mortgagee, as part or all of the purchase price.
       2. Contract for deed–A contract for the sale of real estate wherein the sales price usually is paid in periodic payments until final balance is paid. The purchaser is in possession although the title is retained by the seller.
   I. Assumptions of mortgage or contract–The buyer promises to pay the balance of the seller's obligation to the bank.
       1. Two methods of assumptions.
           a. Assignment–A transfer of rights and/or duties under contract.
           b. Novation–Also a transfer of rights and/or duties under contract.
       2. Special considerations on assumptions.
           a. Alienation clause/due-on-sale–the assumption is not allowable when the original financing documents contain this clause.
           b. FHA/VA assumptions

1. FHA requires novation on all mortgages less than one year old. Any VA loan must follow novation.
2. For FHA mortgages over one year an assignment is allowed. However, the seller is still liable for any default for a period of five years following the assumption.
3. A release of liability on an assumption requires borrower qualification and must be obtained in writing.

III. TYPES OF LOANS

   A. Conventional loans
   1. These are not insured or guaranteed by a government agency.
   2. Security rests on the borrower's ability to pay and the collateral pledged.
   3. As a result of the above, the ratio of loan to value of the property seldom exceeds 80 percent.

   B. Insured conventional loans
   1. Conventional loan in connection with which private insurance is obtained.
   2. Private insurance allows lender to increase loan to value ratio to 90 percent or 95 percent.

   C. FHA-insured loans
   1. The lender is insured against loss by FHA.
   2. Lender provides mortgage loan.
   3. A charge of one-half of one percent of the loan for insurance is required. This one-time mortgage insurance premium is charged to the borrower at closing.
   4. The property must be appraised by an FHA appraiser. The maximum mortgage debt is set by regulation.
   5. Discount points–A fee charged to the parties by the lender to increase mortgage yield.
      a. One point equals one percent of the mortgage.
      b. One point will make up each one-eighth percent difference between the current interest rate and yield ratio. For example, an eight and one-half percent rate vs. a nine percent yield in the market would be offset by four discount points.
   6. The loan to value ratio may be as high as 93–97 percent.
   7. FHA interest rates generally are lower than conventional loans.

   D. Veterans Administration (VA) guaranteed loans
   1. The lender is guaranteed against loss by VA up to the amount of entitlement or 60 percent of the loan, whichever is less.
   2. Lender provides mortgage loan.
   3. Only eligible veterans qualify for the loan and certain unremarried widows and widowers.
   4. Little or no down payment is required. The loan to value can be up to 100 percent.
   5. The limit on the guarantee is set by regulation and can be no more than the appraised value.
   6. A VA one-time funding fee must be paid at closing by buyer or seller or may be added to mortgage at closing. All points must be paid by seller.

FINANCING OF REAL ESTATE

IV. METHODS OF REPAYMENT OF A LOAN
  A. Fixed payment is made in each installment throughout the life of the loan.
    1. Funds are first applied to interest, then to principal.
    2. Debt is amortized.
  B. Graduated payment
    1. Early payments are small, while later payments become larger.
    2. This form accommodates buyers whose ability to pay is greater in later years.
  C. Straight payment plan (term mortgage)
    1. Only the interest is paid during the term of the loan.
    2. The entire principal is due at the end of the term.
  D. Adjustable Rate Mortgage (ARM)
    1. The interest rate on the mortgage adjusts on an annual basis based on a predetermined index and margin.
  E. Loan amortization
    1. Full amortization—Equal payments of principal and interest are scheduled over a period of time (usually 25 or 30 years) until the mortgage balance is at zero.
    2. Partial amortization—Repayment schedule calls for a series of equal payments of principal and interest followed by a balloon payment prior to the balance reading zero (i.e., 30-year amortization will balloon in five years.)
  F. Terms and conditions

V. FORECLOSURE AND REDEMPTION
  A. Foreclosure—Termination of rights of mortgagor after default. Property is sold free of encumbrances (except for possible right of redemption) to collect debt. Three methods of foreclosure exist:
    1. Advertisement (nonjudicial)
      a. Notice of default and public sale is given in the newspaper.
      b. A power-of-sale clause in the mortgage usually is required.
      c. The property is sold to the highest bidder at a public sale.
    2. Action (judicial)
      a. Mortgagee sues mortgagor in court and obtains judgment and court order to sell.
      b. The property is sold to the highest bidder at a public sale.
    3. Strict foreclosure—In this summary procedure, the court may award title to the mortgagee.
  B. Redemption—Through this process the mortgagor regains interest in the property. Two types of redemption exist:
    1. Equitable redemption—Redemption occurs prior to the completion of public sale.

a. The amount currently due plus costs must be paid.
b. The mortgage is reinstated.

2. Statutory redemption—Redemption occurs after the finalized public sale.

a. State law specifies the length of time within which the debtor may redeem his or her property.
b. The debtor pays the mortgage plus the costs set by state statute.
c. If the debtor does not redeem, subordinate creditors may redeem.
d. If the property is not redeemed within the prescribed redemption period, the highest bidder at the public sale generally receives title to the property.

C. Deficiencies—If proceeds from the sale of property are insufficient to pay the mortgage plus foreclosure expenses, the difference is a deficiency. Often the mortgagee can sue the mortgagor for the difference. This process is called suing for a deficiency judgment.

VI. PARTIES TO A MORTGAGE

A. Mortgagor—Borrower, the signer of a pledge
B. Mortgagee—Lender, the receiver of a pledge
C. In some areas, Trustee—A third party to whom property is conveyed in a trust deed.

1. Property is conveyed by the trustor (borrower) for the benefit of the beneficiary (lender).

VII. MORTGAGE INSTRUMENTS—In every mortgage situation, two documents must be executed:

A. Note—Evidence of debt. The debtor agrees to repay the stated loan. The note is a negotiable instrument.
B. Mortgage—Security instrument. It gives the lender a security interest in the property.

VIII. THEORIES OF MORTGAGE LAW

A. Lien theory—Mortgagor remains owner; mortgagee has lien.
B. Title theory—Property is actually conveyed to mortgagee, subject to an agreement to return the property if debt is paid. In some areas, property is actually conveyed to a trustee on behalf of the mortgagee.

IX. OTHER TERMS TO REMEMBER

A. Balloon payment—A final payment on a loan that is larger than all of the other periodic payments.
B. Variable interest rates—The rate of interest over the duration of the loan varies. Usually the rate is tied to changes in the discount rate or the prime lending rate.
C. Prepayment penalty—A penalty for prepaying a mortgage or contract deed. Prohibited on some loans.
D. Acceleration clause—This allows the mortgagee to sue for the entire balance of the mortgage after the mortgagor defaults.
E. Alienation clause—This allows the mortgagee to prevent the purchaser of the

property from assuming the mortgagor's loan, particularly at its old rate of interest. Also referred to as due-on-sale clause.

F. Defeasance clause–When the mortgage note has been fully paid, the mortgagee must execute a release indicating that all interest in the real estate is reconveyed to the mortgagor.
G. Usury–A charge of interest in excess of the maximum rate allowed by law.
H. Contract rate–Rate of interest charged on interest-bearing loans when no interest rate is indicated in the loan agreement.
I. Subordination agreement–Agreement between two creditors that changes the order of priority of their liens.
J. Satisfaction of mortgage or release deed–Document by which a mortgage is acknowledged paid in full and its lien released.
K. Earnest money–Payment made by buyer at time of signing sales agreement to show good faith. It is applied to purchase price; if transaction fails because of seller's breach, it is returned to buyer. If buyer defaults, buyer may forfeit it.
L. Equity–Financial interest of owner of property, that is, the difference between the value of property and the mortgage balance.
M. Fixture–Items of personal property (e.g., appliances) that have been affixed to real estate and therefore become real property.
N. Fixed rate mortgage–The interest remains the same throughout the term of the loan.
O. Adjustable rate mortgage–The interest rate changes periodically during the term of the loan. The rate is tied to changes in a specified index such as U.S. Treasury notes.

DIAGNOSTIC TEST

1. Who is the individual who obtains a real estate loan by signing a note and a mortgage?

   (A) Mortgagor
   (B) Mortgagee
   (C) Optionor
   (D) Optionee

2. Which of the following describes a mortgage that uses both real and personal property as security?

   (A) Blanket mortgage
   (B) Package mortgage
   (C) Purchase-money mortgage
   (D) Wraparound mortgage

3. Which of the following describes a mortgage that requires principal and interest payments at regular intervals until the debt is satisfied?

   (A) Term mortgage
   (B) Amortized mortgage
   (C) First mortgage
   (D) Balloon mortgage

4. What is the clause in a mortgage or trust deed that permits a lender to declare the entire unpaid sum due upon the borrower's default?

   (A) Judgment clause
   (B) Acceleration clause
   (C) Forfeiture clause
   (D) Escalator clause

5. When obtaining a mortgage, the borrower signs a mortgage and a mortgage note. The mortgage note:

    (A) is a negotiable instrument.
    (B) must be signed by the vendor.
    (C) must be signed by the mortgagee.
    (D) must be recorded to be valid.

6. A mortgage must include a power-of-sale clause to be foreclosed:

    (A) by action.
    (B) by advertisement.
    (C) by judicial procedure.
    (D) by the Federal Housing Administration.

7. Discount points on FHA-insured mortgages:

    (A) must be charged to the seller.
    (B) represent the percentage by which the face amount of a mortgage is increased when it is sold to an investor.
    (C) must be paid by the buyer.
    (D) may be added to the mortgage.

8. Which of the following best describes Fannie Mae's function?

    (A) It regulates lending terms and policies of member banks.
    (B) It absorbs any losses incurred by Ginnie Mae.
    (C) It purchases FHA and VA loans.
    (D) It insures FHA loans.

9. In many states, by paying the debt after a foreclosure sale, the mortgagor has the right to regain the property. What is this right called?

    (A) Acceleration   (C) Reversion
    (B) Redemption   (D) Recapture

10. The Real Estate Settlement Procedures Act requires:

    (A) that the closing of a real estate transaction be held within 90 days of the execution of the purchase agreement.
    (B) that disclosure be made of all closing costs prior to the closing.
    (C) the seller's approval of the buyer's statement.
    (D) a qualified buyer.

11. In a lien theory state:

    (A) the mortgagee takes title to the mortgaged property during the term of the mortgage.
    (B) the mortgagor has a lien against the property for the full amount of the mortgage.
    (C) the mortgagor may foreclose only by action.
    (D) the mortgagor holds title to the property during the term of the mortgage.

12. Gloria Stones is qualified to obtain an FHA loan for the purchase of a new home. From which of the following may she obtain this loan?

    (A) Federal Housing Administration
    (B) Federal National Mortgage Association
    (C) A qualified Federal Housing Administration mortgagee
    (D) Federal Home Loan Bank System

FINANCING OF REAL ESTATE

13. A security device that allows the lender to increase the outstanding balance of a loan up to the original sum of the note in order to advance additional funds is called:

    (A) an open-end mortgage.
    (B) a wraparound mortgage.
    (C) an all-inclusive deed of trust.
    (D) interim financing.

14. If the yield on a 30-year loan is ten and one-fourth percent and a mortgage lender charges three points, what is the rate on the mortgage note?

    (A) Nine and one-half percent
    (B) Ten and five-eighth percent
    (C) Ten percent
    (D) Nine and seven-eighth percent

15. A mortgage instrument may include a clause that would prevent the assumption of the mortgage by a new purchaser. What is this clause?

    (A) An alienation clause
    (B) Power of sale
    (C) Defeasance clause
    (D) Certificate of sale

16. The defeasance clause in a mortgage requires the mortgagee to execute a(n):

    (A) assignment of mortgage.
    (B) satisfaction of mortgage.
    (C) subordination agreement.
    (D) partial release agreement.

17. The supply of mortgage credit for single-family homes is regulated by the Federal Reserve System through the use of which of the following?

    (A) Reserve requirements and discount rates
    (B) Federal National Mortgage Association
    (C) Federal Housing Administration
    (D) Housing and Urban Development Corporation

18. Which of the following normally purchase mortgages in the secondary mortgage market?

    (A) Mortgage banking companies, savings and loans, commercial banks and mutual savings banks
    (B) Fannie Mae, Ginnie Mae and Freddie Mac
    (C) Federal Housing Administration
    (D) Veterans Administration

19. John Babbit enters into a contract with Wally Jaansen wherein Babbit will sell his house to Jaansen for $40,000. Jaansen cannot get complete financing, and at the closing Babbit and Jaansen enter into a contract for deed. Upon signing of the contract for deed, Jaansen's interest in the property is that of:

    (A) legal title.
    (B) equitable title.
    (C) joint title.
    (D) mortgagee in possession.

45

ANSWER KEY

Question	Answer	Type of Question	Topic Area	Outline Reference	Page
1.	(A)	Recognition Recall–Definition	Parties to mortgage	VI.A.	42
2.	(B)	Comprehension–Application	Types of mortgages	II.E.	39
3.	(B)	Recognition Recall–Definition	Repayment of loan	IV.E.1.	41
4.	(B)	Recognition Recall–Definition	Terms	IX.D.	42
5.	(A)	Comprehension–Application	Mortgage instruments	VII.A.	42
6.	(B)	Recognition Recall–Definition	Foreclosure	V.A.1.b.	41
7.	(B)	Recognition Recall–Definition	Types of loans	III.C.5.	40
8.	(C)	Recognition Recall–Definition	Sources of mortgage funds	I.B.2.a.	38
9.	(B)	Recognition Recall–Definition	Foreclosure and redemption	V.B.	41
10.	(B)	Recognition Recall–Definition	RESPA	V.C.	50
11.	(D)	Recognition Recall–Definition	Lien theory	VIII.A.	42
12.	(C)	Comprehension–Application	Sources of mortgage funds	I.A.	38
13.	(A)	Recognition Recall–Definition	Types of mortgages	II.F.	39
14.	(D)	Comprehension–Application	Types of loans	III.C.5.b.	40
15.	(A)	Recognition Recall–Definition	Other terms	IX.E.	42
16.	(B)	Recognition Recall–Definition	Other terms	IX.F.	42
17.	(A)	Comprehension–Application	Federal Reserve System		
18.	(B)	Recognition Recall–Definition	Sources of mortgage funds	I.B.2.	38
19.	(B)	Comprehension–Application	Equitable title	II.H.2.	39

FINANCING OF REAL ESTATE

Progress Score

Rating	Percentage	Range	Your Score
EXCELLENT	96% to 100%	19	Financing 19
GOOD	86% to 95%	17–18	Total wrong —
FAIR	76% to 85%	15–16	Total right =
MARGINAL	70% to 75%	13–14	
NEED IMPROVEMENT	69% or less	12 or less	

A.) *Important*: See the Test Question Cross-Reference List on page 135; circle all the questions you missed on the Financing Diagnostic Section.

B.) How many questions did you miss in each area?

   1. Recognition Recall–Definition _____
   2. Comprehension–Application _____

7
Transfer of Property Ownership

REVIEW CHECKLIST

A key part of completing a real estate transaction is the financial and legal close of the property. In this section of the exam you must be able to demonstrate your knowledge of the types of title to real property, the methods of conveying ownership, the legal procedures for dealing with title problems and an understanding of the closing process. This section will cover the following two areas:

Ownership (15 percent of the test)
- Titles to real property
- Settlement procedures

Recognition and Recall

You should know the distinctions between:

- [ ] 1. Warranty deed vs. quitclaim deed
- [ ] 2. Covenant of seisin vs. special warranty deed
- [ ] 3. Absolute delivery of deed vs. delivery in escrow
- [ ] 4. State deed stamps vs. mortgage registration tax
- [ ] 5. Abstract of title vs. Torrens title
- [ ] 6. Joint tenancy vs. tenancy by entirety
- [ ] 7. Trustor vs. trustee
- [ ] 8. Testate vs. intestate
- [ ] 9. RESPA vs. truth in lending

Comprehension

You must understand:

- [ ] 1. The differences among joint tenancy, tenancy in common, tenancy by the entirety and community property rights
- [ ] 2. The basic elements of a deed and the differences among warranty deed, special warranty deed and quitclaim deed
- [ ] 3. Community property rights
- [ ] 4. Ownership in trust
- [ ] 5. The four unities of joint tenancy
- [ ] 6. The passing of title

REAL ESTATE EXAM MANUAL

OUTLINE OF CONCEPTS TO UNDERSTAND

I. PROOF OF TITLE

A. Types of proof of title

1. Abstract of title and lawyer's opinion–Abstract is a history of title, which an attorney searches for flaws.
2. Title insurance–An insurance policy that indemnifies the holder against certain defects, for example, defects in public record, forgery or defective transfers.
   a. In general, extended coverage will cause further checks of the property, the persons in possession, etc., to be made to eliminate additional risks to the client.
   b. Most regular policies exclude coverage against such situations as unrecorded documents, defects the policyholder has knowledge of, questions of survey and persons in possession.
3. Torrens system–A certificate of title is filed with the Registrar's Office, along with the owner's signature. The person whose name appears on the certificate is considered the owner. Torrens property cannot be taken by adverse possession.

II. TYPES OF DEEDS–A deed is the document that conveys title to real estate; It is not a proof of ownership. It must be signed by the grantor or by the attorney-in-fact, pursuant to a power of attorney.

A. Warranty deed–When a seller "conveys and warrants" good title, he or she is providing the buyer with the greatest protection. Basic covenants are:

1. Seisin–The seller has the right to convey ownership.
2. Against encumbrance–The property is free from liens except as noted in the deed.
3. Quiet enjoyment–The buyer can quietly enjoy the property without good claims on it by third parties.
4. Warrant forever–The seller's warranty is good now and forever.
5. Further assurance–The grantor gives assurance with respect to acts of previous owners in the chain of title. For example, grantor Harry Michaels may obtain a quitclaim deed signed by his wife that releases her dower interest.

B. Special warranty deed (Limited warranty deed)

1. The owner warrants only that he or she has not done anything to harm title.
2. This warranty covers only the period of time when the seller owned the property.

C. Quitclaim deed–The seller gives no covenants or warranties, not even that he or she has any interest in the property. The seller is only agreeing to convey whatever interest, if any, he or she has in the property; often used to cure title defects.

D. Other deeds include grant deeds, bargain and sale deeds, deeds involving trusts, administrator's deeds, executor's deeds, trustee's deed or deeds in trust.

TRANSFER OF PROPERTY OWNERSHIP

III. HOW OWNERSHIP IS HELD

  A. Basic ways to hold ownership

  1. In severalty–by a sole owner
  2. Co-ownership–by two or more owners
  3. In trust–by a third party, for one or more persons

  B. Co-ownership

  1. Tenancy in common–Two or more holders own fractions of an undivided interest.

     a. Fractions may differ among owners; for example, one owner may hold two-thirds' interest and the other one-third.
     b. Co-owner may pass interest on to heirs, or sell it.
     c. Co-owner may sue to partition; either divide interest into separate parts, or force a sale to release his or her interest in the property.
     d. If the character of a tenancy is not specified, as in tenancy by entireties or joint tenancy, most states assume tenancy in common.
     e. No right of survivorship.

  2. Joint tenancy–Two or more holders own fractions of an undivided interest.

     a. Fractions are always equal, usually one-half undivided interest.
     b. The right of survivorship applies; that is, survivors absorb deceased's ownership of property.
     c. Four unities are required–title, time, interest and possession.
     d. It can be created only by will or deed; it cannot be implied by law.
     e. A joint tenant may sell or convey his or her interest during his lifetime, but the successor is a tenant in common with the other tenant(s). Only the last surviving tenant can pass property on to his or her heirs by will or descent.
     f. Joint tenants may sue for partition of property.
     g. No dower, curtesy or inheritance rights exist under this type of ownership.

  3. Tenancy by the entirety–This tenancy is similar to joint tenancy except:

     a. Tenants must be husband and wife, each owning one-half undivided interest.
     b. Tenants cannot partition the interest. Title may be sold only when the deed is signed by both parties.
     c. Right of survivorship exists.

  4. Community property rights

     a. Community property: each spouse owns one-half the property acquired during the marriage
     b. Separate property: each spouse may exclusively own property that was, for example, brought to the marriage, or received by one spouse as a gift or inheritance during the marriage

  C. Ownership in trust

  1. Property is transferred from trustor to trustee.

2. The trustee owns for the benefit of beneficiaries designated in the trust document.
3. Land trusts limit the property of trust to real estate alone.

IV. TRANSFER OF MARKETABLE TITLE
   A. Voluntary alienation
      1. By gift
      2. By sale
   B. By involuntary alienation or involuntary taking–The owner does not consent to the transfer of the property.
   C. By will (testate), or transfer by devise
      1. The owner of the property specifies who will inherit it at the time of his or her death.
      2. The will, however, is subject to state laws that give the surviving spouse rights of dower, curtesy or the option to take against the will.
   D. By descent–A person dies without a will, or intestate. State statute determines how the property will be divided. Usually the decedent's closest living relatives inherit the property.

V. REAL ESTATE SETTLEMENT PROCEDURES ACT (RESPA) Requirements
   A. Buyer and seller must have knowledge of all settlement costs prior to closing.
   B. This knowledge should be supplied by:
      1. Banks
      2. Savings and loans
      3. Other lenders whose deposits are insured by FDIC or FSLIC, whose mortgages are insured by FHA, guaranteed by VA or administered by HUD, or who intend to sell mortgages to Fannie Mae, Ginnie Mae or Freddie Mac
   C. RESPA regulations require compliance with the following
      1. A special information booklet, "Settlement Costs and You," must be given to each loan applicant.
      2. A good faith estimate of settlement costs must be supplied to the borrower.
      3. A Uniform Settlement Statement (HUD Form 1) must be used in the loan closing.
      4. Kickbacks are strictly prohibited.

VI. RECORDING DEEDS AND PASSING OF TITLE
   A. In most cases, title and responsibility for risk pass when an executed deed is delivered.
   B. Exceptions:
      1. Closing in escrow–Although title passes when the deed is delivered, the date of passing falls back to the date the deed was placed in escrow. If escrow does not close, however, no title passes.
      2. Torrens property–Title transfers when a certificate of Torrens is registered.
   C. The deed is recorded for protection against a third party.
      1. Recording gives constructive notice to the world of the buyer's interest.

2. When there are conflicting claims to a property, the one that was recorded first usually has priority. Main exceptions are:
   a. Actual notice–Persons who had actual notice, that is, direct information, of an unrecorded document, have a lesser claim.
   b. Possession–By taking possession of a property, an individual gives notice to the world that he or she has an interest in it, even if the deed is not recorded. It is the duty of a prospective buyer to find out what that interest is. If the buyer obtains and records a deed without inspecting the property, he or she has a lesser claim to it than the person possessing it.
3. In order for a deed to be recorded, many states require that it be acknowledged by a notary public or other officer.

VII. ACCOUNTING FOR CHARGES (Debits) and Credits to the Buyer and Seller
   A. Accrued items (expenses)–Items that have been earned during the occupancy or ownership of the seller, but have not been paid, e.g., taxes.
   B. Prepaid items–Items that have been prepaid by the seller, but have not been fully used up, e.g., insurance.
   C. Proration procedures
      1. Determine what the item to be prorated is, e.g., loan interest, fuel bills.
      2. Determine whether it is an accrued item.
      3. Determine whether it is a prepaid item.
      4. Determine which method of calculating prorations should be used.
         a. Statutory method–Assume a 360-day year, 30-day month. This method is usually used in prorating mortgage interest, general real estate taxes and insurance premiums.
         b. Per annum method–Assume a 365-day year, calendar number of days per month.

DIAGNOSTIC TEST

1. Property held by tenancy by the entirety requires which of the following?
   (A) The cotenants must be husband and wife.
   (B) The property in question must be Torrens property.
   (C) Upon the death of a cotenant, the decedent's interest passes to his or her heirs.
   (D) In the event of a dispute the property must be partitioned.

2. Henry Sorvino sold a parcel of real estate to Marlin Kabul and gave Kabul a quitclaim deed. Upon receipt of the deed Kabul may be certain:
   (A) that Sorvino owned the property.
   (B) that there are no encumbrances against the property.
   (C) that Kabul now owns the property subject to certain claims of Sorvino.
   (D) that all interests of Sorvino in the property as of the date of the deed belong to Kabul.

3. Normally, title to property passes when a deed is delivered. Which of the following is an exception to the general rule?
   (A) Title to abstract property is transferred when the deed is recorded.
   (B) Title to Torrens property is transferred when the certificate is registered.
   (C) Title to abstract trust property is transferred upon the death of the beneficiary.
   (D) Title to Torrens property is transferred when the deed is delivered to a licensed realtor.

4. In a community property state:

   (A) the property that a person accumulated prior to marriage is called separate property.
   (B) the property that a person received as a gift during marriage is known as community property.
   (C) all property owned by a married person is called community property.
   (D) the property paid for by the earnings of one spouse during the marriage is known as separate property.

5. All of the following are examples of a proof of title EXCEPT:

   (A) an abstract of title and lawyer's opinion.
   (B) a Torrens certificate.
   (C) title insurance.
   (D) a deed.

6. All of the following are elements of a joint tenancy with right of survivorship EXCEPT:

   (A) it is created only when four unities are present.
   (B) it cannot be created by operation of law.
   (C) each joint tenant may pass on his or her interest to the heirs.
   (D) the land may be the subject of a suit to partition.

7. Boris Short sells certain property to David Janacek and gives Janacek a special warranty deed. Which of the following is true?

   (A) Short is making additional warranties beyond those given in a warranty deed.
   (B) Short's property is Torrens property.
   (C) Short is warranting that no encumbrances have ever been placed against the property that have not been satisfied or released.
   (D) Short's warranties are limited to the time he held the property.

8. Sandy Jacobs and Neva Cole bought a store building and took title as joint tenants with right of survivorship. Cole died testate. Jacobs now owns the store:

   (A) as a joint tenant with rights of survivorship.
   (B) in severalty.
   (C) in absolute ownership under the law of descent.
   (D) subject to the terms of Cole's will.

9. Samantha Hogan sold her house to Buddy Howard. Howard, however, forgot to record this deed. Under these circumstances:

   (A) the transfer of property between Hogan and Howard is ineffective.
   (B) Howard's interest is not fully protected against third parties.
   (C) the deed is invalid after 90 days.
   (D) the deed is invalid after six months.

10. Alonzo Commers, a single person, owned a parcel of land. Subsequent to Commers's death the probate court determined the descent of the parcel of land in accordance with the state statutes. Commers therefore died:

    (A) testate.
    (B) intestate.
    (C) corporeal.
    (D) incorporeal.

TRANSFER OF PROPERTY OWNERSHIP

ANSWER KEY

Question	Answer	Type of Question	Topic Area	Outline Reference	Page
1.	(A)	Comprehension–Application	Tenancy by entirety	III.B.3.	49
2.	(D)	Comprehension–Application	Types of deeds	II.C.	48
3.	(B)	Comprehension–Application	Passing title	VI.B.2.	50
4.	(A)	Recognition Recall–Definition	Community property	III.B.4.b.	49
5.	(D)	Recognition Recall–Definition	Proof of title	I.A.	48
6.	(C)	Comprehension–Application	Joint tenancy	III.B.2.	49
7.	(D)	Comprehension–Application	Special warranty deed	II.B.	48
8.	(B)	Comprehension–Application	Ownership in severalty	III.A.1.	49
9.	(B)	Comprehension–Application	Deed validity	VI.C.	50
10.	(B)	Recognition Recall–Definition	Intestate	IV.D.	50

TRANSFER OF PROPERTY OWNERSHIP

Progress Score

Rating	Percentage	Range	Your Score
EXCELLENT	96% to 100%	10	Ownership 10
GOOD	86% to 95%	8–9	Total wrong —
FAIR	76% to 85%	6–7	Total right =
MARGINAL	70% to 75%	4–5	
NEED IMPROVEMENT	69% or less	3 or less	

A.) *Important*: See the Test Question Cross-Reference List on page 136; circle all the questions you missed on the Transfer of Ownership Diagnostic Section.

B.) How many questions did you miss in each area?

   1. Recognition Recall Definition _____.
   2. Comprehension–Application _____.

8
Real Estate Brokerage

REVIEW CHECKLIST

This section of the examination will evaluate the potential licensee's knowledge of the responsibilities, duties and functions of a real estate salesperson and broker. Because one of the final stages of a real estate transaction is the transfer of ownership, you must have a clear understanding of the expenses involved in closing a transaction and the method of determining the cost and expenses involved in the sale and be able to adjust the settlement expenses to the closing date. In addition, you should be familiar with the functions, responsibilities and duties of a property manager.

As a broker or salesperson you must be able to accurately and properly prepare listing agreements, purchase agreements, leases and options as well as have a basic understanding of mortgages and deeds. Consequently, one area of the ETS examination will evaluate your proficiency in the area of real estate contracts. The objective is to test the potential licensee's ability to comprehend the results and/or consequences of specific details in a real estate contract. You must be prepared to accurately calculate commissions, discount points, down payments, mortgage balances and square footage of an area. This section will test you on the subject areas:

Real Estate Brokerage (25 percent of the test)
- Agency relationship and responsibilities
- Listing of real property
- Negotiating real estate contracts
- Federal laws relating to fair practices

Recognition and Recall

You should be able to distinguish between:

- ☐ 1. Broker vs. fiduciary
- ☐ 2. Principal vs. agent
- ☐ 3. Puffing vs. fraud
- ☐ 4. Price fixing vs. allocation of market
- ☐ 5. Exclusive agency listing vs. exclusive right to sell
- ☐ 6. Open listing vs. net listing

REAL ESTATE EXAM MANUAL

- ☐ 7. Listing agreement vs. multiple-listing service
- ☐ 8. Property manager vs. building manager
- ☐ 9. The six essential elements of a legal contract
- ☐ 10. Treatment of earnest money
- ☐ 11. Assignment vs. novation
- ☐ 12. Legal effect of contract
- ☐ 13. Discharge vs. breach of contract
- ☐ 14. Principal parts of a sales contract, option, listing agreement, lease and escrow agreement
- ☐ 15. Bilateral vs. unilateral contracts
- ☐ 16. Expressed vs. implied contracts
- ☐ 17. Valid vs. void contracts
- ☐ 18. Voidable vs. unenforceable contracts
- ☐ 19. Statute of limitations vs. statute of frauds

Comprehension

You should understand the principles and practices of:

- ☐ 1. Civil Rights Act of 1866 vs. federal housing laws
- ☐ 2. Regulation Z requirements
- ☐ 3. The responsibilities and functions of a salesperson with regard to the principal and broker
- ☐ 4. The law of agency
- ☐ 5. The computation of compensation on a real estate transaction
- ☐ 6. The differences among exclusive right-to-sell listing, open listing, net listing and multiple-listing service
- ☐ 7. The functions of a property manager and principal parts of the management agreement
- ☐ 8. The rights and duties of the parties to a contract
- ☐ 9. The obligations of the broker and seller under a contract
- ☐ 10. The types, functions and advantages of the different listing contracts
- ☐ 11. The rights of the seller and buyer when a contract is revoked or canceled
- ☐ 12. The application of the statute of frauds in a purchase agreement

OUTLINE OF CONCEPTS TO UNDERSTAND

I. LAW OF AGENCY

A. Broker is an agent.
B. Principal may be an owner, lessor, seller or buyer of property. The broker owes fiduciary duty to the principal.
C. The principal may be a prospective buyer or seller of a property. Even though the broker owes fiduciary duty to the principal, the broker is obligated to disclose all facts concerning a property to the other parties to the transaction. It is the seller's responsibility to reveal any latent defects to the buyer.
D. The real estate broker is a special agent; that is, one who works for a principal on one specific transaction only. Brokers are authorized to negotiate contracts, but have no power to buy or sell property, or to bind the principal to a contract.
E. To be entitled to a brokerage fee, a broker must (by statute):

   1. Be licensed during the period of agency

2. Be employed by a principal under a written listing contract
3. Be the procuring cause of the sale
4. Act in good faith

F. To receive a brokerage fee, or commission, you must be employed by the seller and find a ready, willing and able buyer whose offer is accepted by the seller and close the transaction. The commission is due even if:

1. The seller backs out of the transaction.
2. The buyer rescinds because of seller's fraud of which the broker had no knowledge.

G. It is illegal for a broker to share a fee with someone who is not licensed.
H. Dual agency, that is, one broker representing both the buyer and the seller in a single transaction, is prohibited unless the broker obtains both parties' prior consent.
I. The broker must not act as an agent and undisclosed party to a transaction. Any personal interest in property must be made known to and accepted by the other party.
J. The broker must not receive profit, fee or rebate from a transaction without the consent of the principal.
K. The broker must present all offers to the principal.
L. The broker must have a fixed place of business.
M. The broker must keep a trust account for all money in his or her possession belonging to others.
N. Most states prohibit placing blind ads; that is, advertisements that do not indicate the broker is the advertiser. Ads placed by salespeople must also identify their associated or employing broker.
O. Unless the consent of the listing broker is obtained, all negotiations must take place through the listing broker rather than directly with the owner.

II. SALESPERSON

A. The salesperson acts on behalf of the broker.
B. The salesperson has no direct relationship with the principal, but is responsible only to the broker.
C. The salesperson may be either an employee of the broker or an independent contractor working under the broker.

III. ETHICAL CONSIDERATIONS FOR BROKERS

A. Fraud–Puffing vs. fraud

1. Puffing is an opinion.
2. Fraud is a misrepresentation of facts.

B. Violations of antitrust laws

1. Price fixing–Brokers conspire to receive the same fee for services.
2. Allocation of the market–Brokers conspire to restrict competition by dividing the market into exclusive areas of operation. For example, the market may be allocated by geography or by the price of the home.

C. REALTOR'S® canon of ethics

1. Toward the general public

2. Toward clients
3. Toward fellow brokers

IV. TYPES OF LISTING AGREEMENTS
   A. Open listing
      1. Any number of brokers may be retained. The broker who sells the property receives the commission.
      2. If the owner finds a buyer, no broker receives a commission.
   B. Exclusive agency listing
      1. Only one broker is authorized to sell.
      2. If the owner finds a buyer, the broker does not receive a commission.
   C. Exclusive right-to-sell listing
      1. Only one broker is authorized to sell.
      2. If the owner finds a buyer, the broker still receives a commission during the term of agency.
   D. Net listing
      1. The broker's commission is whatever amount is received above a quoted net price.
      2. This arrangement is frowned upon by most states, and outlawed by some.

V. OTHER BROKER SERVICES
   A. Guaranteed sale plan–The broker agrees to buy a house if it is not sold within a specified time for a specified minimum price. The broker's purchase price is the minimum price.
   B. Multiple-listing service
      1. Brokers formally exchange information on listings.
      2. Commissions are split between the listing and selling brokers, according to the individual agreement between them.
      3. Commissions are negotiable
         a. between the seller and broker
         b. between brokers

VI. REAL ESTATE BROKERS
   A. Real estate brokers engage in the sale of real estate.
      1. Agent in sale of real estate
      2. Acts on behalf of principal
      3. Regulated by state statutes

VII. ESSENTIAL ELEMENTS OF A CONTRACT
   A. Competent parties–Both buyer and seller must be of sound mind and legal age.
   B. Offer and acceptance–There must be a meeting of minds on the terms of a contract.
   C. Consideration–Something of value must be exchanged, either money or valuable goods or a promise.
   D. Legal object
   E. Written and signed agreement
   F. Accurate description of the real estate

VIII. CONTRACT CLASSIFICATIONS

A. Bilateral–Contract contains two promises; for example, one party agrees to sell, and the other to buy.
B. Unilateral–Contract contains one promise for a completed act; however, there is no obligation to act.
C. Expressed–Parties' intentions are expressed, either orally or in written form.
D. Executed–Both parties have fulfilled the obligations in the contract.
E. Executory–Something remains to be completed by one or both parties.
F. Implied–Intention is shown by act of a party.

IX. LEGAL EFFECTS OF A CONTRACT

A. Valid–The contract contains all essential elements, and is binding and enforceable by both parties.
B. Void–The contract has no legal effect because it does not contain all essential elements.
C. Voidable–The contract may be disaffirmed by at least one party. It is, however, valid until disaffirmed. Reasons to disaffirm include:
  1. Fraud–The contract can be disaffirmed only by the victim of fraud or duress.
  2. Duress, or undue influence
  3. Minority–The contract is disaffirmed until the party's majority is reached, plus reasonable time.
D. Unenforceable–A party fails to perform, but the other party cannot sue for performance. Either an essential element is missing in the contract, or the second party did not sue before the statute of limitations ran out.

X. PERFORMANCE/DISCHARGE OF A CONTRACT/BREACH OF CONTRACT

A. Contracts are discharged by:
  1. Performance
  2. Substantial performance–Party is not released from liability because of a technical deficiency to complete the terms of a contract.
  3. Mutual agreement releasing performance
  4. Impossibility of performance–For example, destruction of the property or the death of a principal constitutes impossibility of performance.
B. If a contract is not discharged, it is breached; that is, one party has defaulted or failed to perform. The other party has remedy.
  1. When seller has defaulted, the buyer may:
     a. rescind, or terminate, the contract.
     b. sue for specific performance, and force the other party to perform.
     c. sue for damages–This is usually an amount of money that would partially compensate the innocent party.
  2. When buyer has defaulted, the seller may:
     a. perform any of the three preceding options.
     b. in most cases, declare the contract forfeited–In real estate, the seller may retain earnest money and other payments already received.

REAL ESTATE EXAM MANUAL

XI. KEY POINTS TO REMEMBER

A. Statute of limitations–This refers to the length of time within which a party may sue; for example, "x" years from date of breach of contract, or "y" years from date of discovery of fraud.

B. Statute of frauds–Its full name is Statute for Prevention of Fraud and Perjury. It requires:
   1. that certain contracts be in writing before a party can enforce them.
   2. that in real estate, as a general rule, all contracts for sale of land and all leases of more than one year be in writing and signed by all parties.

C. Parol Evidence Rule–This rule states that any prior, or contemporary oral or extraneously written agreements cannot change the terms of a contract.
   1. A complete, written contract must exist for this rule to apply.
   2. The rule does not apply to subsequent oral or written evidence.

D. Assignment–Assignment is a transfer of rights and/or duties under contract.
   1. Rights can be assigned, unless the contract expressly forbids assigning them.
   2. Obligations can often be assigned, but the original party is secondarily liable if the assignee does not perform.
   3. Differs from a sublease in that a sublease is a new second lease that may include new terms.

E. Novation–Novation also is a transfer of rights and/or duties under contract.
   1. The original contract is canceled.
   2. A new contract is renegotiated and redrawn, with same parties or new second party.
   3. The original party, if replaced, is not liable.

F. Offer, acceptance and counteroffer–First party makes an offer to enter into a contract; other party can accept the offer exactly as made, reject the offer or make a counteroffer. Remember that:
   1. the offer remains open until withdrawn or terminated.
   2. the offer may be withdrawn any time before it is accepted.
   3. rejection terminates an offer.
   4. a counteroffer automatically rejects (and terminates) an offer.
   5. once terminated, an offer cannot be reinstated unless it is renegotiated.
   6. the offer is terminated by death of the offeror or destruction of a thing essential to the agreement.

G. Equitable title–The vendee's interest in real estate, when less than full legal title.
   1. Often a person with equitable title eventually will have legal title when all conditions of the sales agreement are fulfilled.
   2. Examples:
      a. Contract for deed (or land contract)–Legal title is conveyed to vendee after contract is paid in full or terms of contract have been met.
      b. Pending sale–This is the period after signing purchase agreement, but before the transfer of title.

H. Earnest money–A deposit made by buyer when entering a sales contract to show good faith. It is applied to the purchase price at closing or returned to the buyer if cancellation is due to no fault of the buyer.
I. Option–An optionee (for example, a prospective buyer) agrees to pay money or consideration to optionor (a prospective seller) for the right to purchase a property for a certain price within a certain period of time.
   1. While the agreement is in effect, the seller must sell to the buyer if he chooses to purchase the property.
   2. The buyer is not obligated to purchase the property.
J. Escrow agreement–An agreement in which parties to a contract empower a third party to assist in carrying out the terms and conditions of the contract.
   1. The escrow agent must ensure that the transaction is closed as required by the sales contract, or by additional changes agreed to by both the purchaser and seller.
   2. Seller must deposit with the escrow agent the deed and other documents relating to the title.
   3. Purchaser must deposit with the escrow agent the purchase price and executed mortgage and note (if applicable).
   4. If the title is unacceptable and the sale is canceled, all parties are restored to their pre-escrow positions.
K. Right of first refusal–An agreement in which an offer must be made to a specific person before it can be made to anyone else.

XII. TYPES OF CONTRACTS USED IN REAL ESTATE
A. Listing agreement–Between seller and broker
B. Real estate sales contract (purchase agreement)–Between seller and buyer
C. Option–Between optionor and optionee
D. Installment contract (contract for deed, land contract)–Between seller and buyer
E. Lease–Between landlord and tenant (lessor and lessee)

XIII. FEDERAL FAIR HOUSING LAWS
A. Civil Rights Act of 1866–Prohibits all racial discrimination, public or private, in the sale or rental of all real or personal property.
B. Fair Housing Law of 1968–Makes it unlawful to discriminate because of race, color, religion, sex, national origin, familial status or handicap.
   1. Prohibited discrimination includes:
      a. refusing to sell, rent or negotiate with any person.
      b. changing the terms of a transaction for certain people.
      c. discriminatory advertisement.
      d. wrongly representing that a house is unavailable.
      e. blockbusting–inducing an owner to sell by representing that minorities will be moving into his or her neighborhood.
      f. redlining–refusing to make loans or provide insurance to persons in certain areas, regardless of their qualifications.
      g. steering–leading prospective homeowners to or away from certain areas in order to create a speculative situation.
      h. denying membership in MLS services or similar organizations.

2. Exemptions from the law
    a. The sale or rental of a single-family home
        1) that is owned by a person who does not own more than three other homes
        2) in which the owner currently is living, or was the most recent occupant
        3) for which no broker was used
        4) about which no discriminatory advertising was used
    b. The rental of a room or unit in an owner-occupied one- to four-family dwelling
    c. Rooms owned by religious organizations may be restricted to people of the same religion.
    d. Private clubs' lodgings–may be restricted to members if the lodgings are not operated commercially.
    e. Commercial and industrial real estate

XIV. OTHER TERMS TO REMEMBER
  A. Lis pendens–This is filed before the conclusion of a lawsuit, giving notice of a possible claim to the property.
  B. Writ of attachment–This is filed during a lawsuit that prevents a debtor from conveying the property involved in the suit.
  C. Incorporeal right–Nonpossessory right
  D. Inchoate right–Incomplete right
  E. State deed stamps–These are transfer stamps to be attached to a deed for valid transfer. The seller often bears the cost of the stamps, which usually are based on the sales price or an adjusted price.
  F. Fixtures–Items of personal property that have been affixed to real property and thus become part of the real property. However, trade fixtures used in a business constitute personal property and can be removed by the lessee.
  G. Quiet title action–Action brought to cure a cloud on title to property.

XV. REGULATION Z–Promulgated under the federal Truth-in-Lending Law, it dictates disclosure requirements in credit transactions.
  A. Where Regulation Z applies
    1. Loans to individuals
        a. All real estate credit transactions for personal, family and household purposes are covered regardless of amount.
        b. Non-real estate credit transactions for personal, family and household purposes are covered up to $25,000. Loans over $25,000 are not covered.
        c. Real estate purchase agreements are not covered.
    2. Business or commercial loans are not covered.
  B. Foremost Regulation Z requirements
    1. Finance charges
        a. All finance charges as well as true interest rate must be disclosed before a transaction is consummated.

b. Finance charges include interest, service charges, loan fees, points, finder's fees, appraisal fees, investigation of credit fees, credit and property insurance.
c. The finance charge must be stated as an annual percentage rate.

2. Liens on residences
   a. Regulation Z requires a "cooling off" period (except on first mortgages) when liens will be placed on principal residence. The customer has the right to rescind the transaction up to midnight of the third business day following the transaction.
   b. The regulation does not apply to mortgages to finance the purchase or construction of a house.
   c. The regulation does not apply to purchase agreements.

3. Restrictions in credit advertising
   a. Regulation Z does not require lenders to advertise credit terms. If, however, lenders advertise some credit details (for example, "nothing down," eight percent interest, or payments of $550 per month), they must make a complete disclosure of terms.
   b. Complete disclosure includes:
      1) cash price or amount of loan.
      2) amount of down payment.
      3) number, amount and due dates of payments.
      4) finance charge as an annual percentage rate.
      5) total of all payments unless the advertisement refers to a first mortgage.
      6) amount of real estate taxes and assessments.
      7) amount of fire insurance required by lender.

DIAGNOSTIC TEST

1. To be entitled to receive a commission, the listing broker must:
   (A) be licensed at the time the sale is consummated to collect the commission.
   (B) be a member of a multiple-listing service.
   (C) have a contract with the selling broker.
   (D) have a seller statement signed.

2. Which of the following best defines "law of agency"?
   (A) The selling of another's property by an authorized agency
   (B) The rules of law that apply to the responsibilities and obligations of a person who acts for another
   (C) The principles that govern one's conduct in business
   (D) The rules and regulations of the state licensing agency

3. Under what circumstances may salespeople advertise a property for sale?
   (A) If they personally listed the property
   (B) If the name of their broker is listed in the ad
   (C) If they personally pay for the ad
   (D) If they are members of the local real estate board

4. Broker Carl North obtained an exclusive agency listing from Rochelle Green. The broker would not be entitled to a commission if:
   (A) North sold the property himself.
   (B) the property were sold through another broker.
   (C) the property were sold through the multiple-listing service.
   (D) the seller sold the property to a neighbor across the street who had her property listed with another broker.

5. The taxes for 1988 are $743.25 and have not been paid. If the sale is to be closed on August 12, 1988, what is the tax proration charged to the seller, based on a 360-day year?
   (A) $463.01
   (B) $458.33
   (C) $437.20
   (D) $425.67

6. What is the relationship of brokers to their listing owners?
   (A) Trustees
   (B) Subagents
   (C) Fiduciaries
   (D) Attorneys-in-fact

7. Broker Alma Corelle had a listing agreement to sell Noah Greenspan's house. Greenspan found a buyer for the house and Corelle collected the brokerage fee. The type of listing agreement Corelle had is:
   (A) an exclusive right-to-sell listing.
   (B) an exclusive agency listing.
   (C) an open listing.
   (D) a net listing.

8. Salesperson Billie Foster was in the employ of broker Jean McKern. While Foster was showing a house to a prospective purchaser she stated that the house "is the best house in the area!" The statement was not true, as there were several in the neighborhood that were better. Because of the statement:
   (A) Foster was guilty of fraud.
   (B) McKern was guilty of fraud because Foster was an employee of McKern, and thus McKern was responsible for her statement.
   (C) Foster was not guilty of fraud but of puffing.
   (D) Foster was guilty of fraud only if the prospective purchaser bought the house.

9. When a transaction will be closed in escrow, what will the buyer deposit with an escrow agent?
   (A) The deed
   (B) Affidavits of title
   (C) Mortgage papers
   (D) Evidence of title

10. The closing statement involves the debits and credits to the parties of the transaction. What is a debit?
    (A) A refund
    (B) An expense
    (C) A closing adjustment
    (D) Proration

11. What are accrued items?
    (A) Items paid in advance
    (B) Items that are unpaid but are due
    (C) Prepaid expenses
    (D) Refunds

12. All of the following are listing contracts EXCEPT a(n):
    (A) open listing.
    (B) exclusive agency.
    (C) exclusive right-to-sell.
    (D) multiple-listing service.

13. A listing agreement may be terminated by all of the following EXCEPT:

    (A) mutual agreement.
    (B) operation of law.
    (C) association.
    (D) impossibility of performance.

14. What is blockbusting?

    (A) Changing the zoning districts of a municipality
    (B) Representing to homeowners that minorities are moving into the area
    (C) Discriminating against minorities by limiting the housing available to them
    (D) Removing property from the tax rolls

15. The Truth-in-Lending Law of 1969 was enacted for the protection of the consumer. How is it commonly referred to?

    (A) Regulation Z
    (B) RESPA
    (C) ECOA
    (D) REIT

16. The federal Fair Housing Law of 1968 prohibits all of the following EXCEPT:

    (A) blockbusting.
    (B) discriminating advertisements in newspapers.
    (C) redlining.
    (D) refusing to sell because of buyer's age.

17. The federal Truth-in-Lending Law:

    (A) requires a lender to estimate a borrower's approximate loan closing charges on residential mortgages.
    (B) regulates advertising that contains information regarding mortgage terms.
    (C) prevents brokers from using phrases like "FHA-VA financing available" in their classified ads.
    (D) dictates that all mortgage loan applications be made on specially prepared government forms.

18. If the seller in a real estate contract breaches the contract, the buyer may do all of the following, EXCEPT:

    (A) sue for damages.
    (B) sue for specific performance.
    (C) rescind the contract.
    (D) declare the contract forfeited.

19. Every enforceable contract for the sale of real estate must be in writing and signed by all parties, in accordance with:

    (A) the Real Estate License Act.
    (B) the Uniform Commercial Code.
    (C) the statute of frauds.
    (D) the Truth-in-Lending Law.

20. The person who is the purchaser in a contract is known as:

    (A) the grantee.
    (B) the vendor.
    (C) the grantor.
    (D) the vendee.

21. An offer to buy may be terminated by:

    (A) acceptance by the seller.
    (B) a counteroffer by the seller.
    (C) the death of the seller.
    (D) default by the buyer.

22. Sandra Hatch and Cyril Adams have entered into a one-year contract wherein Adams has agreed to provide complete lawn care and snow removal services for Hatch. However, after the first snowstorm of the year Adams decides he wants to move south even though the contract has six months left. Eric Bantry wants to provide the services Adams has provided, and the parties agree that Hatch and Bantry will enter into a new contract and that the contract between Hatch and Adams will be canceled. The above is an example of a(n):

    (A) assignment.
    (B) novation.
    (C) unenforceable agreement.
    (D) rejection.

23. If a prospective buyer has an option to purchase a certain parcel of real estate, the prospective buyer has:

    (A) paid consideration for the option right.
    (B) the obligation to purchase the property at a reduced price.
    (C) the right to subject the seller to a new mortgage.
    (D) the obligation to pay existing liens.

24. Victor Hughes enters into a contract to sell certain land to Sally Pettis. During the course of the negotiations, Hughes wrongfully represents the nature of the soil, claiming that it is firm enough to support a building. This contract is:

    (A) void.
    (B) voidable by Pettis because of fraud.
    (C) voidable by Hughes because of mistake.
    (D) voidable by neither because no harm was done.

25. The essential elements of a contract include which of the following?

    (A) A notorial seal
    (B) Mutual agreement
    (C) A three-day cancellation right
    (D) Equal bargaining power

26. What characterizes a bilateral contract?

    (A) Only one of the parties is bound to act.
    (B) The promise of one party is given in exchange for the promise of the other party.
    (C) A restriction is placed by one party to limit the actual performance by the other party.
    (D) Something is to be done by one party only.

27. A contract may be canceled or discharged for any of the following reasons EXCEPT:

    (A) impossibility of performance.
    (B) mutual agreement of the parties to the contract.
    (C) substantial performance.
    (D) a refusal to perform.

28. What characterizes an *executed* contract?

    (A) Only one party to the contract has made a promise.
    (B) At least one party to the contract may still sue for specific performance.
    (C) All of the parties have fully performed their duties.
    (D) One of the conditions of the contract has been completed.

29. Charles Post and Peter Hollub enter into a contract wherein Post agrees to sell his house to Hollub. Post thereafter changes his mind and defaults. Hollub then sues Post to force him to go through with the contract. This is known as a suit for:

    (A) specific performance.
    (B) damages.
    (C) rescission.
    (D) forfeiture.

30. Under the Parol Evidence Rule:
    (A) an oral statement made contemporaneously with the execution of a fully integrated written agreement may not be used to alter the terms of the written agreement.
    (B) a statement made subsequent to the execution of a fully integrated written agreement may be used to alter the terms of the written agreement only if it was in writing.
    (C) any statement that changes the terms of a fully integrated written contract must be made in front of witnesses.
    (D) any statement that changes the terms of a fully integrated written contract must be made in front of a notary.

31. What is the concept that requires that an injured party bring any action within a specific period of time after the injury?
    (A) A variance
    (B) The statute of limitations
    (C) The statute of frauds
    (D) A waiver

32. In order for a deed to be valid:
    (A) the grantor must be legally competent.
    (B) the signature of the grantor must be witnessed.
    (C) the documents must pass through the hands of an escrow agent.
    (D) the grantee must sign the deed.

33. Under the statute of frauds, all contracts for the sale of real estate must be in writing. What is the principal reason for this statute?
    (A) To prevent the buyer from defrauding the seller
    (B) To protect the broker's rights
    (C) To prevent fraudulent proof of a fictitious oral contract
    (D) To protect the public from fraud resulting from unrecorded deeds

34. If either party to a real estate sales contract defaults, usually the other party can:
    (A) bring an action of adverse possession.
    (B) declare a sale canceled.
    (C) serve a notice of redemption.
    (D) carry an unlawful detainer action against him or her.

35. A person must accept an offer to enter into a contract before:
    (A) the payment of any money.
    (B) the death of the offeror.
    (C) the close of the 10th business day following the offer.
    (D) a similar offer is made to a third person.

ANSWER KEY

Question	Answer	Type of Question	Topic Area	Outline Reference	Page
1.	(A)	Recognition Recall–Definition	Requirements for commission	I.E.1.	56
2.	(B)	Comprehension–Application	Law of agency	I.B.	56
3.	(B)	Comprehension–Application	Advertising	I.N.	57
4.	(D)	Comprehension–Application	Exclusive agency listing	IV.B.	58
5.	(B)	Comprehension–Application	Proration		
6.	(C)	Recognition Recall–Definition	Fiduciary	I.B.	56
7.	(A)	Comprehension–Application	Exclusive right-to-sell	IV.C.	58
8.	(C)	Comprehension–Application	Puffing	III.A.1.	57
9.	(C)	Recognition Recall–Definition	Other terms		
10.	(B)	Comprehension–Application	Charges and credits		
11.	(B)	Recognition Recall–Definition	Charges and credits		
12.	(D)	Recognition Recall–Definition	Types of listing agreements	IV.	58
13.	(C)	Recognition Recall–Definition	Performance/discharge	X.A.	59
14.	(B)	Comprehension–Application	Blockbusting	XIII.B.1.c.	61
15.	(A)	Recognition Recall–Definition	Regulation Z	XV.	62
16.	(D)	Recognition Recall–Definition	Federal Fair Housing Law	XIII.B.	61
17.	(B)	Recognition Recall–Definition	Truth-in-Lending Law	XV.B.3.	63
18.	(D)	Recognition Recall–Definition	Discharge and breach	X.B.1.	59
19.	(C)	Recognition Recall–Definition	Other terms	XI.B.	60
20.	(D)	Recognition Recall–Definition	Parties to contract		
21.	(D)	Comprehension–Application	Offer and acceptance	XI.F.	60
22.	(B)	Comprehension–Application	Novation	XI.E.	60
23.	(A)	Recognition Recall–Definition	Option	XI.I.	61
24.	(B)	Comprehension–Application	Legal effect	IX.C.	59
25.	(B)	Recognition Recall–Definition	Essential elements	VII.B.	58
26.	(B)	Recognition Recall–Definition	Contract classifications	VIII.A.	59
27.	(D)	Recognition Recall–Definition	Discharge and breach	X.A.	59
28.	(C)	Comprehension–Application	Contract classifications	VIII.D.	59
29.	(A)	Comprehension–Application	Discharge and breach	X.B.1.6.	59
30.	(A)	Comprehension–Application	Other terms	XI.C.	60
31.	(B)	Recognition Recall–Definition	Other terms	XI.A.	60
32.	(A)	Recognition Recall–Definition	Essential elements	VII.A.	58
33.	(C)	Comprehension–Application	Other terms	XI.B.	60
34.	(B)	Comprehension–Application	Discharge and breach	X.B.	59
35.	(B)	Comprehension–Application	Other terms	XI.F.6.	60

REAL ESTATE BROKERAGE

Progress Score

Rating	Percentage	Range	Your Score	
EXCELLENT	96% to 100%	35	Brokerage	35
GOOD	86% to 95%	33–34	Total wrong	− ___
FAIR	76% to 85%	31–32	Total right	___
MARGINAL	70% to 75%	29–30		
NEED IMPROVEMENT	69% or less	28 or less		

A.) *Important*: See the Test Question Cross-Reference List on page 136; circle all the questions you missed on the Brokerage Diagnostic Section.

B.) How many questions did you miss in each area?

1. Recognition Recall–Definition _____
2. Comprehension–Application _____

9
Specialty Areas

REVIEW CHECKLIST

This section of the examination will evaluate the potential licensee's familiarity with the current tax laws, securities laws affecting real estate, and the functions, responsibilities and duties of a property manager. In addition you should be familiar with the different types of lease agreements.

Specialty Areas (6 percent of the test)
- Current tax laws affecting real estate ownership
- Identification of securities law situations
- Property management
- Lease agreements

Recognition and Recall

You should know:

- [ ] 1. The three types of real estate taxes
- [ ] 2. Real estate broker vs. securities broker
- [ ] 3. Private syndication vs. public syndication
- [ ] 4. General partnership vs. limited partnership
- [ ] 5. Property managers vs. building managers
- [ ] 6. Ground lease vs. net lease
- [ ] 7. Percentage lease vs. net lease
- [ ] 8. Variable lease vs. gross lease

Comprehension

You should understand:

- [ ] 1. The current laws regarding real estate property taxes, the capital gains tax and income taxes
- [ ] 2. Real estate taxes are ad valorem taxes: The tax is according to the value of the property.
- [ ] 3. Limited partnership shares are securities and therefore are subject to regulation by state and federal securities officials.
- [ ] 4. The functions of a property manager and the principal parts of the management agreement

OUTLINE OF CONCEPTS TO UNDERSTAND

I. TYPES OF REAL ESTATE TAXES*

    A. Real property taxes–personal residence
    B. Capital gain taxes–tax on sale
    C. Income taxes

II. SECURITIES LAWS**

    A. Securities laws include provisions to control and regulate the offering and sale of securities.

        1. Real estate securities, unless exempt, must be registered with state officials and/or with the federal Securities and Exchange Commission (SEC). The two most frequently claimed exemptions are:

            a. intrastate exemption–an offering that is directed solely to residents of a single state where the issuer is also a resident and doing business and is exempted from registration with the SEC. The offering must be registered with the state unless it is also exempt from state registration requirements as a private offering.

            b. private offering exemption–designed to exempt an offering that is of a limited scope and directed to such a selected type of investor that the prospective purchasers do not need the protection afforded by the SEC and can save on the expenditure of time and money involved in the registration process.

    B. Real estate investment syndicates–Form of business venture in which a group of people pool resources to own and/or develop a particular piece of property.

        1. Private syndication–Generally involves a small group of closely associated and/or widely experienced investors.
        2. Public syndication–Generally involves a much larger group of investors who may or may not be knowledgeable about real estate as an investment.
        3. Usually organized as either general or limited partnerships

            a. general partnership–all members share equally in the managerial decisions, profits and losses involved with the investment
            b. limited partnership–one party (or parties), usually a property developer or a real estate broker, organizes, operates and takes responsibility for the entire syndicate. This person is the general partner; the other members of the partnership are limited partners.

    C. Salespeople of such real estate securities:

        1. are regulated by federal Securities Act of 1933 and state Blue Sky laws.
        2. are agents in sale of securities.

---

*The ongoing legislative changes regarding this topic make it difficult to present a current outline of concepts. The reader should consult with a tax attorney or an accountant prior to his or her licensing examination to ascertain the most current information regarding real estate taxes.

**Note, Caution: Real estate can be deemed a security if a passive investor relies on the broker's/agent's efforts to ensure a profit, return on investment and management. If so, the real estate agent could not sell the property without a securities license.

SPECIALTY AREAS

        3. may be required to obtain special licenses.
        4. are exempt from real estate license laws in the sale of real estate.

III. PROPERTY MANAGEMENT

    A. Types of managers

        1. Property manager–Oversees the management of a number of properties for various owners.
        2. Building manager–Is involved in the management of one building.
        3. Resident manager–Represents a property management firm; typically, lives on the premises he or she manages.

    B. Functions of the property manager

        1. Developing a management plan that incorporates the owner's purpose
        2. Collecting rents
        3. Maintaining the property
        4. Preparing and executing the budget
        5. Safeguarding the owner's interests in tenant/employee/building matters
        6. Leasing space
        7. Record keeping

    C. Management agreement

        1. Constitutes first step in assuming management of a property.
        2. Should cover:

            a. Property description
            b. Definition of manager's responsibilities
            c. Time period of agreement
            d. Statement of owner's purpose
            e. Degree of manager's authority
            f. Frequency and detail of reporting
            g. Management fee
            h. Allocation of costs between manager and owner

IV. LEASE AGREEMENTS

    A. Classification of leases by method of rent payment

        1. Gross lease–The tenant pays fixed amount of rent.
        2. Net lease–The tenant pays taxes, insurance and/or maintenance in addition to a fixed rent.
        3. Percentage lease–The tenant pays a percent of the income or profits he or she earns from the property as rent. This arrangement often is used in shopping centers.
        4. Ground lease–A long-term lease of land (e.g., 99 years). During the term of the lease the tenant usually operates the property as though it were tenant owned and may construct buildings on it.
        5. Variable lease–Rent changes periodically during lease term. The amount of change could be specified in the lease or depend on an outside index such as the Consumer Price Index.

REAL ESTATE EXAM MANUAL

DIAGNOSTIC TEST

1. In assuming responsibility for the maintenance of a property, the manager is expected to do which of the following?

    (A) Directly or indirectly supervise the routine cleaning and repair work of the building
    (B) Execute an inverse severance contract
    (C) Review all housing disclosure reports
    (D) Approve all exchange agreements

2. A property manager works for the best interest of:

    (A) the tenants.
    (B) the owner.
    (C) the banker.
    (D) government authorities.

3. A management agreement usually covers which of the following items?

    (A) Statement of owner's purpose
    (B) Estoppel certificates
    (C) Joint and several liability
    (D) Waiver of subrogation

4. What is the lease provision that refers to the voluntary surrender of certain rights?

    (A) Access
    (B) Estoppel
    (C) Waiver
    (D) Acknowledgment

5. A lease under which the tenant pays taxes, maintenance and insurance costs, as well as a fixed monthly rental, is known as:

    (A) a gross lease.
    (B) a net lease.
    (C) a percentage lease.
    (D) a graduated lease.

ANSWER KEY

Question	Answer	Type of Question	Topic Area	Outline Reference	Page
1.	(A)	Recognition Recall–Definition	Property management	III.B.	73
2.	(B)	Recognition Recall–Definition	Property management	III.B.5.	73
3.	(A)	Recognition Recall–Definition	Property management	III.C.	73
4.	(C)	Comprehension–Application	Interests in real estate	IV.A.	73
5.	(B)	Recognition Recall–Definition	Net lease	IV.A.2.	73

SPECIALTY AREAS

Progress Score

Rating	Percentage	Range	Your Score
EXCELLENT	96% to 100%	5	Specialty 5
GOOD	86% to 95%	4	Total wrong – __
FAIR	76% to 85%	3	Total right __
MARGINAL	70% to 75%	2	
NEED IMPROVEMENT	69% or less	1 or less	

A.) *Important*: See the Test Question Cross-Reference List on page 000; circle all the questions you missed on the Contract Diagnostic Section.

B.) How many questions did you miss in each area?

1. Recognition Recall–Definition _____
2. Comprehension–Application _____

10
Real Estate Mathematics Review

This review is designed to familiarize you with some basic mathematical formulas that are most frequently used in the computations required on state licensing examinations. These same computations are also important in day-to-day real estate transactions. If you feel you need additional help in working these problems, you may want to order a copy of *Mastering Real Estate Mathematics*, by Ventolo, Allaway and Irby, published by Real Estate Education Company, Chicago.

Percentages

Many real estate computations are based on the calculation of percentages. A percentage expresses a portion of a whole. For example, 50 percent means 50 parts of the 100 parts comprising the whole. Percentages greater than 100 percent contain more than one whole unit. Thus, 163 percent is one whole and 63 parts of another whole. Remember that a whole is always expressed as 100 percent.

In working problems involving percentages, the percentage must be converted to either a decimal or a fraction. To convert a percentage to a decimal, move the decimal two places to the left and drop the percent sign. Thus,

$$60\% = .6 \qquad 7\% = .07 \qquad 175\% = 1.75$$

To change a percentage to a fraction, place the percentage over 100. For example:

$$50\% = \frac{50}{100} \qquad 115\% = \frac{115}{100}$$

These fractions may then be reduced to make working the problem easier. To reduce a fraction, determine the highest number that will evenly divide into the numerator and denominator; divide each of them by that number. For example:

25/100 = 1/4 (both numbers are divided by 25)
49/63 = 7/9 (both numbers are divided by 7)

Percentage problems contain three elements: *percentage, total* and *part*. *To determine a specific percentage of a whole*, multiply the percentage by the whole. This is illustrated by the following formula:

REAL ESTATE EXAM MANUAL

$$percent \times total = part$$
$$5\% \times 200 = 10$$

- A broker is to receive a 7% commission on the sale of a $50,000 house. What will the broker's commission be?

$$.07 \times \$50,000 = \$3,500 \text{ broker's commission}$$

This formula is used in calculating mortgage loan interests, brokers' commissions, loan origination fees, discount points, amount of earnest money deposits and income on capital investments.

A variation, or inversion, of the percentage formula is used to *find the total amount when the part and percentage are known:*

$$total = \frac{part}{percentage}$$

- The Masterson Realty Company received a $3,600 commission for the sale of a house. The broker's commission was 6% of the total sale price. What was the total sale price of this house?

$$\frac{\$3,600}{.06} = \$60,000 \text{ total sale price}$$

This formula is used in computing the total mortgage loan principal still due if the monthly payment and interest rate are known. It is also used to calculate total sales price when the amount and percentage of commission or earnest money deposit are known, rent due if the monthly payment and interest rate are known and market value of property if the assessed value and the ratio (percentage) of assessed value to market value are known.

To determine the percentage when the amounts of the part and the total are known:

$$percent = \frac{part}{total}$$

This formula may be used to determine the tax rate when the taxes and assessed value are known, or the commission rate if the sale price and commission amount are known.

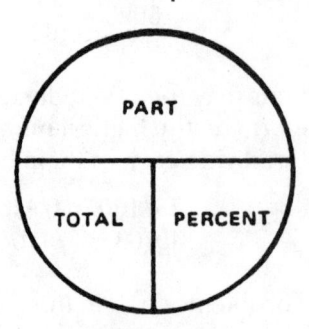

An easy way to remember the formula for part, percent and total is with the above diagram. First draw the circle and divide it in half; then divide the bottom half in half. Put the term "part" in the top half of the circle and the other two terms in the two bottom portions.

Next, replace the words *part, total* and *percent* with the correct figures. The word that remains represents the element you are solving for. If the portions for which you have figures are on the same line, multiply to find the third element; if one figure is above the other, divide the top term by the bottom one.

Rates

Property taxes, transfer taxes and insurance premiums usually are expressed as rates. A rate is the cost expressed as the amount of cost per unit. For example, tax might be computed at the rate of $5 per $100 of assessed value in a certain county. *The formula for computing rates is:*

$$\frac{value}{unit} \times rate\ per\ unit = total$$

- A house has been assessed at $50,000 and is taxed at an annual rate of $2.50 per $100 assessed valuation. What is the yearly tax?

$$\frac{\$50,000}{\$100} \times \$2.50 = total\ annual\ tax$$

$$\$50,000 \div \$100 = 500\ (increments\ of\ \$100)$$

$$500 \times \$2.50 = \$1,250\ total\ annual\ tax$$

Areas and Volumes

People in the real estate profession must know how to compute the area of a parcel of land or to figure the amount of living area in a house. *To compute the area of a square or rectangular parcel, use the formula:*

$$length \times width = area$$

- What is the area of a rectangular lot that measures 200 feet long by 100 feet wide?

$$200' \times 100' = 20,000\ square\ feet$$

Area is always expressed in square units.

To compute the amount of surface in a triangular-shaped area, use the formula:

$$area = ½\ (base \times height)$$

Remember that the arithmetic enclosed by parentheses is always computed before any other arithmetic. The base of a triangle is the bottom, the side on which the triangle rests. The height is an imaginary straight line extending from the point of the uppermost angle straight down to the base:

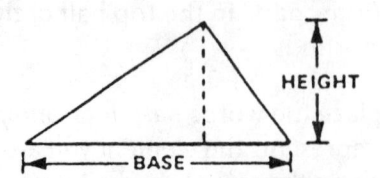

- A triangle has a base of 50 feet and a height of 30 feet. What is its area?

    ½ (50' × 30') = area in square feet
    ½ (1500) = 750 square feet

To compute the area of an irregular room or parcel of land, divide the shape into regular rectangles, squares or triangles. Next, compute the area of each regular figure and add the areas together to obtain the total area.

Problem: Compute the area of the hallway in the following figure:

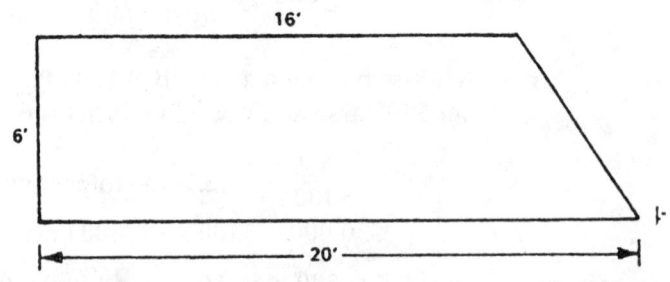

First, make a rectangle and a triangle by drawing a single line through the figure as shown:

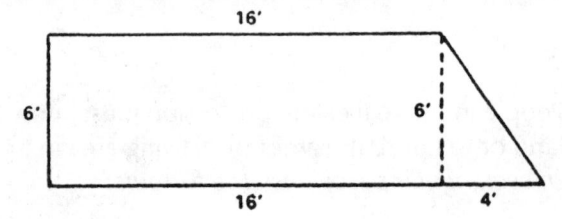

Compute the area of the rectangle:

    area = length × width   16' × 6' = 96 square feet

Compute the area of the triangle:

    area = ½ (base × height)   ½ (4' × 6') = ½ (24) = 12 square feet

Total the two areas:

    96 + 12 = 108 square feet in total area

Volume. The cubic capacity of an enclosed space is expressed as volume. Volume is used to describe the amount of space in any three-dimensional area and, for example, would be used in measuring the interior airspace of a room to determine what capacity heating unit is required. *The formula for computing cubic or rectangular volume is:*

volume = length × width × height

Volume is always expressed in cubic units.

- The bedroom of a house is 12 feet long and 8 feet wide, and has a ceiling height of 8 feet. How many cubic feet does the room enclose?

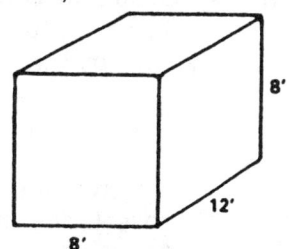

$$8' \times 12' \times 8' = 768 \text{ cubic feet}$$

To compute the volume of a triangular space, such as the airspace in an A-frame house, use the formula:

volume = ½ (base × height × width)

Problem: What is the volume of airspace in the house shown below?

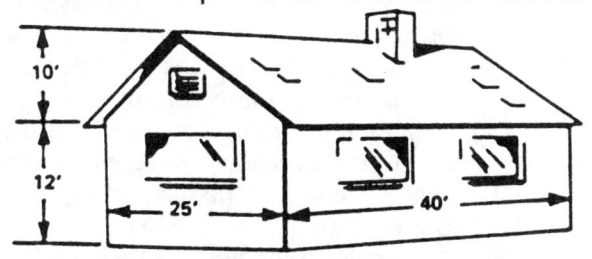

First, divide the house into two shapes, triangular and rectangular, as shown:

Find the volume of T:

volume = ½ (base × height × width)
½ (25' × 10' × 40') = ½ (10,000) = 5,000 cubic feet

Find the volume of R:

25' × 40' × 12' = 12,000 cubic feet

Total volumes T and R:

5,000 + 12,000 = 17,000 cubic feet of airspace in the house

REAL ESTATE EXAM MANUAL

Cubic measurements of volume are used to compute the construction costs per cubic foot of a building, the amount of airspace being sold in a condominium unit or the heating and cooling requirements for a building.

Ensure that, when you compute either area or volume, all dimensions are in the same unit of measure. For example, you may not multiply 2 feet by 6 inches to get the area; you have to multiply 2 feet by ½ foot.

Prorations

The prorating of taxes, interest and other items is customary when a real estate transaction is closed. Part V: Broker Examination contains a discussion of proration mathematics.

TYPE OF MATH QUESTIONS

Although test questions may have variations and often require more than one mathematical step in order to arrive at the correct answer, problems containing math can generally be categorized into a number of specific classifications. The categories are as follows:

A. *General Math*–Involves your ability to master basic mathematical thought processes.
B. *Measurements*–Involves the determination of the square footage and the lineal size of designated premises.
C. *Real Estate Commissions*–Involves the relationship between the commission received by a real estate agent and the price of the property.
D. *Interest*–Involves the relationship between the interest paid as a loan and the principal amount of the loan.
E. *Mortgage Fundamentals*–Involves the relationship of a mortgage with the value of the property and mortgage payments.
F. *Taxes*–Involves the relationship between a property's market value, its assessed value and the taxes paid in connection with it.
G. *Cash at Closing*–Involves the determination of the non-financed portion of a purchase price and the costs to be borne by a party at the time of closing.
H. *Proration*–Involves the dividing of due or prepaid expenses and/or income between a seller and a buyer.
I. *Relative Value of a Property*–Involves the appreciation or depreciation of a particular property over time and the profit or loss that the owner of the property incurs.
J. *Capitalization*–Involves the return on investment received from income-producing property. A percentage ratio between a building value and the net income it produces.

MATHEMATICS REVIEW TEST

1. Broker Sally Smith of Happy Valley Realty recently sold Jack and Jill Hawkins's home for $43,500. Smith charged the Hawkinses a 6½% commission and will pay 30% of that amount to the listing salesperson and 25% to the selling salesperson. What amount of commission will the listing salesperson receive from the Hawkins sale?

   (A) $1,555.13   (C) $848.25
   (B) $1,272.38   (D) $706.88

2. Susan Silber signed an agreement to purchase a condominium apartment from Perry and Marie Morris. The contract stipulated that the Morrises replace the damaged bedroom carpet. The carpet Silber has chosen costs $11.95 per square yard plus $2.50 per square yard for installation. If the bedroom dimensions are as illustrated below, how much will the Morrises have to pay for the job?

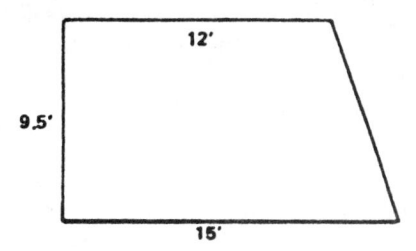

   (A) $170.28   (C) $205.91
   (B) $189.20   (D) $228.79

3. Hal Peters, Olive Gamble, Ron Clooney and Marvin Considine decided to pool their savings and purchase some commercial real estate for $125,000. If Peters invested $30,000 and Gamble and Clooney each contributed $35,000, what percentage of ownership was left for Considine?

   (A) 20%   (C) 28%
   (B) 24%   (D) 30%

4. Harold Barlow is curious to know how much money his son and daughter-in-law still owe on their mortgage loan. Barlow knows that the interest portion of their last monthly payment was $291.42. If the Barlows are paying interest at the rate of 8¼%, what was the outstanding balance of their loan before that last payment was made?

   (A) $43,713.00   (C) $36,427.50
   (B) $42,388.36   (D) $34,284.70

5. Nick and Olga Stravinski bought their home on Sabre Lane a year ago for $68,500. Property in their neighborhood is said to be increasing in value at a rate of 12% annually. If this is true, what is the current market value of the Stravinskis' real estate?

   (A) $76,720   (C) $77,405
   (B) $77,063   (D) none of the above is within $50

6. The DeHavilands' home on Dove Street is valued at $65,000. Property in their area is assessed at 60% of its value, and the local tax rate is $2.85 per hundred. What is the amount of the DeHavilands' monthly taxes?

   (A) $1,111.50   (C) $111.15
   (B) $ 926.30   (D) $ 92.63

REAL ESTATE EXAM MANUAL

7. The Fitzpatricks are planning to construct a patio in their backyard. An illustration of the surface area to be paved appears below. If the cement is to be poured as a 6-inch slab, how many cubic feet of cement will be poured into this patio?

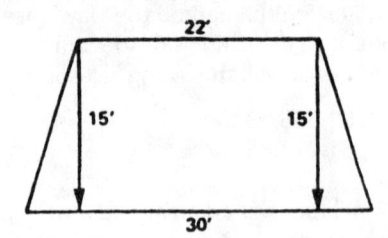

```
         22'
     ┌─────────┐
    /           \
 15'/             \15'
  /               \
 /_____\
         30'
```

(A) 660 cubic feet (C) 330 cubic feet
(B) 450 cubic feet (D) 195 cubic feet

8. Happy Morgan receives a monthly salary of $500 plus 3% commission on all of his listings that sell and 2½% on all his sales. None of the listings that Morgan took sold last month, but he received $3,675 in salary and commission. What was the value of the property Morgan sold?

(A) $147,000 (C) $122,500
(B) $127,000 (D) $105,833

9. The Salvatini residence has proved difficult to sell. Salesperson Martha Kelley suggests it might sell faster if they enclose a portion of the backyard with a privacy fence. If the area to be enclosed is as illustrated below, how much would the fence cost at $6.95 per linear foot?

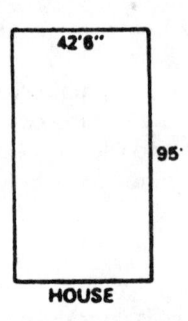

```
      42'6"
   ┌─────────┐
   │         │
   │         │95'
   │         │
   │         │
   └─────────┘
     HOUSE
```

(A) $1,911.25 (C) $1,615.88
(B) $1,654.10 (D) $ 955.63

10. Andrew McTavish leases the 12 apartments in the Overton Arms for a total monthly rental of $3,000. If this figure represents an 8% annual return on McTavish's investment, what was the original cost of the property?

(A) $450,000 (C) $45,000
(B) $360,000 (D) $36,000

84

REAL ESTATE MATHEMATICS REVIEW

ANSWER KEY

1. $43,500 sale price × 6½% commission =
   $43,500 × .065 = $2,827.50, Happy Valley's commission
   $2,827.50 × 30% = $2,827.50 × .30 = $848.25, listing salesperson's commission
   Correct answer–(C) $848.25

2.

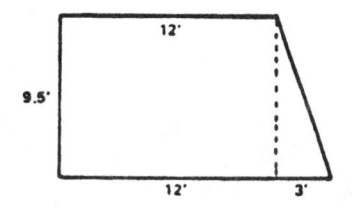

   ```
            12'
        ┌─────────╲
   9.5' │          ╲
        └──────────┘
            12'     3'
   ```

   12' × 9.5' = 114 square feet, area of rectangle
   ½ (3' × 9.5') = ½ (28.5) = 14.25 square feet, area of triangle
   114 + 14.25 = 128.25 square feet
   to convert square feet to square yards divide by 9
   128.25 ÷ 9 = 14.25 square yards
   $11.95 carpet + $2.50 installation = $14.45 cost per square yard
   $14.45 × 14.25 square yards = $205.9125
   Correct answer–(C) $205.91

3. $30,000 Peters + $35,000 Gamble + $35,000 Clooney = $100,000
   $125,000 − $100,000 = $25,000, Considine's contribution
   $\frac{part}{total}$ = percent
   $25,000 ÷ $125,000 = .20 or 20%
   Correct answer–(A) 20%

4. $291.42 × 12 = $3,497.04, annual interest
   $\frac{part}{percent}$ = total
   $3,497.04 ÷ 8¼% = $3,497.04 ÷ .0825 = $42,388.363
   Correct answer–(B) $42,388.36

5. $68,500 × 12% = $68,500 × .12 = $8,220, annual increase in value
   $68,500 + $8,220 = $76,720, current market value
   Correct answer–(A) $76,720

REAL ESTATE EXAM MANUAL

6. $65,000 × 60% = $65,000 × .60 = $39,000, assessed value
   divide by 100 because tax rate is stated per hundred dollars
   $39,000 ÷ 100 = $390
   $390 × $2.85 = $1,111.50, annual taxes
   divide by 12 to get monthly taxes
   $1,111.50 ÷ 12 = $92.625
       Correct answer–(D) $92.63

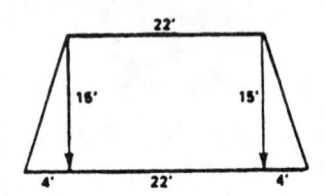

7.

   22' × 15' = 330 square feet, area of rectangle
   ½ (4' × 15') = ½ (60) = 30 square feet, area of each triangle
   30 × 2 = 60 square feet, area of two triangles
   330 + 60 = 390 square feet, surface area to be paved
   6" deep = ½ foot
   390 × ½ = 195 cubic feet, cement needed for patio
       Correct answer–(D) 195 cubic feet

8. $3,675 − $500 salary = $3,175 commission on sales
   $3,175 ÷ 2.5% = $3,175 ÷ .025 = $127,000, value of property sold
       Correct answer–(B) $127,000

9. two sides of 95' plus one side of 42'6"
   95' × 2 = 190 feet
   42'6" = 42.5 feet
   190 + 42.5 = 232.5 linear feet
   232.5 × $6.95 = $1,615.875
       Correct answer–(C) $1,615.88

10. $3,000 × 12 = $36,000 annual rental
    $36,000 ÷ 8% = $36,000 ÷ .08 = $450,000, original cost of property
        Correct answer–(A) $450,000

11
Sample Examinations

These sample exams test your general real estate knowledge and test-taking ability. Simulate as closely as possible the actual test conditions (see Chapter 1, "Use of the Manual"); eliminate distractions and use only those tools allowed by your jurisdiction. Each of these exams contains 80 questions; remember that the ETS exam includes an additional portion of 30 to 40 questions that test your knowledge of your jurisdiction's laws on real estate licensure, condominiums, subdivisions and fair housing and on administrative hearing procedures.

After completing and grading the first sample exam, carefully analyze your results. Did you complete all the questions in the allotted time? Did you answer a minimum of 65 questions correctly? You will probably find it useful at this point to mark off all the questions you missed in the Test Question Cross-Reference List under Sample Exam 1, beginning on page 134. All the questions are keyed to topics under Chapters 4–10: Salesperson Examination's content outline. The pattern of your errors should immediately suggest which areas require additional study.

Once you feel you have mastered your problem areas, repeat this procedure with the other two sample exams, filling out the forms that follow each exam. As a final check, you may wish to review all test questions in the guide relating to a given topic. Do not hesitate to test and retest yourself. The greater your familiarity with the scope and style of the ETS exam, the better you are likely to perform.

SAMPLE EXAMINATION I

The questions that follow are similar to those found on the ETS real estate licensing exams. You may use this 80-question exam to evaluate your real estate knowledge. Score one point for each correct answer; consider a total of 60 or better to be a passing grade.

1. Which of the following is a lien on real estate?

    (A) Easement
    (B) Recorded mortgage
    (C) Encroachment
    (D) Restrictive covenant

2. A contract agreed to under duress is:

    (A) voidable.
    (B) breached.
    (C) discharged.
    (D) void.

3. The landlord of tenant Caligula has sold his building to the state so that an expressway can be built. Mr. Caligula's lease is up, but the landlord is letting him remain until the time the building will be torn down; Caligula continues to pay the same rent as prescribed in his lease. What is Caligula's tenancy called?

    (A) Holdover tenancy
    (B) Month-to-month tenancy
    (C) Tenancy at sufferance
    (D) Tenancy at will

4. When a form of real estate sales contract has been agreed to and signed by a purchaser and spouse and given to the seller's broker with an earnest money check:

    (A) this transaction constitutes a valid contract in the eyes of the law.
    (B) the purchaser can sue the seller for specific performance.
    (C) this transaction is considered an offer.
    (D) the earnest money will be returned if the buyer defaults.

5. In establishing priorities for liens:

    (A) a mechanic's lien is always first in priority.
    (B) the date on which the lien was recorded determines priority.
    (C) the date on which the debt was incurred determines priority.
    (D) a broker's lien is automatically in first priority.

6. A seller gives an open listing to several brokers, specifically promising that if one of the brokers finds a buyer for the seller's real estate, the seller will then be obligated to pay a commission to that broker. Which of the following describes this offer by the seller?

    (A) Executed agreement
    (B) Discharged agreement
    (C) Unilateral agreement
    (D) Bilateral agreement

7. A broker receives a check for earnest money from a buyer and deposits the money in an escrow or trust account. He does this to protect himself from the charge of which of the following?

    (A) Commingling
    (B) Novation
    (C) Lost or stolen funds
    (D) Embezzlement

8. An escrow agent requires the seller to deposit all of the following with him before the specified date of closing EXCEPT:

    (A) the deed.
    (B) title evidence.
    (C) affidavits of title (if required).
    (D) existing liability insurance policies.

9. The advantages of closing a real estate transaction in escrow include all of the following EXCEPT:

    (A) assurance to the seller that he or she will receive the earnest money.
    (B) assurance to the buyer that the title is delivered as agreed.
    (C) the broker is paid a commission.
    (D) assurance the buyer will not default on the lease.

10. If the broker holds the earnest money in a trust account, when does the seller of a piece of property receive it?

    (A) At the time the offer is made
    (B) At the time of the settlement
    (C) After the settlement
    (D) Upon acceptance of the purchase agreement

11. What is a mortgage loan that requires monthly payments of $175.75 for 20 years and a final payment of $5,095 known as?

    (A) A wraparound mortgage
    (B) An accelerated mortgage
    (C) A balloon mortgage
    (D) A variable mortgage

12. By paying his debt after a foreclosure sale, the mortgagor has the right to regain his property. What is such right called?

    (A) Acceleration
    (B) Redemption
    (C) Reversion
    (D) Recovery

13. Which of the following relates to a mortgage loan?

    (A) Acceleration clause
    (B) Covenant of further assurance
    (C) Writ of execution
    (D) Vested interest

14. What type of mortgage loan allows a buyer to obtain financing from a seller without assuming the seller's first mortgage?

    (A) A wraparound mortgage
    (B) An open-end mortgage
    (C) A balloon mortgage
    (D) An accelerated mortgage

15. In a sale-and-leaseback arrangement:

    (A) the seller/vendor retains title to the real estate.
    (B) the buyer/vendee gets possession of the property.
    (C) the sale is disallowed in most states.
    (D) the buyer/vendee is the lessor.

16. The mortgagor computed the interest he was charged for the previous month on his $60,000 mortgage loan balance as $412.50. What is his rate of interest?

    (A) 7½%
    (B) 7¾%
    (C) 8¼%
    (D) 8½%

17. In which of the following markets may a lender sell a loan that a bank had previously originated?

    (A) Primary market
    (B) Secondary market
    (C) Mortgage market
    (D) Investor market

18. Fannie Mae (FNMA) was established by:

    (A) the federal government.
    (B) the Federal Home Loan Bank Board.
    (C) a group of large institutional investors.
    (D) FHA

19. Fannie Mae and Ginnie Mae (GNMA):

    (A) work together as primary lenders.
    (B) are both federal agencies.
    (C) are both private agencies.
    (D) are both involved in the secondary market.

20. A quitclaim deed:

    (A) carries no covenant or warranty.
    (B) may not transfer the seller's title.
    (C) carries full warranty.
    (D) provides a limited warranty.

21. What is the kind of deed that carries with it five covenants?

    (A) Warranty deed
    (B) Quitclaim deed
    (C) Grant deed
    (D) Deed in trust

22. A deed in trust creates a trust for which:

    (A) public records do not indicate the beneficial owner's identity.
    (B) the time limit is usually 25 years.
    (C) the time limit is 10 years.
    (D) none of the above

23. You cannot create an easement by:

    (A) a grant.
    (B) reservation.
    (C) condemnation.
    (D) consideration.

24. What is steering?

    (A) Leading prospective homeowners to or away from certain areas
    (B) Refusing to make loans to persons in certain areas
    (C) A requirement to join MLS
    (D) A practice of setting commissions

25. Mrs. Hogan grants a life estate to her grandson and stipulates that upon her grandson's death the title will pass to her son-in-law. What is this second estate called?

    (A) An estate in reversion
    (B) An estate in remainder
    (C) An estate for years
    (D) An estate in recapture

26. Under joint tenancy:

    (A) there is a right of survivorship.
    (B) only two people can own real estate.
    (C) the fractional undivided interest may differ.
    (D) all of the above

27. The Fair Housing Law of 1968 does not apply to:

    (A) rental housing.
    (B) vacant land sales.
    (C) single family sales.
    (D) commercial or industrial properties.

28. Condominium owners:

    (A) hold common elements as tenants in common.
    (B) hold common elements as joint tenants.
    (C) hold individual elements only.
    (D) none of the above

29. A licensed broker:

    (A) is generally due a commission if a sale is not consummated because of the principal's default.
    (B) can disclose any truthful information received from the principal.
    (C) is responsible to present only offers acceptable to the principal.
    (D) all of the above

30. A licensed salesperson is authorized by law to:

    (A) sign a closing statement.
    (B) collect a commission directly from a principal for performing assigned duties.
    (C) advertise property under own name.
    (D) act under the supervision of a real estate broker.

31. Licensed salespeople can receive compensation or commission:

    (A) only from their employing brokers.
    (B) from the principals.
    (C) from other brokers.
    (D) from a landlord for renting property.

32. What is a datum?

    (A) An undersized or fractional section
    (B) An imaginary line from which heights are measured
    (C) A primary township
    (D) An imaginary line that measures longitude

33. An insurance premium has been paid in advance by the seller of a house. The policy, worth $50,000, has a premium of $400 for a three-year period, beginning January 1, 1988, ending on December 31, 1990. The closing date for the sale of the house is July 15, 1989. The amount to be reimbursed is:

    (A) $194.46.
    (B) $215.46.
    (C) $201.58.
    (D) $95.89.

34. In some states, a lender is the owner of mortgaged land. These states are known as:

    (A) title theory states.
    (B) lien theory states.
    (C) statutory share states.
    (D) dower rights states.

35. A deficiency judgment can take place when:

    (A) a foreclosure sale does not produce sufficient funds to pay a mortgage debt in full.
    (B) not enough taxes have been paid on a piece of property.
    (C) a foreclosure sale is not completed.
    (D) all of the above

36. What is a tenancy at will?

    (A) A tenancy with the consent of the landlord
    (B) A tenancy that expires on a specific date
    (C) A tenancy created by the death of the owner
    (D) A tenancy created by the testator

37. Which of the following represents transfer of marketable title?

    (A) Transfer by delivery
    (B) Transfer by devise
    (C) Transfer by dedication
    (D) Transfer by disintermediation

38. An option is a contract that:

    (A) sets a time limit in which to accept an offer.
    (B) is an open-end agreement.
    (C) does not set the sale price for the property.
    (D) transfers title when it is signed by the seller.

39. The market value of a piece of land:

    (A) is an estimate of the present worth of future benefits.
    (B) includes a measure of past expenditures.
    (C) is what a buyer pays for the property.
    (D) is the same as the market price.

40. Capitalization rates are:

    (A) determined by the gross rent multiplier.
    (B) the rates of return a property will produce on the owner's investment.
    (C) a mathematical value of a property determined by the sale price.
    (D) determined by the amount of depreciation on the property.

41. A house with outmoded plumbing is suffering from:

    (A) functional obsolescence.
    (B) curable physical deterioration.
    (C) incurable physical deterioration.
    (D) depreciation.

42. Police powers include all of the following EXCEPT:

    (A) zoning.
    (B) liens.
    (C) building codes.
    (D) subdivision regulations.

43. Joe O'Boyle built a building that has six stories. In 1983, several years later, an ordinance was passed banning any building six stories or higher in the area. This instance represents:

    (A) a nonconforming use.
    (B) a situation in which the building would have to be demolished.
    (C) a conditional use.
    (D) a variance.

SAMPLE EXAMINATIONS

44. A seller wants to net $65,000 on his house after paying the broker's fee of 6%. His gross selling price will be:

    (A) $69,149.
    (B) $68,093.
    (C) $67,035.
    (D) $66,091.

45. An acre contains:

    (A) 43,560 square feet.
    (B) 36 sections.
    (C) 360 degrees.
    (D) 640 square feet.

46. Wilma Banke is buying a condominium in a new subdivision and obtaining financing from a local savings and loan association. In this situation, which of the following best describes Banke?

    (A) Vendor
    (B) Mortgagee
    (C) Grantor
    (D) Mortgagor

47. Assume listing and selling brokers split their commission evenly. What was the sales price of a house if the listing broker received $2,593.50 and the total commission rate was 6.5%?

    (A) $88,400
    (B) $79,800
    (C) $76,200
    (D) $39,900

48. According to the statute of frauds, an oral lease for five years is:

    (A) a long-term lease.
    (B) renewable.
    (C) legal.
    (D) unenforceable.

49. A mortgage on real estate given by the buyer to the seller as security for financing is a:

    (A) conventional mortgage.
    (B) purchase-money mortgage.
    (C) package mortgage.
    (D) land contract or contract for deed.

50. Under the concept of the parol evidence rule:

    (A) prior oral evidence cannot vary the terms of a written contract.
    (B) all contracts must be in writing to be valid.
    (C) all leases of real property must be in writing to be valid.
    (D) all contracts must be executed within one year.

51. A mortgage lender intends to lend money at 9¾%, and if the lender intends to yield 10⅜%, how many points should the lender charge?

    (A) Eight points
    (B) Five points
    (C) One-half point
    (D) Four points

52. Unless a mortgage note is to be repaid without interest, a rate should be specified. If not, most state statutes will impose a rate known as:

    (A) the contract rate.
    (B) the usury rate.
    (C) the statutory rate.
    (D) the imposed rate.

53. An eligible veteran made an offer of $50,000 to purchase a home to be financed with a VA-guaranteed loan. Four weeks after the offer was accepted, a certificate of reasonable value (CRV) for $47,000 was issued for the property. In this case the veteran may:

    (A) withdraw from the sale with a 1% penalty.
    (B) purchase the property with a $3,000 down payment.
    (C) not withdraw from the sale.
    (D) withdraw from the sale upon payment of $3,000.

54. The current value of a property is $40,000. The property is assessed at 40% of its current value, with an equalization factor of 1.5 applied to the assessed value. If the tax rate is $4 per $100 of assessed value, what is the amount of tax due on the property?

    (A) $640
    (B) $960
    (C) $1,600
    (D) $2,400

55. If a house sold for $40,000, and the buyer obtained an FHA mortgage in the amount of $38,500, how much money would be paid for points if the lender charged four points?

    (A) $1,500
    (B) $385
    (C) $1,540
    (D) $1,600

56. Dick Middleton decided he could make more money from his tree farm by dividing it into small parcels and selling the parcels to numerous individuals. Subsequently, Middleton entered into a series of purchase agreements in connection with which Middleton agreed to continue to operate the property and distribute proceeds from its income to the buyers. Under the circumstances, Middleton has sold:

    (A) real estate because the object of the sale was land.
    (B) securities because the buyers were investors relying on Middleton's activities to generate a profit from the premises purchased.
    (C) real estate because the property was subdivided first before the sales took place.
    (D) securities because the object of the purchase was trees and the underlying land merely was incidental to the sale.

57. A building was sold for $60,000. Buyer Kelly Golding put up 10% in cash and obtained a loan for the balance. The lending institution charged a 1% loan fee. What was the total cash used by Golding for this purchase?

    (A) $6,540
    (B) $6,600
    (C) $540
    (D) $6,000

58. Find the area of the lot sketched below.

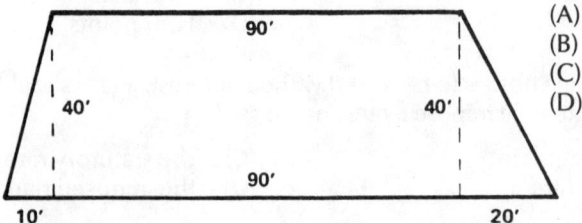

    (A) 3,800 square feet
    (B) 4,000 square feet
    (C) 4,200 square feet
    (D) 3,600 square feet

59. After the snowstorm of the century, Warren Pace offers to pay $6 to whoever will shovel his driveway. This is an example of which of the following?

    (A) An implied contract
    (B) A bilateral contract
    (C) A license
    (D) A unilateral contract

60. Peter Studney wishes to net $46,000 after the broker has deducted 8% of the selling price of his home. What must the selling price be to accommodate Studney?

    (A) $48,920
    (B) $49,680
    (C) $50,000
    (D) $40,000

61. All of the following situations are in violation of the Federal Fair Housing Law of 1968 EXCEPT:

    (A) the refusal of property manager Joe Kelley to rent an apartment to a Catholic couple who are otherwise qualified.
    (B) the general policy of the Locust Loan Company, which avoids granting home improvement loans to individuals in "changing" neighborhoods.
    (C) the intentional neglect of broker Harvey Hall to show a black family any property listings of homes in all-white neighborhoods.
    (D) the insistence of Agnes Taylor, a widow, on renting her spare bedroom only to another woman.

62. Your commission on a sale is 7¾% of $50,000. What is the dollar amount of your commission?

    (A) $3,500
    (B) $4,000
    (C) $4,500
    (D) $3,875

63. If a house is sold under an FHA plan for $50,000, and the required down payment was set at 3% for the first $25,000 and 5% for any amount over $25,000, what is the amount of the down payment?

    (A) $2,000
    (B) $2,750
    (C) $1,250
    (D) $1,500

64. In an FHA transaction:

    (A) points may be paid by the seller or the buyer.
    (B) origination fee must be paid by seller.
    (C) the mortgage insurance premium must be paid in cash at settlement.
    (D) the mortgage insurance premium must be paid by the seller.

65. All of the following will terminate an offer EXCEPT:

    (A) revocation of the offer before acceptance.
    (B) death of the offeror before acceptance.
    (C) a counteroffer by the offeree.
    (D) an offer from a third party.

66. If a house sold for $95,900 (a price $13,160 more than market value for tax purposes) and the assessed value of the house was $16,548, what is the assessment ratio?

    (A) 18%
    (B) 20%
    (C) 22%
    (D) 24%

67. An offeree has which of the following rights?

    (A) The right to reject an offer
    (B) The right to revoke an offer
    (C) The right to rescind an offer
    (D) The right to release an offer

REAL ESTATE EXAM MANUAL

68. Ellen Glamis is purchasing a house under a contract for deed. Until the contract is paid, Glamis has:

   (A) legal title to the premises.
   (B) no interest in the property.
   (C) a legal life estate in the premises.
   (D) equitable title in the premises.

69. All of the following are true about subdivided real estate EXCEPT:

   (A) once land has been subdivided it may not be resubdivided.
   (B) a subdivision plat may be recorded.
   (C) subdivided land is broken down into lots and blocks.
   (D) the legal description should always include the name of the county and state.

70. Emma Anderson and Chuck Benson enter into an agreement wherein Benson will mow Anderson's lawn every two weeks during the course of the summer. Shortly thereafter, Benson decides to go into a different business. Jimmy Nealis would like to assume Benson's duties mowing the lawn. Anderson agrees, and enters into a new contract with Nealis. Anderson and Benson tear up the original agreement. This is known as:

   (A) an assignment.
   (B) a novation.
   (C) a secondary agreement.
   (D) a sublease.

71. Joe and Gloria Bileski borrowed $4,000 from a private lender, using the services of a broker. After deducting the loan costs, the Bileskis received $3,747. What was the face amount of this note?

   (A) $4,000
   (B) $4,253
   (C) $3,747
   (D) $7,747

72. A real estate sales contract becomes valid or in effect when it has been signed by which of the following?

   (A) Buyer
   (B) Buyer and seller
   (C) Seller
   (D) Broker and buyer

73. Wilfred J. Bannister has just made the final payment on his mortgage loan to the Unity American National Savings and Loan Association. Regardless of this fact, the savings and loan association will still hold a lien on Bannister's mortgaged property until which of the following is recorded?

   (A) Satisfaction of the mortgage instrument
   (B) Reconveyance of the mortgage instrument
   (C) Alienation of the mortgage instrument
   (D) Reversion of the mortgage instrument

74. If a storage tank that measures 12 feet by 9 feet by 8 feet was designed to store natural gas, and the cost of natural gas is $1.82 per cubic foot, what does it cost to fill the tank to one-half its capacity?

   (A) $864.00
   (B) $1,572.48
   (C) $786.24
   (D) $684.58

75. If the annual net income from certain commercial property is $22,000, and the capitalization rate is 8%, what is the value of the property using the income approach?

   (A) $275,000
   (B) $176,000
   (C) $200,000
   (D) $183,000

76. If two-thirds of an assessment is for improvements and one-third for the land, what is the assessed value of the improvements if the tax rate is $8.50 per $100 and monthly taxes are $62.00?

    (A) $6,200.00
    (B) $5,835.30
    (C) $8,752.94
    (D) $2,917.65

77. If the assessment ratio is 40%, the semiannual tax payment is $920 and the tax rate is $11.50 per $100, what is the market value of a parcel of real estate?

    (A) $40,000
    (B) $42,240
    (C) $20,000
    (D) $37,350

78. Broker Allen enters into a listing agreement with seller Bennett wherein Bennett will receive $12,000 from the sale of a vacant lot and Allen will receive any sale proceeds over and above that amount. The type of listing agreement into which Allen and Bennett entered is:

    (A) called a gross listing.
    (B) a highly popular method of listing property in most states.
    (C) called an exclusive agency.
    (D) called a net listing.

79. Robert and Dorothy Jamieson, no longer needing their large house, decide to sell the house and move into a cooperative apartment building. Under the cooperative form of ownership, the Jamiesons will:

    (A) become stockholders in a corporation.
    (B) never lose their apartment if they pay their share of the cooperative's taxes.
    (C) take out a new mortgage on their unit.
    (D) receive a 20-year lease for their unit.

80. Joseph Barclay owns a large parcel of undeveloped property, in severalty, very near a large urban area. Developer Edward Longworth, who believes the property could be developed for commercial purposes, enters into an agreement with Barclay to purchase the property. Longworth insists that Barclay's wife join in the deed. The purpose of obtaining Mrs. Barclay's signature is to:

    (A) terminate any rights Mrs. Barclay may have in the property.
    (B) defeat any curtesy rights.
    (C) provide the developer with a sale/leaseback agreement.
    (D) subordinate Barclay's wife's interest to that of Longworth.

REAL ESTATE EXAM MANUAL

SOLUTIONS TO SAMPLE EXAM I

The solutions to Sample Examination I contain the question number, the correct answer choice, the type of question and the topic area as well as the page number and outline reference number where the student may refer for information on the material covered in the question. The computations for the math problems have been worked out and may be found immediately following the solutions.

Question	Answer	Type of Question	Topic Area	Outline Reference	Page
1.	(B)	Comprehension, Transfer of Ownership	Lien	IV. A. 1. a. 1. b.	23
2.	(A)	Definition, Brokerage	Voidable contract	IX. C. 2.	59
3.	(D)	Comprehension, Laws Relating to Ownership	Tenancy at will	III. B. 2. a. 3.	20
4.	(C)	Comprehension, Brokerage	Offer	XI. F.	60
5.	(B)	Comprehension, Laws Relating to Ownership	Liens	IV. A. 1. a.	22
6.	(C)	Comprehension, Brokerage	Unilateral contract	VIII. B.	59
7.	(A)	Comprehension, Brokerage	Earnest money	XI. H.	61
8.	(D)	Definition, Brokerage	Escrow agreement	XI. J. 2.	61
9.	(D)	Comprehension, Brokerage	Escrow agreement	XI. J.	61
10.	(B)	Comprehension, Brokerage	Earnest money	XI. H.	61
11.	(C)	Definition, Financing	Balloon payment	IX. A.	42
12.	(B)	Definition, Financing	Redemption period	V. B.	41
13.	(A)	Definition, Financing	Acceleration clause	IX. D.	42
14.	(A)	Definition, Financing	Types of mortgage	II. G.	39
15.	(D)	Definition, Financing	Sale and leaseback	Glossary	186
16.	(C)	Comprehension, Math	Compute the interest rate	Math Review	77-82
17.	(B)	Definition, Financing	Sources of mortgage dollars	I. B. 1.	38
18.	(A)	Comprehension, Financing	Secondary market	I. B. 2. a.	38
19.	(D)	Definition, Financing	Secondary market	I. B. 2.	38
20.	(A)	Definition, Transfer of Ownership	Types of deeds	II. C.	48
21.	(A)	Definition, Transfer of Ownership	Types of deeds	II. A.	48
22.	(A)	Comprehension, Transfer of Ownership	How ownership is held	II. D.	49
23.	(D)	Comprehension, Laws Relating to Ownership	Easement	IV. B. 1.	23
24.	(A)	Comprehension, Brokerage	Fair Housing	XIII. B. 1. g.	62
25.	(B)	Definition, Transfer of Ownership	Life estate	III. B. 1. c. 5.	20
26.	(A)	Comprehension, Laws Relating to Ownership	How ownership is held	III. B. 2. b.	49
27.	(D)	Comprehension, Brokerage	Fair Housing	XIII. B. 2.	62
28.	(A)	Comprehension, Transfer of Ownership	Condominiums	III. C. 1.	20
29.	(A)	Comprehension, Brokerage	Law of agency	I. F.	57
30.	(D)	Comprehension, Brokerage	Law of agency	II.	57
31.	(A)	Comprehension, Brokerage	Salesperson	II. C.	57
32.	(B)	Comprehension, Valuation	Datum	VII. A.	33

SAMPLE EXAMINATIONS

#	Ans	Category	Topic	Ref	Page
33.	(D)	Comprehension, Math	Compute proration of insurance	Math Review	77-82
34.	(A)	Definition, Financing	Mortgage theories	VIII. B.	42
35.	(A)	Comprehension, Financing	Deficiencies	V. C.	42
36.	(A)	Comprehension, Laws Relating to Ownership	Leasehold estate	III. 2. a. 3.	20
37.	(B)	Definition, Transfer of Ownership	Transfer of title	IV. C.	50
38.	(A)	Definition, Contracts	Option	XI. H.	61
39.	(A)	Comprehension, Valuation	Present worth, Income stream	I. C.	32
40.	(B)	Definition, Valuation	Capitalization	I. C. 1.	32
41.	(A)	Definition, Valuation	Depreciation	I. B. 3.	32
42.	(B)	Definition, Laws Relating to Ownership	Police power	V. A.	24
43.	(A)	Comprehension, Laws Relating to Ownership	Zoning	V. A. 1. c.	24
44.	(A)	Comprehension, Math	Compute sale price	Math Review	77-82
45.	(A)	Definition, Valuation	Acre		
46.	(D)	Definition, Financing	Mortgagor	VI. A.	42
47.	(B)	Comprehension, Math	Compute sale price	Math Review	77-82
48.	(D)	Definition, Brokerage	Statute of frauds	XI. B.	60
49.	(B)	Comprehension, Financing	Purchase money mortgage	II. C.	39
50.	(A)	Definition, Brokerage	Parol evidence	XI. C.	60
51.	(B)	Comprehension, Financing	Discount points	III. C. 5.	40
52.	(A)	Definition, Financing	Contract rate	IX. H.	43
53.	(B)	Comprehension, Financing	V.A. loan	III. D.	40
54.	(B)	Comprehension, Math	Compute tax, based on assessed value	Math Review	77-82
55.	(C)	Comprehension, Financing	Discount points	III. C. 5.	40
56.	(B)	Comprehension, Brokerage	Type of Broker		
57.	(A)	Comprehension, Math	Compute amount of cash needed	Math Review	77-82
58.	(C)	Comprehension, Math	Compute area in sq. feet	Math Review	77-82
59.	(D)	Comprehension, Brokerage	Unilateral	VIII. B.	58
60.	(C)	Comprehension, Math	Compute sale price	Math Review	77-82
61.	(D)	Definition, Brokerage	Fair Housing	XIII. B. 2.	61
62.	(D)	Comprehension, Math	Compute commission	Math Review	77-82
63.	(A)	Comprehension, Math	Compute down payment	Math Review	77-82
64.	(A)	Definition, Financing	Points	III. C. 5.	40
65.	(D)	Comprehension, Brokerage	Termination	X.	59
66.	(B)	Comprehension, Math	Compute assessment ratio	Math Review	77-82
67.	(A)	Comprehension, Contracts	Offeree		
68.	(D)	Definition, Contracts	Equitable title		
69.	(A)	Comprehension, Valuation	Subdivided land		
70.	(B)	Comprehension, Brokerage	Novation	XI. E.	60
71.	(A)	Comprehension, Math	Compute the face amount of the note	Math Review	77-82
72.	(B)	Comprehension, Brokerage	Valid	VII. E.	59
73.	(A)	Comprehension, Financing	Mortgage satisfaction	IX. J.	43

REAL ESTATE EXAM MANUAL

74.	(C)	Comprehension, Math	Compute cubic feet and cost per cubic foot	Math Review	77–82
75.	(A)	Comprehension, Math	Compute the value of property	Math Review	77–82
76.	(B)	Comprehension, Math	Compute assessed value	Math Review	77–82
77.	(A)	Comprehension, Math	Compute market value	Math Review	77–82
78.	(D)	Comprehension, Brokerage	Net listing	IV. D.	58
79.	(A)	Comprehension, Laws Relating to Ownership	Cooperative	III. C. 2.	22
80.	(A)	Comprehension, Laws Relating to Ownership	Legal life estates	III. 3.	21

SOLUTION TO MATH QUESTIONS

Sample Examination 1

16) $412.50 monthly interest × 12 = $4,950.00 annual interest; $4,950 interest ÷ $60,000 loan = .0825 or 8¼% interest rate

33) determine policy period 3 years × 360 days a year = 1080 days; buyer responsible for July 15, 1986–December 31, 1987 = 525 days; $400 premium ÷ 1080 days = cost of $.3704/day; $.3704 × 525 = $194.46 reimbursed

44) if commission = 6%, the seller's net = 94%; therefore $65,000 = 94% of selling price; $65,000 ÷ .94 = $69,149.00 selling price

47) ½ of commission = $2,593.50; $2,593.50 × 2 = $5,187 total commission; $5,187 ÷ .065 commission rate = $79,800 price of house

51) 9¾% is same as 9⅝%; 10⅜% − 9⅝% = ⅝%; one point charged for each ⅛% = 5 points

54) $40,000 market value × 40% or .40 = $16,000 assessed value; × 1.5 equalization factor = $24,000; $24,000 ÷ 100 × $4.00 = $960 tax due

55) 1 point = 1% of mortgage; 4 points = 4% of mortgage; $38,500 mortgage × .04 or 4% = $1,540 charged for points

57) $60,000 sale price × .10 = $6,000 down payment; $60,000 sale price − $6,000 down payment = $54,000 mortgage; $54,000 × .01 = $540 loan fee; $6,000 down payment + $540 loan fee = $6,540 cash used by buyer

58) area of left triangle = ½(10 × 40) = 200 sq. feet; area of center rectangle = 90 × 40 = 3,600 sq. feet; area of right triangle = ½(20 × 40) = 400 sq. feet; add areas together 200 + 3,600 + 400 = 4,200 sq. feet

60) commission = 8%; therefore net to seller = 92%; $46,000 = 92%; $46,000 ÷ .92 = $50,000 sale price

62) $50,000 price of house × 7¾% or .0775 commission rate = $3,875 commission

63) down payment on first $25,000 is $25,000 × .03 = $750; sale price in excess of $25,000 is $50,000 − $25,000 = $25,000; down payment or excess is $25,000 × .05 = $1,250; add parts of down payment $750 + $1,250 = $2,000 down payment

66) sale price of $95,900 − $13,160 = market value of $82,740; $16,548 assessed value ÷ $82,740 market value = .20 or 20% assessment ratio

74) total storage room is 12 × 9 × 8 = 864 cubic feet; 864 × $1.82 cost per cubic foot = $1,572.48; $1,572.48 × .5 (tank ½ full) = $786.24

75) $22,000 income ÷ .08 capitalization rate = $275,000 value of property

76) $62.00 monthly taxes × 12 = $744 annual taxes; $744 × 100 and ÷ $8.50 = $8,752.94 assessed value; $8,752.94 × ⅔ (proportion allowable to improvements) = $5,835.30 assessed value of improvements

77) $920 semiannual payment × 2 = $1,840 annual taxes; $1,840 × 100 and ÷ $11.50 = $16,000 assessed value; $16,000 ÷ .40 assessment ratio = $40,000 market value

SAMPLE EXAM I

Progress Score

Rating	Percentage	Range	Your Score
EXCELLENT	96% to 100%	77–80	Exam I 80
GOOD	86% to 95%	69–76	Total wrong −
FAIR	76% to 85%	61–68	Total right =
MARGINAL	70% to 75%	56–60	
NEED IMPROVEMENT	69% or less	55 or less	

SAMPLE EXAMINATION II

1. An oral sales contract involving the sale of real estate can:

    (A) be enforced through a court action.
    (B) be assigned to a third party.
    (C) be subject to a real estate commission.
    (D) be voidable.

2. Assume a house sold for $82,500 subject to the following terms: earnest money of $1,000, which would be applied to the purchase price at the time of closing; $10,000 down payment; a first mortgage of $65,200 at 10¼% interest amortized over 25 years; a second mortgage for the balance with interest of 8% payable monthly in arrears and principal payable in full at the end of 30 months. How much must the buyer pay in connection with the second mortgage in the payment due at the end of 30 months?

    (A) $6,342.00
    (B) $7,884.33
    (C) $7,300.00
    (D) $7,348.67

3. Discount points are a cost to the seller or buyer and are:

    (A) limited by government regulations.
    (B) determined by the FHA.
    (C) only charged on conventional loans.
    (D) determined by the money market.

4. Henry Kargol defaulted and had his property sold under foreclosure proceedings at a sheriff's sale. What is the period of time after the sale during which he has the right to regain his interest in the land known as?

    (A) Equitable redemption period
    (B) Statutory redemption period
    (C) Informal redemption period
    (D) Formal redemption period

5. At the time the original colonies were settled, land was transferred and deeded by:

    (A) metes and bounds.
    (B) rectangular survey.
    (C) colonial plat.
    (D) government deed.

6. What would it cost to lay a new floor in a den measuring 15 by 20 feet if the cost of materials is $6.95 per square yard and the cost of labor an additional $250.00?

    (A) $231.67
    (B) $481.67
    (C) $610.33
    (D) $2,335.00

7. What is the legal procedure or action brought by either the buyer or the seller to enforce the terms of a contract?

    (A) An injunction
    (B) Specific performance
    (C) Lis pendens
    (D) An attachment

8. A defect or a cloud on the title to property may be cured by:

    (A) obtaining quitclaim deeds from all other interested parties.
    (B) bringing an action to register title.
    (C) paying cash for the property at the closing.
    (D) bringing an action to repudiate title.

9. Under a gross lease the lessee may be requested to pay:

   (A) maintenance.
   (B) real estate taxes.
   (C) insurance.
   (D) a percent of sales.

10. Sally DeLaSalle is in the process of purchasing Jack Kerwood's house. To protect its interest, Mrs. DeLaSalle's mortgagee decides to take out title insurance. The title insurance policy:

    (A) may act as the instrument of transfer.
    (B) indemnifies the holder against some, but not all, of the possible defects in title.
    (C) protects DeLaSalle from some defects in title.
    (D) protects Kerwood from a lawsuit.

11. The Federal Fair Housing Law of 1968 makes it illegal to discriminate because of:

    (A) age.
    (B) marital status.
    (C) public assistance.
    (D) religion.

12. What is the difference between a general and a specific lien?

    (A) A general lien cannot be enforced in court, while a specific lien can be enforced.
    (B) A specific lien is held by one person, while a general lien is held by at least two persons.
    (C) A general lien is a lien against all of the debtor's property, while a specific lien covers only a certain piece of the real property.
    (D) A specific lien is a lien against real estate, while a general lien is a lien against personal property.

13. Under the condominium form of ownership, the interest of the owner in the apartment unit he or she posseses would normally be:

    (A) a life estate.
    (B) a fee simple interest.
    (C) a proprietary leasehold interest.
    (D) a reciprocal proprietary easement interest.

14. In an option to purchase real estate, the optionee:

    (A) must purchase the property, but may do so at any time within the option period.
    (B) has no obligation to purchase the property.
    (C) as a matter of right is limited to a refund of the option consideration if the option is exercised.
    (D) is the prospective seller of the property.

15. The most important factor in determining whether a property that is sold should be classified as real estate or a security is:

    (A) the passiveness of the buyers with regard to the operation of the property.
    (B) the number of vendors involved in the sales.
    (C) the intent of the seller in entering into the purchase agreements.
    (D) the license held by the broker involved in the transactions.

16. An individual seeking to be excused from the dictates of a zoning ordinance should request a:

    (A) building permit.
    (B) certificate of alternate usage.
    (C) restrictive covenant.
    (D) variance.

17. How many acres are in the N½ of the SW¼ plus the NE¼ of the SE¼ of a section?

    (A) 120 acres
    (B) 5 acres
    (C) 10 acres
    (D) 20 acres

18. Acceleration is a term associated with which of the following?

    (A) Listings
    (B) Sale contracts
    (C) Mortgages
    (D) Leases

19. Broker Len Ikoma receives a deposit with a written offer that includes a ten-day acceptance clause. On the fifth day, and prior to acceptance by the seller, Carla Mitchell, buyer Fergus Lambert notifies the broker he is withdrawing his offer and demands that his deposit be returned. In this situation:

    (A) Lambert cannot withdraw the offer—it must be held open for the full ten-day period.
    (B) Lambert has the right to revoke his offer and secure the return of the deposit at any time before he is notified of Mitchell's acceptance.
    (C) Ikoma notifies Mitchell that Lambert is withdrawing his offer, and Ikoma and Mitchell each retain one-half of the deposit.
    (D) Ikoma declares the deposit forfeited and retains it for his services and commission.

20. Mark Holt and Cliff Walden entered into a contract for the sale of certain lands. Walden breaches the contract. Holt's attorney informs him that while, at one time, he had the right to sue Walden for performance, he no longer has that right. Chances are:

    (A) the statute of frauds has not been satisfied.
    (B) the statute of limitations has run out.
    (C) the parol evidence rule would prevent effective testimony.
    (D) Walden has signed a specific performance waiver.

21. Amanda Cayman and George Green are joint tenants. Green sells his interest to Percy Foote. What is the relationship of Cayman and Foote with respect to the land?

    (A) They are joint tenants.
    (B) They are tenants in common.
    (C) There is no relationship, because the sale from Green to Foote of joint tenancy property is ineffective.
    (D) Each owns a divided one-half interest.

22. A mechanic's lien:

    (A) is a lien on all property of the debtor.
    (B) may have priority over a lien for unpaid taxes.
    (C) has priority over a prerecorded mortgage.
    (D) may be held by a person who supplied materials.

23. Deed restrictions are a means whereby:

    (A) local zoning laws are enforced.
    (B) the planning commission's work is made effective.
    (C) villages and cities can control construction details.
    (D) the seller can limit or control the buyer's use.

24. If the assessed value of a parcel of real estate is $14,500, the equalization factor is 1.50, and the tax rate is $5.00 per $100, then the tax bill will be:

    (A) $1,707.50.
    (B) $1,087.50.
    (C) $725.00.
    (D) $1,074.00.

25. Sam Olafson and Henry Walters orally enter into a one-year lease. If Walters defaults, Olafson:

    (A) may not bring a court action because of the parol evidence rule.
    (B) may not bring a court action because of the Statute of Frauds.
    (C) may bring a court action because one-year leases need not be in writing to be enforced.
    (D) may bring a court action because the statute of limitations does not apply to oral leases.

26. A government-sponsored loan that insures the lender against loss is a(n):

    (A) FHA (Federal Housing Administration) mortgage.
    (B) VA (Veterans Administration) mortgage.
    (C) Adjustable Rate Mortgage.
    (D) Graduated Payment Mortgage.

27. On Monday, Victor Tinberg offers to sell his vacant lot to Leona Winters for $12,000. On Tuesday, Winters counteroffers to buy the lot for $10,500. On Friday, Winters withdraws her counteroffer of $10,500 and accepts Tinberg's original price. Under these conditions:

    (A) there is a valid agreement, because Winters accepted Tinberg's offer exactly as it was made.
    (B) there is not a valid agreement, because Winter's counteroffer was a rejection of Tinberg's offer, and once rejected, it cannot be accepted later.
    (C) there is a valid agreement, because Winters accepted before Tinberg advised her that the offer was withdrawn.
    (D) there is not a valid agreement, because Tinberg's offer was not accepted within 72 hours.

28. Property over which an easement runs in favor of another parcel of real estate is known as:

    (A) prescriptive tenement.
    (B) dominant tenement.
    (C) condemned tenement.
    (D) servient tenement.

29. If the quarterly interest at 7.5% is $562.50, what is the principal amount of the loan?

    (A) $7,500
    (B) $75,000
    (C) $30,000
    (D) $90,000

30. Assuming a state deed transfer tax rate of $1.10 per $500.00 or fraction thereof, what is the amount of transfer tax due on the sale of a house if the purchase price was $84,500 and a new mortgage of $26,500 was obtained by the buyer?

    (A) $188.10
    (B) $37.40
    (C) $169.00
    (D) $185.90

31. Assume a house sold for $84,500 and the commission rate was 7%. If the commission is split 60/40 between the selling broker and the listing broker, and each broker splits his share of the commission evenly with his salesperson, how much will the listing salesperson earn from the sale of the house, according to the sales contract?

    (A) $1,774
    (B) $1,183
    (C) $1,020
    (D) $2,366

32. Justin Time and Lotta Time enter into a purchase agreement with Henry and Susan Butler to buy the Butlers' house for $84,500. The buyers pay $2,000 in earnest money and obtain a new mortgage of $67,600. The purchase agreement provides for a March 15, 1984, closing. The buyers and sellers prorate 1984 taxes of $1,880.96, which have been prepaid. The Times have closing costs of $1,250 and the Butlers have closing costs of $850. How much cash must the buyers bring to the closing?

    (A) $17,239.09
    (B) $17,637.70
    (C) $16,541.87
    (D) $19,639.09

33. If in the above problem the taxes that were prorated were not prepaid, and the buyers had to pay the taxes on or before November 30, 1984, how much cash would the buyers have to bring to the closing?

    (A) $15,758.50
    (B) $16,150.00
    (C) $14,660.91
    (D) $15,052.78

34. If a mortgage on a house is 80% of the appraised value and the mortgage interest of 8% amounts to $460 per month, what is the appraised value of the house?

    (A) $86,250
    (B) $71,875
    (C) $69,000
    (D) $92,875

35. The proper description of the township section that is shaded is:

    (A) T4N R2W
    (B) T2W R4N
    (C) T4N R2E
    (D) T2E R4N

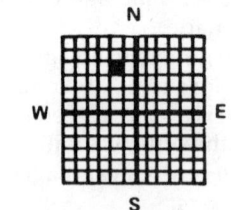

36. Gus Bollin purchases a $37,000 property, depositing $3,000 earnest money. If he can obtain a 75% mortgage (loan-to-value rates), and no additional items are prorated, how much more cash will he need to close?

    (A) $5,500
    (B) $9,250
    (C) $6,250
    (D) $3,250

37. Local zoning ordinances often regulate all of the following EXCEPT:

    (A) the height of buildings in an area.
    (B) the density of population.
    (C) the use of the property.
    (D) the price of the property.

38. Broker Mary Andrews took a listing and later discovered that her client had previously been declared incompetent by a court of law. The listing is now:

    (A) binding, as the broker was acting as the owner's agent in good faith.
    (B) of no value to the broker because it is void.
    (C) the basis for recovery of a commission if the broker produces a buyer.
    (D) renegotiable.

39. Alberta Seneca and Broderick Hampstead secretly enter into an agreement to blow up David Lessing's house. This agreement is:

    (A) voidable if there was duress or undue influence.
    (B) unenforceable unless it was the free and voluntary act of both Seneca and Hampstead.
    (C) void because the object was illegal.
    (D) void because Lessing did not know of the agreement.

40. FHA and VA loans differ from conventional mortgage loans in many ways. Which of the following statements is correct?

    (A) FHA loans are made at higher loan-to-value ratios than VA loans, but at lower loan-to-value ratios than conventional loans.
    (B) All three types of loans must be either insured or guaranteed.
    (C) Conventional mortgage interest rates are generally lower than FHA or VA loan rates, but conventional loans are not always guaranteed or insured.
    (D) Conventional mortgages are usually made at lower loan-to-value ratios, while FHA and VA interest rates are generally lower.

41. The value of Faye Barlow's real estate exceeds her mortgage debt. Her interest is called:

    (A) equality.
    (B) escrow.
    (C) surplus.
    (D) equity.

42. Perry Blacke defaulted on his home mortgage loan payments, and the lender obtained a court order to foreclose on the property. At the foreclosure sale, however, Blacke's house sold for only $29,000; the unpaid balance on the loan at the time of foreclosure was $40,000. What must the lender do to recover the $11,000 Blacke still owes?

    (A) Sue for damages
    (B) Sue for specific performance
    (C) Seek a judgment by default
    (D) Seek a deficiency judgment

43. Jay Brudner, an unmarried man, signed a contract to purchase real estate. The contract included a clause providing that Brudner's liability would terminate and his deposit be refunded if a duplicate of the contract signed by the seller is not delivered to him within two days of the contract date. Owner Saul Feldman signed the contract the next day. The broker attempted to deliver the signed copy to Brudner, but learned that he had since died as the result of an accident. In these circumstances:

    (A) since the seller had accepted the offer within the time limit, the estate of the deceased buyer is liable for completion of the contract.
    (B) the contract, by its terms, is unenforceable.
    (C) death cancels all real estate contracts.
    (D) there is no valid contract.

44. All of the following are exemptions to the Federal Fair Housing Law of 1968 EXCEPT:

    (A) the sale of a single-family home where the listing broker does not advertise the property.
    (B) the rental of a unit in an owner-occupied, three-family dwelling where an advertisement is placed in the paper.
    (C) the restriction of noncommercial lodgings by a private club to members of that club.
    (D) the restriction of noncommercial housing in a convent where a certified statement has not been filed with the government.

45. In an appraisal of a building constructed in 1912, the cost approach would be the least accurate appraisal method because of:

    (A) difficulties in estimating changes in material costs.
    (B) difficulties in finding 1912 building codes.
    (C) difficulties in estimating changes in labor rates.
    (D) difficulties in estimating depreciation.

46. A broker holds a listing on a vacant lot measuring 100 feet wide by 125 feet deep at a listing price of $250 per front foot. The commission that the broker will collect on the deal is set in the listing agreement at 8%. If the property sells for its full asking price, what will the broker's fee be?

    (A) $2,500
    (B) $2,000
    (C) $1,500
    (D) $1,250

47. Normally, a deed will be considered valid even if:

    (A) signed by attorney-in-fact rather than the seller.
    (B) the grantor was not a legal entity.
    (C) the grantor was a minor.
    (D) the grantor did not deliver the deed.

48. The Torrens system is a system of land registration in which:

    (A) the person whose name appears on a certificate of title at the title registrar's office is the owner of the land.
    (B) title is transferred by the delivery of a Torrens deed to the purchaser.
    (C) ownership can be taken by adverse possession.
    (D) title is proven by an abstract.

49. On behalf of Frank Cathay, Sal Hepworth had been offering Cathay's house for sale at the price of $47,900. Mr. and Mrs. Cortez, a Mexican couple, saw the house and were interested in purchasing it. When Mrs. Cortez asked Hepworth what the price of the house was, Hepworth said $53,000. Under the Federal Fair Housing Law of 1968, such a statement is:

    (A) legal, because all that is important is that Mr. and Mrs. Cortez be given the right to buy the house.
    (B) legal, because the representation was made by broker Hepworth and not by Cathay.
    (C) illegal, because the difference in the offering price and the quoted price was greater than $5,000.
    (D) illegal, because the terms of the sale were changed for Mr. and Mrs. Cortez.

50. Sarah Goodhue and Tony Antczak, who are not married, jointly own a parcel of real estate. Each owns an undivided interest; Goodhue's share is two-thirds and Antczak's share is one-third. The form under which Goodhue and Antczak own the real estate is:

    (A) tenancy in common.
    (B) joint tenancy.
    (C) tenancy by the entirety.
    (D) tenancy in severalty.

51. Frances Benjamin moved into a condominium that boasted of many common facilities, including a swimming pool, tennis courts and a putting green. Under a typical condominium arrangement, these common elements are owned by:

    (A) an association of homeowners in the condominium.
    (B) a corporation in which Benjamin and the owners of the other units in the condominium own stock.
    (C) Benjamin and the owners of the other units in the condominium in the form of undivided percentage interest.
    (D) Benjamin and the owners of the other units in the condominium in the form of divided interests.

52. Professional appraiser Herman Franks has just been contracted to analyze a parcel of vacant land to estimate its market value. In doing so, his first consideration will be to establish:

    (A) the price at which the land can be purchased.
    (B) the price at which the land should be listed.
    (C) capitalization of gross income.
    (D) the highest and best use of the land.

53. George McKee sold his house to Sylvia Woods. In the form of deed that was used in the transaction, McKee's only guarantee was that the property was not encumbered during the time he held title except as noted in the deed. The type of deed McKee gave to Woods is a:

    (A) general warranty deed.
    (B) quitclaim deed.
    (C) special warranty deed.
    (D) limited quitclaim deed.

54. Julie Smith has just been hired to prepare a mortgage value appraisal of a property. The property includes an elegant old mansion that is now used as an insurance company office. Which approach to value would Smith principally rely on in making this appraisal?

    (A) Income approach
    (B) Gross rent multiplier approach
    (C) Market data approach
    (D) Replacement cost approach

55. A deed must be signed by which of the following?

    (A) The grantor
    (B) The grantee
    (C) Grantor and grantee
    (D) The grantee and two witnesses

56. Any of the following can be a fiduciary EXCEPT:

    (A) principal.
    (B) broker.
    (C) lawyer.
    (D) banker.

57. A graduated payment loan is one in which:

    (A) mortgage payments decrease.
    (B) mortgage payments balloon in five years.
    (C) mortgage payments increase.
    (D) the interest rate on the loan adjusts annually.

58. If the amount of a loan is $13,500, and the interest rate is 7½%, what is the amount of the semiannual interest payment?

    (A) $596.55
    (B) $506.25
    (C) $602.62
    (D) $457.14

59. Which of the following items is not usually prorated between buyer and seller at the closing?

    (A) Recording charges
    (B) General taxes
    (C) Rents
    (D) Utility bills

60. As an entity operating in the Secondary Mortgage Market, the Federal Home Loan Mortgage Corporation was established to assist the:

    (A) Federal Housing Administration.
    (B) Federal National Mortgage Association.
    (C) Federal Savings and Loans.
    (D) Federal banks.

61. Jack Twilley feels that he has been the victim of an unfair discriminatory practice committed by a local real estate broker. In accordance with federal regulations, he must file a complaint against the broker within:

    (A) 90 days of the alleged discrimination.
    (B) 180 days of the alleged discrimination.
    (C) nine months of the alleged discrimination.
    (D) one year of the alleged discrimination.

62. Which of the following is true about a term mortgage?

    (A) All interest is paid at the end of the term.
    (B) The entire principal is due at the end of the term.
    (C) The debt is partially amortized over the term.
    (D) The term is limited by state statutes.

63. A mortgage using both real and personal property as security is a:

    (A) blanket mortgage.
    (B) package mortgage.
    (C) a dual mortgage.
    (D) a wraparound mortgage.

64. Discount points are a cost to the seller or the buyer. If a buyer obtains a mortgage for $50,000 and points are at four, how much will be charged by the lender at closing?

    (A) $6,000
    (B) $200
    (C) $2,000
    (D) $600

65. Signe Ferguson wishes to net $96,000 after deducting 8% of the selling price of her home. What must the selling price be to accommodate Ferguson?

    (A) $112,800
    (B) $134,380
    (C) $104,348
    (D) $40,000

66. Zoning ordinances control the use of privately owned land by establishing land-use districts. Which one of the following is not a usual zoning district?

    (A) Residential
    (B) Commercial
    (C) Industrial
    (D) Rental

67. Which of the following is true in both an installment contract (land contract) sale and a sale financed by a purchase-money mortgage?

    (A) The buyer is given possession.
    (B) The seller executes and delivers a deed at closing.
    (C) The buyer executes and delivers a mortgage at settlement.
    (D) The seller delivers title at settlement.

68. A borrower obtained a second mortgage loan for $7,000. The loan called for payments of $50 per month, including 6% interest over a period of five years, with the final installment made as a balloon payment including the remaining outstanding principal. What type of loan is this?

    (A) Fully amortized loan
    (B) Straight loan
    (C) Partially amortized loan
    (D) Accelerated loan

69. The proper description of the shaded area is which of the following?

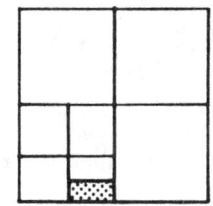

    (A) W½ of the SE¼ of the SW¼
    (B) S½ of the SW¼ of the SE¼
    (C) E½ of the SW¼ of the SW¼
    (D) S½ of the SE¼ of the SW¼

70. If using the following property at its highest and best use would yield an annual income of $3.35 per square foot, how much income would a person be able to earn from this property in a two-year period?

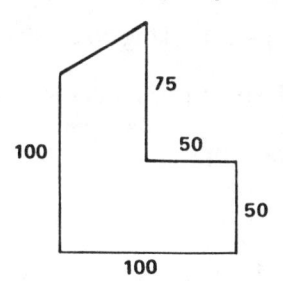

    (A) $8,125.00
    (B) $27,218.75
    (C) $16,250.00
    (D) $54,437.50

71. Michael Buckley owned property in a secluded area adjacent to the Atlantic Ocean. Shortly after he bought the property, he noticed that people from town often walked along the shore in front of his property. He later learned that the locals had been walking along this beach for years. Thereafter, Buckley went to court to try to stop people from walking along the water's edge in front of his property. Buckley is likely to be:

    (A) unsuccessful, because the local citizens were walking there before he bought the property, and thus had an easement.
    (B) unsuccessful, because under the doctrine of littoral rights, Buckley owned the property only to the high-water mark, and the public can use the land below the high-water mark.
    (C) successful, because of the doctrine of Riparian Rights.
    (D) successful, because he has the right to control access to his own property.

72. Frank La Coeur, who desires to sell his house, enters into a listing agreement with broker Effie Berouka. Broker Nora Williamson finds a buyer for the house, and Berouka does not receive the commission. The listing agreement La Coeur and Berouka signed could have been:

    (A) an exclusive right-to-sell listing.
    (B) an exclusive agency listing.
    (C) an open listing.
    (D) a multiple listing.

73. What is the cost of constructing a fence 6 feet 6 inches high around a lot measuring 90 feet by 175 feet, if the cost of erecting the fence is $1.25 per linear foot and the cost of material is $.825 per square foot of fence?

    (A) $2,083.56
    (B) $2,053.75
    (C) $1,752.31
    (D) $3,504.63

74. All of the following are true about the law of agency in real estate EXCEPT:

    (A) the broker is an agent.
    (B) the agent owes a duty to the fiduciary.
    (C) a broker may not act as a dual agent unless the consent of all parties is received.
    (D) to receive a commission a broker must have been the procuring cause of the sale.

75. The manager of a commercial building carries out many duties in connection with the operation and maintenance of the structure. The manager would normally be considered the agent of:

    (A) the lessor of the building.
    (B) the lessee in the building.
    (C) the lessor and lessee.
    (D) the investors.

76. All of the following are true about the concept of adverse possession EXCEPT:

    (A) the person taking possession of the property must do so without the consent of the owner of the property.
    (B) occupancy of the property by the person taking possession must be continuous over a specified period of time.
    (C) the person taking possession of the property must compensate the owner at the end of the adverse possession period.
    (D) the person taking possession of the property may end up owning the property.

77. Broker Jane Dalton signed a listing agreement with the owner of a house. After the house sold for $82,000, broker Dalton wound up with a commission of $3,000 and broker Donald Travis wound up with a commission of $2,600. Because broker Dalton did not get the full commission, it would appear that she:

    (A) belonged to a multiple-listing service.
    (B) had an open listing.
    (C) had an exclusive agency listing.
    (D) did not represent the seller.

78. Sally Bosworth, a salesperson associated with Ocean Front Brokerage, obtained the signature of the owners of a unit in Atlantic Towers Condominium on a listing agreement. Bosworth in this transaction:

    (A) has a direct contractual relationship with the owners of the unit.
    (B) acts on behalf of Ocean Front Brokerage.
    (C) acts on behalf of Atlantic Towers Condominium.
    (D) must find a buyer to obtain a share of the commission.

79. Broker Sam Tillman has an exclusive right-to-sell listing with Ned Kulver. While Kulver is out of town on business, Tillman finds a buyer who is interested in buying Kulver's house if Kulver will take a purchase-money mortgage. However, the buyer must have a commitment from the seller prior to Kulver's scheduled return to the city. Under these circumstances:

    (A) Tillman may enter into a binding agreement on behalf of Kulver.
    (B) Tillman may collect a commission even if the transaction falls through due to Kulver's absence from the city.
    (C) the buyer is deemed to have an option Kulver signs.
    (D) Tillman must obtain the signature of Kulver in order to get a commission.

80. Antitrust laws prohibit all of the following EXCEPT:

    (A) real estate companies agreeing on fees charged to sellers.
    (B) brokers allocating markets based on value of homes.
    (C) real estate companies allocating market based on the location of commercial buildings.
    (D) salespersons allocating markets based on location of homes.

REAL ESTATE EXAM MANUAL

SOLUTIONS TO SAMPLE EXAM II

The solutions to Sample Examination II contain the question number, the correct answer choice, the type of question and the topic area as well as the page number and outline reference number where the student may refer for information on the material covered in the question. The computations for the math problems have been worked out and may be found immediately following the solutions.

Question	Answer	Type of Question	Topic Area	Outline Reference	Page
1.	(D)	Comprehension, Brokerage	Voidable contracts	IX. C.	59
2.	(D)	Comprehension, Math	Compute payment due	Math Review	77-82
3.	(D)	Comprehension, Financing	Discount points	III. C. 5.	40
4.	(B)	Definition, Financing	Statutory redemption	V. B. 2.	42
5.	(A)	Definition, Laws Relating to Ownership	Metes & bounds	II. A. 1.	19
6.	(B)	Comprehension, Math	Area and cost per sq. yard	Math Review	77-82
7.	(B)	Definition, Brokerage	Specific performance	X. B. 1. b.	59
8.	(A)	Comprehension, Transfer of Ownership	Cloud on title	II. C.	48
9.	(D)	Definition, Specialty Areas	Gross lease	IV. A.	73
10.	(B)	Definition, Transfer of Ownership	Title insurance	I. A. 2.	48
11.	(D)	Definition, Brokerage	Fair Housing	XIII. B.	61
12.	(C)	Comprehension, Laws Relating to Ownership	Lien	IV. A. 1. a.	22
13.	(B)	Definition, Laws Relating to Ownership	Condominium	III. C. 1.	21
14.	(B)	Definition, Brokerage	Option	XI. 1.	61
15.	(A)	Comprehension, Specialty Areas	Securities	II. B.	72
16.	(D)	Definition, Laws Relating to Ownership	Zoning ordinance	V. A. 1.	24
17.	(A)	Comprehension, Laws Relating to Ownership	Section of land	II. A. 2. f.	19
18.	(C)	Definition, Financing	Acceleration	IX. D.	42
19.	(B)	Comprehension, Brokerage	Acceptance of contract	XI. F.	60
20.	(B)	Comprehension, Brokerage	Statute of limitations	XI. A.	60
21.	(B)	Comprehension, Transfer of Ownership	Tenants in common	III. B.	49
22.	(D)	Definition, Laws Relating to Ownership	Mechanic's lien	IV. A. 1. a.	23
23.	(D)	Definition, Laws Relating to Ownership	Deed restrictions	V. B.	24
24.	(B)	Comprehension, Math	Compute amount of tax	Math Review	77-82
25.	(C)	Comprehension, Brokerage	Statute of frauds	XI. B.	60
26.	(A)	Definition, Financing	FHA mortgage	III. C.	40
27.	(B)	Comprehension, Brokerage	Valid contract	IX. A.	59
28.	(D)	Definition, Laws Relating to Ownership	Servient tenement	IV. A. 1. b.	23
29.	(C)	Comprehension, Math	Compute loan amount	Math Review	77-82

114

SAMPLE EXAMINATIONS

#	Ans	Category	Topic	Ref	Page
30.	(D)	Comprehension, Math	Compute state deed stamps	Math Review	77-82
31.	(B)	Comprehension, Math	Compute commission	Math Review	77-82
32.	(B)	Comprehension, Math	Compute amount of cash	Math Review	77-82
33.	(A)	Comprehension, Math	Compute amount prorated	Math Review	77-82
34.	(A)	Comprehension, Math	Compute appraised amount	Math Review	77-82
35.	(A)	Comprehension, Laws Relating to Ownership	Section	II. A. 2. d.	19
36.	(C)	Comprehension, Math	Compute loan to value and cash amount	Math Review	77-82
37.	(D)	Definition, Laws Relating to Ownership	Zoning ordinances	V. A. 1.	24
38.	(B)	Definition, Brokerage	Void contract	IX. B.	59
39.	(C)	Comprehension, Brokerage	Void contract	IX. B.	59
40.	(D)	Comprehension, Financing	FHA financing	III. C.	40
41.	(D)	Definition, Financing	Equity	IX. L.	43
42.	(D)	Comprehension, Financing	Deficiency judgment	V. C.	42
43.	(D)	Comprehension, Brokerage	Valid contract	IX. A.	59
44.	(A)	Comprehension, Brokerage	Fair Housing	VIII. B. 2.	62
45.	(D)	Comprehension, Valuation	Cost approach	I. B.	32
46.	(B)	Comprehension, Math	Compute commission and cost per front foot	Math Review	77-82
47.	(A)	Comprehension, Transfer of Ownership	Power of attorney	II.	48
48.	(A)	Definition, Transfer of Ownership	Torrens system	I. A. 3.	48
49.	(D)	Comprehension, Brokerage	Fair Housing	XIII. B. 1. b.	61
50.	(A)	Comprehension, Transfer of Ownership	Tenancy in common	III. B. 1.	49
51.	(C)	Comprehension, Laws Relating to Ownership	Condominium	III. C. 1.	21
52.	(D)	Comprehension, Valuation	Highest and best use	II. B. 6.	33
53.	(C)	Comprehension, Transfer of Ownership	Limited warranty	II. B.	48
54.	(A)	Comprehension, Valuation	Income approach	I. C.	32
55.	(A)	Definition, Transfer of Ownership	Deed	II.	48
56.	(A)	Definition, Brokerage	Fiduciary	I. B.	56
57.	(C)	Definition, Financing	GPM	IV. B.	41
58.	(B)	Comprehension, Math	Compute semiannual interest	Math Review	77-82
59.	(A)	Comprehension, Transfer of Ownership	Proration	VII.	51
60.	(C)	Definition, Financing	F.H.L.M.C.	I. B.	38
61.	(B)	Definition, Brokerage	Fair Housing	XIII.	61
62.	(B)	Definition, Financing	Term mortgage	IV. C.	41
63.	(B)	Definition, Financing	Package mortgage	II. E.	39
64.	(C)	Comprehension, Financing	Discount points	III. C. 5.	40
65.	(C)	Comprehension, Math	Compute sale price	Math Review	77-82

115

66.	(D)	Comprehension, Laws Relating to Ownership	Zoning ordinance	V. A. 1. b.	24
67.	(A)	Comprehension, Financing	Seller financing	II. H.	39
68.	(C)	Comprehension, Financing	Partially amortized loan	IV. E. 2.	41
69.	(D)	Comprehension, Laws Relating to Ownership	Rectangular survey	II. A. 2.	19
70.	(D)	Comprehension, Math	Compute income/sq. feet and total income	Math Review	77-82
71.	(B)	Comprehension, Laws Relating to Ownership	Littoral rights	IV. B. 2.	24
72.	(C)	Definition, Brokerage	Open listing	IV. A.	58
73.	(D)	Comprehension, Math	Compute cost per linear foot and cost per sq. foot	Math Review	77-82
74.	(B)	Definition, Brokerage	Law of agency	I.	56
75.	(A)	Comprehension, Specialty	Property management	III.	73
76.	(C)	Definition, Laws Relating to Ownership	Adverse possession	III. B. 4.	21
77.	(A)	Comprehension, Brokerage	Multiple listing service	V. B. 2.	58
78.	(B)	Comprehension, Brokerage	Law of agency	I.	56
79.	(D)	Comprehension, Brokerage	Authority of broker	I. D.	56
80.	(D)	Definition, Brokerage	Antitrust	III. B.	57

Sample Examination II Math Solutions

2) $82,500 price of house − $10,000 down payment ($1,000 earnest money is included in down payment) = $72,500 amount financed; $72,500 − $65,200 first mortgage = $7,300 second mortgage; $7,300 × .08 = $584 annual interest; $584 ÷ 12 = $48.67 monthly interest; last payment on second mortgage = principal + 1 month interest or $7,300 + $48.67 = $7,348.67

6) 15 × 20 = 300 sq. feet; 300 ÷ 9 = 33.33 sq. yards; 33.33 × $6.95 = $231.67 cost of materials; add cost of materials and cost of labor $231.67 + $250.00 = $481.67

24) $14,500 assessed value × 1.5 equalization factor = $21,750; $21,750 ÷ 100 and × $5 = $1,087.50 annual taxes

29) $562.50 quarterly interest × 4 = $2,250 annual interest; $2,250 ÷ .075 interest rate = $30,000 amount of loan

30) $84,500 purchase price ÷ $500 = 169 units; 169 × $1.10 = $185.90 state deed tax

31) $84,500 price × 7% or .07 commission rate = $5,915 total commission; $5,915 × .40 listing broker's share = $2,366; $2,366 × .50 share of listing salesperson = $1,183

32) $84,500 price − $2,000 earnest money and − $67,600 mortgage = $14,900 cash toward house brought to closing; $1,250 = buyer's closing costs; $1,880.96 annual taxes ÷ 360 days = $5.22 per day; buyer's share is March 15 to December 31 or 285 days; $5.22 × 285 = $1,487.70 for taxes; add 3 components $14,900 + $1,250 + $1,489.09 = $17,637.70 buyer's cash for closing

SAMPLE EXAMINATIONS

33) $14,900 cash toward house and $1,250 closing costs are same as in question 32; seller's share of taxes is $5.22 × 75 days = $391.50; cash needed by buyer is $14,900 + $1,250 − $391.50 (credit for seller's taxes to be paid later by buyer) = $15,758.50

34) $460 monthly interest × 12 = $5,520 annual interest; $5,520 ÷ .08 interest rate = $69,000 amount of mortgage; $69,000 ÷ .80 ratio = $86,250 value of house

36) $37,000 price × .75 = $27,750 amount of mortgage; $37,000 − $27,750 = $9,250 amount of down payment; $9,250 − $3,000 earnest money = $6,250 cash brought to closing

46) 100 (width of property) × $250 = $25,000 price of lot; $25,000 × .08 commission rate = $2,000 commission

58) $13,500 loan × .075 or 7½% interest rate = $1,012.50 annual interest; $1,012.50 ÷ 2 = $506.25 semiannual interest

64) 1 point = 1% of mortgage; 4 points = 4% of mortgage; $50,000 mortgage × .04 = $2,000 charged by lender

65) seller wants $96,000 after deducting 8% of selling price; therefore $96,000 = 92% of selling price; $96,000 ÷ .92 = $104,348 selling price

70) divide property into square, rectangle and triangle; area of square is 50 × 50 = 2,500 sq. feet; area of rectangle is 50 × 100 = 5,000 sq. feet; area of triangle is ½(50 × 25) = 625 sq. feet; add three parts together 2,500 + 5,000 + 625 = 8,125 sq. feet; 8,125 × $3.35 income per square foot = $27,218.75 annual income; $27,218.75 × 2 = $54,437.50 income in 2 years

73) perimeter of lot (length of fence) is 90 + 175 + 90 + 175 = 530 feet; 530 × $1.25 = $662.50 cost of labor; 530 length × 6.5 height (6 feet 6 inches = 6.5 feet) = 3,445 square footage of fence material; 3,445 × $.825 = $2,842.13 cost of material; add cost of labor and cost of material $662.50 + $2,842.13 = $3,504.63 cost of fence

SAMPLE EXAM II

Progress Score

Rating	Percentage	Range
EXCELLENT	96% to 100%	77–80
GOOD	86% to 95%	69–76
FAIR	76% to 85%	61–68
MARGINAL	70% to 75%	56–60
NEED IMPROVEMENT	69% or less	55 or less

Your Score
Exam II   80
Total wrong   −
Total right   ___

SAMPLE EXAMINATION III

1. The gross rent multiplier is used in connection with which of the following?

    (A) Single-family homes
    (B) Retail space
    (C) Industrial plant
    (D) Commercial property

2. Which shaded area depicts the NE¼ of the SE¼ of the SW¼?

    (A) Area 1
    (B) Area 2
    (C) Area 3
    (D) Area 4

3. Kay Woodhue owns an apartment building. Using a capitalization rate of 8%, Woodhue's building is valued at $100,000. Due to a change in the economic climate, investors now demand a capitalization rate of 10% for this type of building. With the new cap rate, the value of the property will:

    (A) increase by 20%.
    (B) increase less than 20%.
    (C) decrease less than $10,000.
    (D) decrease more than $10,000.

4. The major intent of zoning regulations is to:

    (A) demonstrate the police power of the state.
    (B) ensure the health, safety and welfare of the community.
    (C) set limits on the amount and kinds of businesses in a given area.
    (D) protect residential neighborhoods from encroachment by business and industry.

5. Reconciliation is an appraisal term used to describe:

    (A) the appraiser's determination of a property's highest value.
    (B) an average of real estate values for properties similar to the one being appraised.
    (C) the appraiser's analysis and comparison of the results of each appraisal approach.
    (D) the method used to determine a property's most appropriate capitalization rate.

6. Currently, FNMA's activities include all of the following EXCEPT:

    (A) buying and selling FHA-VA mortgages.
    (B) buying and selling conventional mortgages.
    (C) buying and selling mortgages at full face value.
    (D) buying and selling mortgages at discounted values.

7. The market price on real estate is generally the same as:

    (A) sale price.
    (B) market value.
    (C) highest and best use.
    (D) assessed value.

8. All of the following are basic principles of value EXCEPT:

    (A) highest and best use.
    (B) anticipation.
    (C) substitution.
    (D) novation.

SAMPLE EXAMINATIONS

9. All of the following are true about townships EXCEPT:

    (A) each township is composed of 36 sections.
    (B) a township square and a township strip are not the same.
    (C) there are 640 acres in a township.
    (D) townships are located by reference to principal meridians and base lines.

10. In consideration of $50, Jim Pascucci gives Charles Gutman the right to purchase certain described real estate for $2,000 if Gutman enters into an agreement to purchase it within 60 days. Gutman is:

    (A) an optionor.
    (B) an escrowee.
    (C) an optionee.
    (D) a remainder.

11. Assume a house sold for $95,900 and the commission rate was 7%. The listing and selling brokers split the commission fifty-fifty. The listing broker gives the listing salesperson 30% of his commission, and the selling broker gives the selling salesperson 35% of his commission. How much does the selling salesperson earn from the sale after deducting advertising expenses of $35?

    (A) $1,139.78
    (B) $1,174.78
    (C) $971.95
    (D) $1,183.88

12. Allan and Ella Gator entered into a purchase agreement to buy a house owned by Cindy and Donald Smith for $95,900. The purchase agreement provides for an earnest money deposit of $2,000, the assumption of an existing mortgage with a current balance of $45,850, and a second mortgage of $25,000. Assuming a calendar tax year and annual taxes of $2,234, payable in two equal installments on May 30 and November 30, if the Smiths' closing costs are $800 and the Gators' closing costs are $950, how much cash must the Gators bring to a closing to be held on September 15?

    (A) $22,694.58
    (B) $25,384.58
    (C) $23,384.58
    (D) $23,534.25

13. A house sold for $95,900. The buyer purchased the house by making a cash down payment of $25,050, assuming an existing mortgage of $45,850, and obtaining a new second mortgage of $25,000. If $1,500 of the house's purchase price represented the reasonable value of identifiable personal property that was included in the sale, what is the amount of state deed tax payable if the tax rate is $1.10 per $500 or fraction thereof?

    (A) $111.10
    (B) $210.00
    (C) $218.90
    (D) $107.80

14. When a mortgage loan has been paid in full, which of the following is the most important thing for the borrower to do?

    (A) Put the paid note and all canceled papers in a safe-deposit box
    (B) Arrange to receive and pay future real estate tax bills
    (C) Be sure mortgagee signs a Satisfaction of Mortgage
    (D) Record the Satisfaction of Mortgage

15. In most states, for a contract for deed to be recorded it must:

    (A) be in the form of a memorandum agreement.
    (B) be notarized.
    (C) be for a term of at least 3 years.
    (D) be witnessed.

16. Normally, the priority of general liens is determined by:

    (A) the order in which they are filed or recorded.
    (B) the order in which the cause of action arose.
    (C) the size of the claim.
    (D) the court.

17. When property is held in tenancy by the entirety:

    (A) the owners must be husband and wife.
    (B) either owner may sell his or her own interest separately to a third party by signing a quitclaim deed.
    (C) there is no right of survivorship.
    (D) the property may be partitioned.

18. Greg Chambers listed his home for sale with the XYZ Brokerage Company under an open listing agreement. After the sale of the property, a dispute arose between XYZ Brokerage and Sunnyday Brokerage; both claimed they were entitled to a commission. In this situation, the commission should be paid to the broker who:

    (A) listed the property.
    (B) advertised the property.
    (C) obtained the first offer.
    (D) was the procuring cause of the sale.

19. Regulation Z applies to:

    (A) business loans.
    (B) real estate purchase agreements.
    (C) commercial loans under $10,000.
    (D) personal-use real estate credit transactions over $25,000.

20. What is a mortgage loan that requires monthly payments of $213.75 for 20 years and a final payment of $5,350?

    (A) A wraparound mortgage
    (B) An accelerated mortgage
    (C) A balloon mortgage
    (D) A variable mortgage

21. The practice of channeling potential buyers of one race into one area and potential buyers of another race into a second area is known as:

    (A) canvassing.
    (B) blockbusting.
    (C) redlining.
    (D) steering.

22. A broker who is entitled to collect a commission when the sellers sell their own property:

    (A) has an exclusive agency listing contract with the sellers.
    (B) has a net listing contract with the sellers.
    (C) has an exclusive right-to-sell listing contract with the sellers.
    (D) has an open listing contract with the sellers.

23. Under the doctrine of riparian rights, the owners of property adjacent to navigable rivers or streams have the right to use the water, and:

    (A) may erect a dam across the navigable river or stream if the owners on each side agree.
    (B) are considered to own the submerged land to the center point of the river.
    (C) are considered owners of the water adjacent to the land.
    (D) are considered to own the land to the edge of the water.

24. The word *improvement* refers to all of the following EXCEPT?

    (A) Streets
    (B) Sewer and drainage systems
    (C) Land in urban areas
    (D) Retaining wall

25. In the decade prior to the passage of the Fair Housing Law of 1968, several executive orders and congressional acts were passed covering limited areas of the housing industry. Areas covered by these orders and acts prohibited discrimination in:

    (A) housing projects that receive state funding.
    (B) house sales involving FHA or VA loans.
    (C) home sales involving down payments of more than $250,000.
    (D) homes worth less than $40,000.

26. Norman Henson sells his house and moves into a condominium. Shortly after moving in he learns that Taylor Bainbridge, his next-door neighbor, has failed to pay his real estate taxes. If Bainbridge does not pay his taxes:

    (A) there is a general lien against the condominium, including Henson's apartment.
    (B) the only lien that can be placed against the property is a lien against Bainbridge's apartment and Bainbridge's interest in the common areas.
    (C) there is no lien against Henson's apartment, but a lien is placed against the common areas.
    (D) the only lien that can be placed against the property is against Bainbridge's apartment. No lien can be placed against any interest in the common areas, because of the interests of condominium owners who have paid their taxes.

27. Sheila Horning listed a property under a valid written listing agreement. After the sale was completed, the owner refused to pay the broker's fee. Which of the following can Horning do?

    (A) She can take the seller to court and sue for the commission.
    (B) She is entitled to a lien on the seller's property for the amount of the commission.
    (C) She can go to court and stop the transaction until she is paid.
    (D) She can collect the commission from the buyer.

28. Terence Keane lent money to Rena Bushman and in return took a mortgage as security for the debt. Keane immediately recorded the mortgage. Thereafter, Omar Rooney lent money to Bushman, took a mortgage and recorded it. Bushman later defaulted, and a court determined that Rooney's interest had priority over Keane's interest. Under these circumstances, chances are:

    (A) Keane knew Rooney was going to make a loan prior to making his own loan.
    (B) Rooney's loan was larger than Keane's loan.
    (C) Keane had signed a subordination agreement in favor of Rooney.
    (D) Rooney had signed a satisfaction.

29. How many acres are in the S½ of the NW¼ of the SE¼ of a section?

    (A) 10 acres
    (B) 20 acres
    (C) 40 acres
    (D) 120 acres

30. All of the following are tests for determining a fixture EXCEPT:

    (A) intent of the parties.
    (B) size of the item.
    (C) method of attachment of the item.
    (D) adaptation of the item to the particular real estate.

31. All of the following are agencies operating in the secondary market EXCEPT:

    (A) the Federal National Mortgage Association.
    (B) the Federal Savings and Loan Insurance Corporation.
    (C) the Government National Mortgage Association.
    (D) the Federal Home Loan Mortgage Corporation.

32. Al Jones, Harold Murphy and Josh Hagstrom are joint tenants owning a parcel of land. Hagstrom conveys his interest to his friend, Bill Phillips. After the conveyance, Jones and Murphy:

    (A) become tenants in common.
    (B) remain joint tenants owning an undivided two-thirds interest in the land.
    (C) become joint tenants with Phillips.
    (D) continue to be joint tenants with Hagstrom.

33. If an individual needs to net $50,000 after a sale, and the costs incurred in selling the house include a 7% commission and other expenses that total $1,200, what must the house sell for?

    (A) $54,700.00
    (B) $54,963.44
    (C) $55,053.76
    (D) $55,633.25

34. Mortgagor Carmen Nyro computed the interest he was charged last month on his $27,500 mortgage loan balance as $189.06. His rate of interest is which of the following?

    (A) 7½%
    (B) 7¾%
    (C) 8¼%
    (D) 8½%

35. Assume that listing and selling brokers split a commission fifty-fifty and that they then split their shares of the commission fifty-fifty with their respective salespeople. If a house sold for $86,500 and the salesperson of the realty company that sold the house received a commission of $1,297.50, what is the commission rate on the sale?

    (A) 3%
    (B) 5%
    (C) 6%
    (D) 7%

36. When real estate is sold under an installment land contract, possession is usually given to the buyer. Title is:

    (A) subject to a purchase-money mortgage.
    (B) always required to be transferred to a land trust.
    (C) kept by the seller until the full purchase price is paid.
    (D) also given to the buyer.

37. A seller has a 3-year, $25,000 insurance policy expiring April 7, 1989, for which she paid a premium of $78.50. What was the amount of unearned premium allowed to the seller when the sale was closed on February 15, 1988?

    (A) $29.66
    (B) $28.73
    (C) $27.89
    (D) $26.03

38. To start a condominium, a developer will normally file which of the following?

    (A) Judgment
    (B) Lien
    (C) Certificate
    (D) Declaration

39. The seller's mortgage balance assumed by the purchaser was $17,672 at 6¾% interest and had been paid through December 31, 1988. What was the proration of accrued interest when the sale was closed on January 17, 1989?

    (A) $52.78
    (B) $54.01
    (C) $56.27
    (D) $57.20

40. Tenant Olga Smithers and landlord Harry Dubois enter into a lease. The agreement provides that Dubois will remove a fence that had been built prior to the tenant's taking possession. A dispute over the fence arises, and Dubois argues that after the lease had been typed, but several days before it was executed by the parties, the two parties agreed that Smithers would remove the fence. Which of the following doctrines will come into play?

    (A) The statute of limitations
    (B) Novation
    (C) The rule of 78's
    (D) The parol evidence rule

41. A licensed real estate broker:

    (A) becomes an agent of the vendee upon obtaining a valid listing.
    (B) can disclose any truthful information received from the principal.
    (C) becomes an agent of the vendor when a buyer is found.
    (D) must disclose all material facts to the principal.

42. George Barstow agrees to buy Elaine Clark's real estate for $53,000. Barstow signs a sales contract and deposits $5,300 earnest money with broker Stuart Donovan. Clark is unable to show good title, and Barstow demands the return of his earnest money from Donovan, as provided in the contract. What should Donovan do?

    (A) Deduct his commission and return the balance to Barstow
    (B) Deduct his commission and pay the balance to Clark
    (C) Return the entire amount of the earnest money to Barstow
    (D) Pay the entire amount to Clark to dispose of as she sees fit

43. A homestead exemption protects against judgments:

    (A) of unsecured creditors.
    (B) that result from unpaid taxes.
    (C) that result from foreclosure of a mortgage.
    (D) that result from cost of improvements.

44. If the annual rate of interest on a mortgage loan is 8½%, and the monthly interest payment is $201.46, what is the principal amount of the loan?

    (A) $2,417.52
    (B) $28,441.41
    (C) $2,844.14
    (D) $14,270.00

45. In the event the parties to a contract wish to delete a provision in the printed agreement form, they should:

    (A) execute a supplement to the purchase agreement.
    (B) cross out the provisions to be deleted.
    (C) have their signatures notarized.
    (D) arrive at an oral agreement to make the changes.

46. If a house was sold for $55,000 and an FHA mortgage was obtained for $50,000, how many points were charged to the seller if the seller had to pay $2,000?

    (A) Two points
    (B) Three and one-half points
    (C) Four points
    (D) Five points

47. All of the following are contracts between an agent and a principal EXCEPT:

    (A) open listing.
    (B) net listing.
    (C) multiple listing.
    (D) exclusive listing.

48. Hobart Lucas is a tenant with a lease that has five years to run. The premises, however, have become too small for Lucas's business. Morley Knight is interested in possessing the premises for three years. Which of the following agreements would Lucas and Knight execute to effect Knight's wishes?

    (A) An assignment
    (B) A novation
    (C) A sublease
    (D) A tenancy at sufferance

49. If a mortgage is placed upon a parcel of real estate valued at $87,500 in an amount equal to 80% of its value, what is the interest rate of the mortgage if the monthly interest is $510.42?

    (A) 8¼%
    (B) 8½%
    (C) 8¾%
    (D) 9%

50. A listing agreement can be terminated by:

    (A) partial performance.
    (B) unilateral revocation.
    (C) mutual agreement.
    (D) execution of a holdover clause.

51. Mary Kanasaki and Dudley Peters enter into a contract wherein Peters will build a building for Kanasaki on some vacant land. After agreeing upon a price and entering into the agreement, Peters begins work and finds that because of the nature of the soil, the supports for the building will have to be dug much deeper than he had thought. The additional work will cause Peters to lose money on the project. Under these circumstances:

    (A) Peters does not have to continue with the contract, under the doctrine of impossibility.
    (B) Peters does not have to continue with the contract, because Kanasaki does not have the right to force Peters to lose money.
    (C) Peters can force Kanasaki to renegotiate the contract because of Peter's mistake, if the mistake was reasonable.
    (D) Peters will be liable for breach of contract if he fails to perform, and the fact that the job is now more difficult than Peters had expected is irrelevant.

52. According to the following plat of Indian Hills, which lot(s) is (are) described here? "Beginning at the intersection of the west line of White Road and the north line of Red Road, and running due west a distance of 120 feet, then due north a distance of 100 feet, thence northwesterly on a course of N 35°W a distance of 120 feet, then due east a distance of 200 feet, thence due south a distance of 200 feet to the point of beginning."

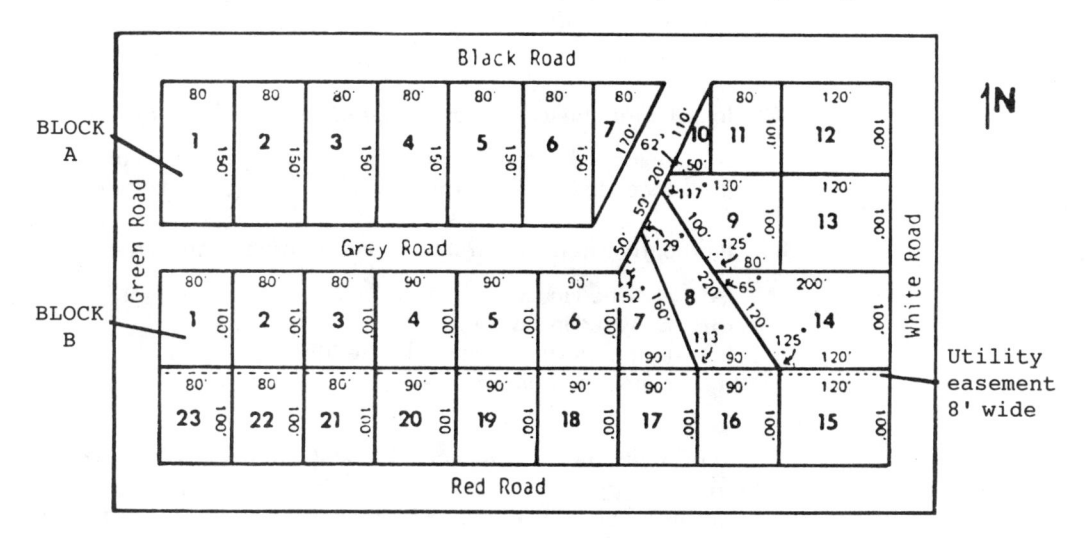

(A) Lots 8 and 14 in Block B
(B) Lot 14 in Block B
(C) Lots 14 and 15 in Block B
(D) Lot 15 in Block B

53. Mary Pannell and Dick Kuhl are salespeople in the brokerage firm of Farnsworth-Schmidt Realty. One day over coffee they decide that Pannell will specialize in houses on the east side of town and Kuhl will specialize in houses on the west side of town. Such a practice is:

(A) legal, because the prohibition against allocation of market does not apply to salespeople working for the same brokerage.
(B) legal, because the agreement was not in writing.
(C) illegal, because it is a violation of the antitrust laws.
(D) illegal, because only brokers may agree to restrict competition.

54. Broker Carol Steingart has several salespeople employed at her office. Early one day, one member of the sales staff brought in a written offer with an earnest money deposit on a house listed with the broker. Later the same day, another salesperson brought in a higher written offer on the same property, also including an earnest money deposit. Broker Steingart, in accordance with the policy of her office, did not submit the second offer to the seller until the first had been presented and rejected so the seller was not informed of the second offer. In this situation, the broker's actions are:

(A) permissible, providing the commission is split between the two salespeople.
(B) permissible, if such an arrangement is written into the salespeople's employment contracts.
(C) not permissible, because the broker must submit all offers to the seller.
(D) not permissible, because the broker must notify the second buyer of the existence of the first offer.

55. Brice and Judy Rucker purchased their home three years ago. They made a $20,000 down payment and obtained a mortgage loan to finance the balance of their purchase. The Ruckers have paid $14,400 in mortgage payments over the last three years, $10,000 of which has been used to pay the mortgage interest. The $24,400 that the Ruckers have invested in their home over the last three years is referred to as their:

    (A) homestead.
    (B) profit.
    (C) redemption.
    (D) equity.

56. In order for title to pass to the grantee of a deed, the deed must be:

    (A) delivered to the grantee.
    (B) recorded by the grantee.
    (C) executed by the grantor.
    (D) executed by the grantee.

57. If property was owned solely by one spouse the property:

    (A) is owned in trust.
    (B) is owned in severalty.
    (C) is immune from seizure by creditors.
    (D) cannot be homesteaded.

58. Tom Jasaitis has a claim affecting the title to Bill Shipley's property. Shipley has been trying to sell the property, and Jasaitis is concerned about the possibility of a bona fide purchaser buying it before he obtains a judgment. To protect himself during the course of the court action, Jasaitis should:

    (A) file a lis pendens.
    (B) publish a notice in a newspaper.
    (C) bring a quick summary proceeding.
    (D) notify Shipley that any attempt to sell the property will be considered fraud.

59. After the statute of limitations has run out, a contract that has been breached is which of the following?

    (A) Unenforceable
    (B) Rescinded
    (C) Terminated
    (D) Discharged

60. After a neighborhood had been hit by vandals on a number of occasions, Nolan Wilcox offered to pay $100 to anyone providing information leading to the arrest and conviction of the guilty party. Shortly thereafter, Eileen O'Brian supplied the needed information and received the reward. This is an example of:

    (A) a gift.
    (B) an option.
    (C) a unilateral contract.
    (D) a voidable contract.

61. John Allen offers to sell Naomi Summers certain undeveloped land in the country and represents to Summers that a new freeway will run right by the land, even though Allen knows that the plans for the new freeway have been dropped. Summers, relying on the representation, purchases the land from Allen. Under these circumstances:

    (A) Allen can be forced to proceed with the sale even though there was fraud.
    (B) the contract is voidable at the option of Allen.
    (C) the misrepresentation automatically voids the contract.
    (D) Summers may not proceed with the purchase after discovery of the fraud.

62. If a house was sold for $37,500 with an FHA mortgage, and the required down payment was set at 3% for the first $25,000 and 5% for any amount over $25,000, what was the amount of the mortgage?

    (A) $1,375
    (B) $1,425
    (C) $36,125
    (D) $35,850

63. A joint tenancy may be created:

    (A) automatically, if the property is distributed to surviving children.
    (B) by presumption, if the form of ownership is not described.
    (C) by deed or by will.
    (D) only by a deed executed by both spouses.

64. Howard Klutch agrees to buy Thomas Frazier's land for $5,000. Klutch deposits the purchase price with Joanna Holland, and Frazier deposits the deed with Holland. Holland is instructed to record the deed when Frazier shows good title to the land. Holland is to pay the $5,000, less appropriate deductions, to Frazier when Klutch has good title. What is this procedure called?

    (A) A provisional sale
    (B) A sale upon condition
    (C) An option
    (D) An escrow

65. Broker Kate Meletos pays her salespeople 20% of the commission for listing a property and 40% of the commission for selling it. The commission rate is 5%. What was the selling price of a house if the salesperson who both listed and sold it received $3,600?

    (A) $120,000
    (B) $200,000
    (C) $72,000
    (D) $100,000

66. If the market value of a house is $84,500, the assessment ratio is 35% and the tax rate is 30 mills, what are the monthly taxes?

    (A) $887.25
    (B) $942.50
    (C) $73.94
    (D) $87.72

67. If Richard Ine seeks relief from zoning regulations on the ground of nonconforming use, effective arguments to the zoning authorities would include all of the following EXCEPT:

    (A) that the nonconforming use existed prior to the passing of the zoning ordinance.
    (B) that he would earn more by using the property for purposes that do not conform with the zoning ordinance.
    (C) that the nonconforming use didn't harm the public health, safety and general welfare.
    (D) that conforming to the zoning ordinance would create an undue hardship.

68. Which of the following is a loan in which only interest is payable during the term of the loan and all principal is payable at the end of the loan period?

    (A) An amortized loan
    (B) A flexible loan
    (C) A fixed installment loan
    (D) A term loan

69. If the interest rate for conventional loans is 10¼%, and a FHA-insured lender must charge five points in order to equalize the yield, what is the interest rate on the FHA loan?

    (A) 9⅝%
    (B) 9⅞%
    (C) 5¼%
    (D) 10⅞%

70. When property fails to sell at a court foreclosure for an amount sufficient to satisfy the mortgage debt, the mortgagee may usually sue for which of the following?

    (A) A judgment by default
    (B) A deficiency judgment
    (C) A satisfaction of mortgage
    (D) Damages

71. A mortgagor can get direct financing from all of the following EXCEPT:

    (A) mortgage banking companies.
    (B) savings and loan associations.
    (C) commercial banks.
    (D) Fannie Mae.

72. A property manager normally is charged with all of the following duties EXCEPT:

    (A) renting space to tenants.
    (B) preparing a budget.
    (C) developing a management plan.
    (D) repairing a tenant's fixture.

73. Which of the following transfers is an involuntary alienation of property?

    (A) Quitclaim
    (B) Inheritance
    (C) Eminent domain
    (D) Gift

74. Brenda Montgomery is a tenant under a leasehold estate for years. Under such an estate:

    (A) the term of the lease must be for at least one year.
    (B) no notice is required to terminate the lease.
    (C) a 30-day notice is required to terminate the lease.
    (D) the lessee is deemed to hold a freehold estate.

75. Joe Spapperi is purchasing a parcel of real estate that has been registered as Torrens property. In connection with the purchase:

    (A) Spapperi should have an attorney review the abstract and render an opinion about prior transfers.
    (B) the Torrens certificate is a proof of ownership.
    (C) Spapperi should check for adverse possession.
    (D) the execution of the deed will transfer title.

76. Gregory Mitsakopoulos is purchasing property from Sam Lee and is taking a quitclaim deed for the same. Under the assurances of such a deed, Mitsakopoulos can be certain:

    (A) that Lee had good title to the property.
    (B) that Lee's title to the property at the time is being transferred to Mitsakopoulos.
    (C) that Lee will convey after-acquired title.
    (D) that there are no liens against the property that will adversely affect marketable title.

77. Seller Henry Abbott and Broker Walter Hall enter into an open listing agreement. Under such an agreement:

    (A) Abbott must inform Hall of all potential buyers.
    (B) Abbott does not have to pay Hall a commission if Abbott finds a buyer for the property.
    (C) Abbott must pay Hall a commission if Abbott or Hall finds a buyer.
    (D) Abbott must pay Hall a commission if anyone but Abbott finds a buyer.

78. Developer Emil Robbins placed a mortgage on his housing development. When he sold a lot to purchaser Sandy Bielman, a partial release was obtained for the lot she purchased. The mortgage Robbins had obtained would have been:

   (A) a blanket mortgage.
   (B) a purchase-money mortgage.
   (C) a package mortgage.
   (D) an open-end mortgage.

79. All of the following are required by the Real Estate Settlement Procedures Act EXCEPT:

   (A) lenders must provide borrowers with a good-faith estimate of loan closing costs.
   (B) a uniform form must be used in loan closings.
   (C) the borrower must be given five days to back out of the loan transaction after receiving the required settlement information.
   (D) no kickbacks may be given to any party in connection with the loan transaction.

80. All of the following represent a transfer of property that takes place upon the death of the owner of real estate EXCEPT:

   (A) transfer by devise.
   (B) transfer by dedication.
   (C) transfer by descent.
   (D) escheat.

SOLUTIONS TO SAMPLE EXAM III

The solutions to the Sample Examination III contain the question numbers, the correct answer choice, the type of questions and the topic area as well as the page number and outline reference number where the student may refer for information on the material covered in the question. The computations for the math problems have been worked out and may be found immediately following the solutions.

Question	Answer	Type of Question	Topic Area	Outline Reference	Page
1.	(A)	Definition, Valuation	Gross rent multiplier	I. C. 2.	32
2.	(B)	Comprehension, Laws Relating to Ownership	Rectangular survey	II. A. 2.	19
3.	(D)	Comprehension, Valuation	Capitalization rate	I. C.	32
4.	(B)	Definition, Laws Relating to Ownership	Zoning regulations	V.	24
5.	(C)	Definition, Valuation	Reconciliation	VII. H.	33
6.	(C)	Definition, Financing	F.N.M.A.	I. B.	38
7.	(A)	Comprehension, Valuation	Market price	II. D.	33
8.	(D)	Definition, Valuation	Value	II. B.	32
9.	(C)	Definition, Laws Relating to Ownership	Rectangular survey	II. A. 2.	19
10.	(C)	Comprehension, Brokerage	Option	XI. 1.	61
11.	(A)	Comprehension, Math	Compute commission	Math Review	77-82
12.	(D)	Comprehension, Math	Compute cash required	Math Review	77-82
13.	(D)	Comprehension, Math	Compute state deed stamps	Math Review	77-82
14.	(C)	Definition, Financing	Release deed	IX. J.	43
15.	(B)	Definition, Transfer of Ownership	Recording deed	VI. C. 3.	51
16.	(A)	Definition, Laws Relating to Ownership	Liens	IV. A. 1. a.	22
17.	(A)	Definition, Transfer of Ownership	Tenancy by entirety	III. B. 3.	49
18.	(D)	Comprehension, Brokerage	Open listing	IV. A.	58
19.	(D)	Definition, Brokerage	Regulation Z	XV.	62
20.	(C)	Definition, Financing	Balloon mortgage	IX. A.	42
21.	(D)	Definition, Brokerage	Fair Housing	XIII. B. 1. g.	61
22.	(C)	Definition, Brokerage	Exclusive-right-to-sell	VI. C.	58
23.	(D)	Definition, Laws Relating to Ownership	Riparian rights	IV. B. 1.	23
24.	(C)	Comprehension, Laws Relating to Ownership	Real property	I. A.	18
25.	(B)	Comprehension, Brokerage	Fair Housing	XIII.	61
26.	(B)	Comprehension, Laws Relating to Ownership	Condominiums	III. C. 1. b.	21
27.	(A)	Comprehension, Brokerage	Law of agency	I. F.	57
28.	(C)	Comprehension, Financing	Subordination agreement	IX. 1.	43
29.	(B)	Comprehension, Laws Relating to Ownership	Rectangular survey	II. A. 2.	19
30.	(B)	Definition, Laws Relating to Ownership	Fixtures	I. C.	18
31.	(B)	Definition, Financing	Secondary market	I. B. 2.	38

SAMPLE EXAMINATIONS

32.	(B)	Comprehension, Transfer of Ownership	Joint tenants	III. B. 2.	49
33.	(C)	Comprehension, Math	Compute sale price	Math Review	77-82
34.	(C)	Comprehension, Math	Compute rate	Math Review	77-82
35.	(C)	Comprehension, Math	Compute commission	Math Review	77-82
36.	(C)	Definition, Financing	Contract for deed	II. H. 2.	39
37.	(A)	Comprehension, Math	Compute refund	Math Review	77-82
38.	(D)	Definition, Laws Relating to Ownership	Condominiums	III. C. 1. f.	21
39.	(C)	Comprehension, Math	Compute interest	Math Review	77-82
40.	(D)	Comprehension, Brokerage	Parol evidence rule	XI. C.	60
41.	(D)	Definition, Brokerage	Law of agency	I. C.	56
42.	(C)	Comprehension, Brokerage	Earnest money	XI. H.	61
43.	(A)	Definition, Laws Relating to Ownership	Homestead	III. B. 3. b.	21
44.	(B)	Comprehension, Math	Compute mortgage	Math Review	77-82
45.	(A)	Comprehension, Brokerage	Purchase agreement	VII.	58
46.	(C)	Comprehension, Financing	Discount points	III. C. 5.	40
47.	(C)	Definition, Brokerage	Listing contract	IV.	58
48.	(C)	Comprehension, Brokerage	Sublease	XI. D. 3.	60
49.	(C)	Comprehension, Math	Compute interest rate	Math Review	77-82
50.	(C)	Definition, Brokerage	Discharge	X. A.	59
51.	(D)	Comprehension, Brokerage	Breach of contract	X.	59
52.	(C)	Comprehension, Laws Relating to Ownership	Metes and bounds	II. A. 1.	19
53.	(A)	Comprehension, Brokerage	Antitrust laws	III. B.	57
54.	(C)	Comprehension, Brokerage	Law of agency	I. K.	57
55.	(D)	Comprehension, Financing	Equity	IX. L.	43
56.	(A)	Definition, Transfer of Ownership	Deed	VI. A.	50
57.	(B)	Definition, Transfer of Ownership	Sole owner	III. A. 1.	49
58.	(A)	Comprehension, Brokerage	Lis pendens	XIV. A.	62
59.	(A)	Definition, Brokerage	Statute of limitations	XI. A.	60
60.	(C)	Comprehension, Brokerage	Unilateral contract	VIII. B.	59
61.	(A)	Comprehension, Brokerage	Voidable contract	IX. C. 1.	59
62.	(C)	Comprehension, Math	Compute down payment and mortgage	Math Review	77-82
63.	(C)	Definition, Transfer of Ownership	Joint tenancy	III. B. 2.	49
64.	(D)	Comprehension, Transfer of Ownership	Escrow	VI. B. 1.	50
65.	(A)	Comprehension, Math	Compute sale price	Math Review	77-82
66.	(C)	Comprehension, Math	Compute tax	Math Review	77-82
67.	(B)	Definition, Laws Relating to Ownership	Zoning	V. A. 1.	24
68.	(D)	Definition, Financing	Term loan	IV. C.	41
69.	(A)	Comprehension, Financing	Discount points	III. C. 5. b.	40
70.	(B)	Definition, Financing	Deficiency judgment	V. C.	42
71.	(D)	Definition, Financing	Secondary market	I. B. 2.	38
72.	(D)	Definition, Specialty Areas	Property management	III. B.	73
73.	(C)	Definition, Laws Relating to Ownership	Eminent domain	VII. F.	25
74.	(B)	Definition, Laws Relating to Ownership	Leasehold estates	III. B. 2. a. 1.	20

REAL ESTATE EXAM MANUAL

75.	(B)	Comprehension, Transfer of Ownership	Torrens title	I. A. 3.	48
76.	(B)	Comprehension, Transfer of Ownership	Quitclaim deed	II. C.	48
77.	(B)	Definition, Brokerage	Open listing	IV. A.	58
78.	(A)	Definition, Financing	Blanket mortgage	II. D.	39
79.	(C)	Definition, Transfer of Ownership	RESPA	V.	50
80.	(B)	Definition, Transfer of Ownership	Transfer of title	IV.	50

Sample Examination III Math Solutions

3) $100,000 (current value) × .08 present capitalization rate = $8,000 annual income; $8,000 ÷ .10 revised capitalization rate = $80,000 (revised value); $100,000 − $80,000 = $20,000 decrease in value; therefore decreased more than $10,000

11) $95,900 price × .07 commission rate = $6,713 commission; $6,713 × .50 share of selling broker = $3,356.50 commission of selling broker; $3,356.50 × .35 share of selling salesperson = $1,174.78 commission of selling salesperson; $1,174.78 − $35.00 advertising expenses = $1,139.78 net to selling salesperson

12) $95,900 price of house − $2,000 earnest money = $93,900; $93,900 − $45,850 assumed mortgage = $48,050; $48,050 − $25,000 second mortgage = $23,050 cash brought to closing toward house; $950 = buyer's closing costs; annual taxes = $2,234; unpaid taxes as of closing date = $1,117 (½ of total taxes); unpaid taxes cover July 1 to December 31; $1,117 ÷ 180 days = $6.21 per day; days that seller is responsible for = 75 (July 1—September 15); $6.21 × 75 = $465.75 seller taxes to be credited to buyer at closing; combine 3 components $23,050 + $950 − $465.75 = $23,534.25 buyer's cash for closing

13) $95,900 price − $45,850 assumed mortgage = $50,050; $50,050 − $1,500 personal property = $48,550 price on which tax based; $48,550 ÷ $500 = 97.1 units; round up to 98; 98 × $1.10 = $107.80 state deed tax

33) commission = 7% of price; therefore net to seller + other expenses = 93% of price; $50,000 net to seller + $1,200 other expenses = $51,200; $51,200 = 93% of price; $51,200 ÷ .93 = $55,053.76

34) $189.06 monthly interest × 12 = $2,268.72 annual interest; $2,268.72 ÷ $27,500 loan balance = .0825 or 8¼% interest

35) $1,297.50 commission share of selling salesperson ÷ .50 = $2,595 commission share of selling broker; $2,595 ÷ .50 = $5,190 total commission; $5,190 ÷ $86,500 price = .06 or 6% commission

37) policy covers 3 years or 1,080 days; $78.50 premium ÷ 1,080 = $.072 cost per day; number of days between closing and termination date of policy = 412 days (315 in year of closing + 97 in following year); 412 × $.072 = $29.66 unearned premium

39) $17,672 mortgage balance × .0675 (6¾%) interest rate = $1,192.86 annual interest; $1,192.86 ÷ 360 days = $3.31 interest per day; closing on January 17 and interest paid through end of prior year; therefore 17 days accrued interest; $3.31 × 17 = $56.27 accrued interest

SAMPLE EXAMINATIONS

44) $201.46 monthly interest × 12 = $2,417.52 annual interest; $2,417.52 ÷ .085 (8½%) interest rate = $28,441.41 principal amount of loan

46) $2,000 amount paid for points ÷ $50,000 mortgage = .04 ratio of points to mortgage; 1 point = 1% of mortgage; .04 or 4% = 4 points

49) $87,500 value of real estate × .80 ratio = $70,000 amount of mortgage; $510.42 monthly interest × 12 = $6,125.04 annual interest; $6,125.04 ÷ $70,000 = .0875 or 8¾% interest rate

62) down payment on first $25,000 is $25,000 × .03 = $750; sale price in excess of $25,000 is $37,500 − $25,000 = $12,500; down payment or excess is $12,500 × .05 = $625; add points of down payment $750 + $625 = $1,375 down payment; $37,500 price of house − $1,375 down payment = $36,125 mortgage

65) salesperson received 60% of commission (20% + 40%); $3,600 salesperson's commission ÷ .60 = $6,000 total commission; $6,000 ÷ .05 commission rate = $120,000 price of house

66) $84,500 market value × .35 (35%) assessment ratio = $29,575 assessed value; 1 mill is $.001, therefore 30 mills = $.030; $29,575 × $.030 = $887.25 annual taxes; $887.25 ÷ 12 = $73.94 monthly taxes

69) 10¼% = 10²⁄₈%; 5 points charged, therefore FHA interest rate is ⅝% less than conventional rate; 10²⁄₈ − ⅝ = 9⅝% interest rate on FHA loan

SAMPLE EXAM III

Progress Score

Rating	Percentage	Range	Your Score
EXCELLENT	96% to 100%	77–80	Exam III 80
GOOD	86% to 95%	69–76	Total wrong −
FAIR	76% to 85%	61–68	Total right
MARGINAL	70% to 75%	56–60	
NEED IMPROVEMENT	69% or less	55 or less	

REAL ESTATE EXAM MANUAL

TEST QUESTION CROSS-REFERENCE LIST

The following table cross-references questions from the diagnostic tests and the three sample exams to topics in the concept outlines. The table works two ways:

1.) If you wish to review test questions relating to a certain subject, scan the left-hand column, entitled "concepts," until you find it. Reading across the page, you will find the question numbers in each of the tests that deal with that subject. For example, *options* is covered in question 7 in the Contracts diagnostic pretest, question 38 in Sample Exam 1, question 14 in Sample Exam II and question 10 in Sample Exam III;

2.) If you wish to find what topic in the concept outlines a particular question relates to, scan the top of the table. Locate the test in which the question occurred. Just below the test name, find the range that includes the question number you are researching, and read down that column until you come to the number. The concept in the left-hand column in that line is the subject of your question. You can then review the outline or additional real estate texts for more information.

SAMPLE EXAMINATIONS

TEST QUESTION CROSS-REFERENCE LIST

CONCEPTS	DIAGNOSTIC TEST	SAMPLE EXAM I	SAMPLE EXAM II	SAMPLE EXAM III
Real Property and Laws Relating to Ownership				
condominiums and cooperatives	2	28, 79	13, 51	26, 38
freehold estates	6	25, 80		43
leasehold estates	3	3, 15, 36	9	74
liens and encumbrances	5, 13	1, 5, 23, 56	12, 22, 28	16
terms	18	32	8	24, 30, 58
water rights	8		71	23
title transfer–voluntary and involuntary	1, 9, 10		76	73
control of land use	13	42, 43	16, 23, 37, 66	4, 67
legal descriptions	12	45, 69	5, 17, 35, 69	2, 9, 52
Valuation of Real Property				
appraising	1, 2, 3, 4, 5, 6	39, 40, 41	45, 52, 54	1, 3, 5, 7, 8
Financing of Real Estate				
foreclosure and redemption	6, 9	12, 35	4, 42	70
loan repayment	7		62, 68	68
mortgage instruments	5	71		
mortgage theories	11	34		
parties to mortgage	1	46		
sources of mortgage funds	12, 13, 18	17, 18, 19	57, 60	6, 31, 71
terms	5, 10, 15, 16, 17	11, 13, 52, 73	18, 41	14, 20, 28, 55
types of loans	7, 14	51, 53, 64	3, 26, 40	
types of mortgages	2, 13	14, 49	63, 67	36, 78

REAL ESTATE EXAM MANUAL

CONCEPTS	DIAGNOSTIC TEST	SAMPLE EXAM I	SAMPLE EXAM II	SAMPLE EXAM III
Transfer of Property Ownership				
co-ownership	2, 6	26	21, 50	17, 32, 63
ownership in severalty				57
proof of title	7		10, 48	75
recording and passing of title	3		15	15, 56
types of deeds	2	20, 21, 22	53, 55	76
title transfer by descent and will	10	37		80
RESPA				79
escrow agreement	13 (Brokerage) 25	8, 9		64
Real Estate Brokerage				
federal fair housing	3, 15	24, 27, 61	11, 44, 49, 61	21, 25
charges and credits	10, 11		59	
ethical considerations	8, 14		80	53
law of agency	2	7, 29	56, 74, 79	27, 41, 54
listing agreements	4, 7, 12	6, 78	72, 77	18, 22, 47
Regulation Z	15, 17			19
assignment and novation	5	70		
contract classifications	28	59		60
discharge and breach	13, 18, 27, 29			50, 51
earnest money		10		42
elements of a contract	9, 20, 25, 32	72	1, 38, 47	45
equitable title	6	68		
legal effects	24	2	39	61
offer and acceptance	13, 21		19, 27, 58	5, 23
options	23	38	14	10
other listing agreement	4, 7, 12	50		6
parol evidence			30	40
parties to contract	20	48		
statute of frauds			25	
statute of limitations	23		20	59
types of contracts				48
Specialty Areas				
property management	1, 2, 3		75	72
net lease	5			
Math				
arithmetic ability	6 (Brokerage), 24 (Contracts)	16, 33, 44, 47, 54, 55, 57, 58, 60, 62, 63, 66, 74, 75, 76, 77	2, 6, 24, 29, 30, 31, 32, 33, 34, 36, 46, 58, 64, 65, 70, 73	11, 12, 13, 29, 33, 34, 35, 37, 39, 44, 46, 49, 62, 65, 66, 69

12
Broker Examination

The Educational Testing Service broker examination, like the salesperson exam, consists of two individual examinations: an 80-question uniform exam and a 30- to 40-question state exam. The uniform exam covers generic real estate brokerage practices on a national scale. The state exam details state real estate practices as well as license law and rules and regulations.

The uniform portion of the broker examination contains 80 questions, in the subject areas outlined below:

- Real Property and Laws Relating to Ownership (23%)
- Valuation of Real Property (13%)
- Federal Income Tax Laws Affecting Real Estate (7%)
- Financing of Real Estate (20%)
- Settlement (12%)
- Real Estate Practice (25%)

To test your knowledge of these topics, take the examination that follows. Then analyze your performance, checking to see whether you finished the test within the allotted time and whether you answered at least 65 questions correctly.

THE SETTLEMENT STATEMENT

In addition, since the broker is responsible for completing the real estate transaction, accounting for earnest money and necessary expenses and transferring title, ETS expects students to be knowledgeable about the principles and practices of settlement procedures. Although actually filling out the settlement statement is no longer part of the ETS exam, you should know how to compute and charge expenses to the seller and the buyer when closing a transaction. These costs can be broken down into closing costs and prepaid expenses. To assist you in mastering this subject area, beginning on page 155 a sample settlement statement is included with instructions teaching you how to fill it out. A quiz on closing follows. (The statements used in your jurisdiction may vary in format from those reproduced here, but they will contain the same general information.)

BROKER SAMPLE EXAMINATION

1. When a buyer signs a purchase agreement and the seller accepts, the buyer acquires an interest in the real estate, prior to closing, known as:

   (A) equitable title.
   (B) equitable rights.
   (C) statutory rights.
   (D) servient tenement.

2. Which of the following documents would be used when the seller is to receive a down payment, regular periodic payments and, in accordance with the contract terms, deliver the deed at settlement?

   (A) Installment contract
   (B) Purchase-money mortgage
   (C) FHA mortgage
   (D) Contract for deed

3. Which of the following illustrates a mortgage lien?

   (A) Voluntary lien
   (B) Involuntary lien
   (C) Statutory lien
   (D) Escrow lien

4. Which of the following is an example of a general lien?

   (A) Mortgage lien
   (B) Mechanic's lien
   (C) Vendee's lien
   (D) Franchise tax lien

5. How may title to real estate be transferred?

   (A) By descent and distribution
   (B) By involuntary alienation
   (C) Purchase agreement
   (D) all of the above

6. All of the following are intended to convey title to real estate EXCEPT:

   (A) warranty deed.
   (B) deeds of trust.
   (C) trustee's deed.
   (D) deed in trust.

7. The ABC Real Estate Co. listed a piece of real estate at $4.50 per square foot. The land dimensions were 50 feet by 137 feet. If the commission rate was set at 7¼%, what amount would the seller pay the ABC Real Estate Co.?

   (A) $1,005.50
   (B) $2,234.81
   (C) $22,348.12
   (D) $10,055.00

8. Assume the FHA interest rate is set at 10%, points are at six and the mortgage banker must yield 10¾%. If points drop to four, what will happen to the interest rate?

   (A) It will drop by ½%.
   (B) It will increase by ¼%.
   (C) It will decrease by ¼%.
   (D) It will increase by ½%.

9. To purchase a home, a buyer obtained a $42,500 mortgage at 9¾% interest for 25 years. The mortgage was closed on June 15; however, the monthly payment was adjusted to the first of the month. At the closing, which of the following occurred?

   (A) The buyer paid a $172.66 interest adjustment.
   (B) The seller paid a $172.66 interest adjustment.
   (C) The seller paid a $345.31 interest adjustment.
   (D) The buyer paid a $345.31 interest adjustment.

10. A home was sold for $95,000. The seller had a first mortgage of $27,567 with a rate of 8%. The home was purchased with the use of a wraparound purchase-money mortgage with $15,000 down at an 11½% rate. What is the amount of the second mortgage?

   (A) $80,000
   (B) $95,000
   (C) $27,567
   (D) $15,000

11. The words *to have and to hold* in a deed define the ownership being transferred. This phrase is known as:

   (A) the granting clause.
   (B) the habendum clause.
   (C) the alienation clause.
   (D) the distributor clause.

12. To be valid, a deed can be signed by which of the following?

   (A) The grantors
   (B) An attorney at law
   (C) The grantees
   (D) The broker

13. In order to have a valid conveyance, all of the following are necessary EXCEPT:

   (A) legal capacity to execute.
   (B) recital of consideration.
   (C) designation of any limitations.
   (D) proof of heirship.

14. The Federal Fair Housing Law prohibits discriminatory acts. Which of the following is exempted from this law?

   (A) The rental of rooms in an owner-occupied one-to-four family dwelling
   (B) Alteration of the terms or conditions of a mortgage
   (C) Property for sale above $250,000
   (D) Property sold on an installment sales contract

15. Which of the following requires that finance charges be stated as an annual percentage rate?

   (A) Regulation Z
   (B) Real Estate Settlement Procedures Act
   (C) Equal Credit Opportunity Act
   (D) Fair Housing Act

16. Jack Dobson owns an apartment building in a large city. After discussing the matter with his advisers, Dobson decided to alter the type of occupancy in the building from rental to condominium status. This procedure is known as:

   (A) amendment.
   (B) partition.
   (C) conversion.
   (D) disclosure.

17. In the preceding question, after checking the applicable laws Dobson found that in connection with the change to condominium status he must initially offer to sell each unit to the tenant who currently occupied the unit. If the tenant does not accept the offer, Dobson may then offer the unit for sale to the general public. The requirement that Dobson first offer the property to the tenant is known as:

   (A) a conditional restriction.
   (B) a right of first refusal.
   (C) a covenant of prior acceptance.
   (D) conditional sales option.

REAL ESTATE EXAM MANUAL

18. Joe Thornton Enterprises manages a number of income-producing properties for a large landholder in the city. The management agreement provides that the property manager shall be responsible for finding new tenants and maintaining the property. The fee Thornton Enterprises may charge for its services might be:

   (A) a percentage of the net income earned from the property.
   (B) a percentage of the total expenses incurred in maintaining the property.
   (C) both A and B
   (D) neither A nor B

19. On a settlement statement, the commission owed to the broker in a real estate transaction is treated as:

   (A) a debit to the sellers and a credit to the buyers.
   (B) a debit to the buyers.
   (C) a credit to the sellers and a debit to the buyers.
   (D) a credit to the buyers.

20. Stewart Branning recently entered into a purchase agreement to sell his house to Larry and Connie Manders. The closing is scheduled to take place April 15. In January Branning paid the taxes for the entire year, although the Manders are assuming responsibility for taxes attributable to the period following the closing. At the closing, on the settlement statement the adjustment made for property taxes will appear as:

   (A) a debit to the buyer and a credit to the seller.
   (B) a credit to the buyer and a debit to the seller.
   (C) a credit to the buyer.
   (D) a debit to the seller.

21. In the preceding question, the amount of the adjustment for taxes that would appear in the settlement statement would be:

   (A) the total annual taxes appearing on the tax statement.
   (B) the prorated share of annual taxes attributable to the period prior to the closing.
   (C) the prorated share of annual taxes attributable to the period after the closing.
   (D) none of the above

22. Harry and Edith Jones have entered into a purchase agreement to sell their house. Some time ago, a special assessment was levied against their property for sidewalk and street improvements in front of their house. Under the agreement with the purchaser, the buyers will not assume the special assessment. Assuming that the assessment had not been paid off prior to the closing, the amount remaining due on the special assessment would appear:

   (A) as a credit to the buyer.
   (B) as a debit to the seller.
   (C) as a credit to the seller and a debit to the buyer.
   (D) as a debit to the seller and a credit to the buyer.

23. Expenses involved in the closing of a real estate transaction would be shown on the settlement as:

   (A) a debit to the buyers or the sellers.
   (B) a credit to the buyers or the sellers.
   (C) a debit to both buyer and seller.
   (D) a credit to both buyer and seller.

24. Items to be prorated at a closing that represent prepaid expenses should be shown on the settlement statement as:

    (A) credit to the seller and debit to the buyer.
    (B) debit to the seller and credit to the buyer.
    (C) a credit to buyer.
    (D) a debit to seller.

25. Joe and Janet Atkinson entered into an agreement to sell a rental property they own. The closing is to take place September 15. On September 1 the Atkinsons received a rent payment for the month of September from the tenant. Under the terms of the purchase agreement, the buyers are entitled to any rent received covering the period subsequent to the closing. At the closing the prepaid rent will appear as:

    (A) a credit to the seller and a debit to the buyer.
    (B) a debit to the seller and a credit to the buyer.
    (C) a credit to buyer.
    (D) a debit to seller.

26. The requirements of the Real Estate Settlement Procedures Act apply to any residential real estate transaction that takes place:

    (A) in a state that had adopted RESPA.
    (B) involving a federally related mortgage loan.
    (C) involving any mortgage financing less than $100,000.
    (D) involving any sale price less than $100,000.

27. Under the provisions of the Real Estate Settlement Procedures Act, certain disclosures are required from:

    (A) the seller in a residential real estate transaction.
    (B) the buyer in a residential real estate transaction.
    (C) the lender in a residential real estate transaction.
    (D) the closer in a residential real estate transaction.

28. Which of the following real estate documents would least likely be recorded at the county recorder's office?

    (A) A contract form deed
    (B) A long-term lease
    (C) An option agreement
    (D) A purchase agreement

29. A purchaser of property can be assured of receiving good title to the property if at the closing he or she receives:

    (A) a general warranty deed.
    (B) a quitclaim deed.
    (C) contract for deed.
    (D) none of the above

30. In the process of valuating real estate, the concept of depreciation is probably most important to the purchaser of which of the following parcels of real estate?

    (A) A residential single-family dwelling
    (B) An apartment building
    (C) An industrial plant
    (D) A shopping center

REAL ESTATE EXAM MANUAL

31. In determining whether to extend a loan to the purchaser of a house, lending institutions normally consider:

    (A) the sale price.
    (B) the stability of the purchaser's business position.
    (C) the appraised value.
    (D) the term of the loan.

32. In a township there are 36 sections. Which of the following statements is true about those sections?

    (A) Section 16 lies to the north of Section 21.
    (B) Section 18 is by law set aside for school purposes.
    (C) Section 6 lies in the northeast corner of the township.
    (D) Section 31 lies to the east of section 32.

33. Broker Betty Singleton represented the seller in a transaction. Her client informed her that he did not want the deed to recite the actual consideration that was paid for the house. Under the Realtors'® Code of Ethics Singleton:

    (A) must inform her client that only the actual price of the real estate may appear on the deed.
    (B) may show a price on the deed other than the actual price, provided the variance is not greater than 10% of the purchase price.
    (C) may show consideration of $10 on the deed.
    (D) should inform the seller that either the full price should be stated in the deed or all references to consideration should be removed from the deed.

34. Salesperson Harry Kellner is proposing an advertisement for a house on which he obtained a listing for broker Dick Wallace. In the ad, Kellner:

    (A) need not show Wallace's name if Kellner's phone number appears.
    (B) must show his association with Wallace if his own name appears.
    (C) must show the sale price of the property.
    (D) all of the above

35. Broker Sally Fulton obtained a listing agreement to act as the agent in the sale of Dan Hamilton's house. A buyer has been found and agreements signed. It is Fulton's duty to assure herself that:

    (A) the buyer will make loan application.
    (B) the buyer has a copy of all written agreements.
    (C) the buyer is qualified for the mortgage.
    (D) the buyer has inspected the home.

36. Broker Sandra Freeman represents a buyer interested in a house that has been listed with broker Jack Butler. Freeman feels that Butler is often very difficult to negotiate with. Therefore, Freeman may inform her client:

    (A) to carry on negotiations with the seller directly.
    (B) to inform the buyer that builder is difficult to deal with.
    (C) to write an offer below the listed price.
    (D) that general principles under which REALTORS® operate prohibit her from talking to the seller directly.

37. Broker Jane Barnes is trying to expand her business. In the course of her work she has become friendly with two salespeople working for broker Frank Langdon. Before soliciting these two salespeople to work for her, Barnes must:

    (A) inform broker Langdon that she intends to solicit his employees.
    (B) wait until all listings that either salesperson has obtained for broker Langdon have been sold or have expired before she makes an offer to that salesperson.
    (C) send a letter to the Board of REALTORS® with notification of solicitation.
    (D) provide Langdon with a referral fee upon release of the agent.

38. Sellers Gwen and Thomas Manchester have executed three open listings with three brokers around town. All three brokers would like to place "for sale" signs on the sellers' property. Under these circumstances:

    (A) a broker does not have to obtain the seller's permission before placing a sign on the property.
    (B) only one "for sale" sign may be placed on the property at one time.
    (C) upon obtaining the seller's written consent, all can place "for sale" signs on the property.
    (D) the first listing broker must consent to all signs.

39. If a dispute develops between two realtors over the entitlement to a commission, the controversy should be:

    (A) submitted to arbitration.
    (B) appealed to a court of law if a broker is not satisfied with a decision.
    (C) settled by an equal split of the commission.
    (D) settled by the decision of the seller.

40. For a parcel of real estate to have value, it must have:

    (A) utility.   (C) transferability.
    (B) scarcity.   (D) all of the above

41. In determining the value of real estate via the cost approach, the appraiser should:

    (A) estimate the replacement cost of the building.
    (B) deduct an amount for depreciation of the land and improvements.
    (C) determine original cost and adjust for inflation.
    (D) review the sale price of other buildings.

42. All of the following are variables on a yield table EXCEPT:

    (A) interest rate.   (C) payback rate.
    (B) size of balloon.   (D) term.

43. Timesharing is a concept of real estate ownership that has developed in recent years, particularly in resort areas. In connection with a timesharing sale:

    (A) the selling broker must be a licensed security broker.
    (B) each of the various owners of a timeshared unit has the right of occupancy of the unit for a specific period of time each year.
    (C) the vendee.
    (D) the selling agent must be an employee of the developer.

REAL ESTATE EXAM MANUAL

44. Under the income approach to estimating the value of real estate, the capitalization rate is:

    (A) the rate at which the property will increase in value.
    (B) the rate of return the property will earn on an investment.
    (C) the rate of capital required to keep a property operating by its most effective method.
    (D) the maximum rate of return allowed by law on an investment.

45. Robert Rizzon was asked to value a single-family home in order to determine the proposed sale price. Rizzon found five comparable houses that had recently been sold, and must now make adjustments to the sale prices of the comparables to reflect differences from the subject property. Adjustments should be made to reflect differences in:

    (A) location, physical condition and amenities of the property.
    (B) gross rent multiplier of other properties.
    (C) expired properties.
    (D) current listed properties.

46. The gross rent multiplier is most closely related to the:

    (A) variable payment schedule.
    (B) sale and leaseback.
    (C) amortization of payment.
    (D) capitalization rate.

47. When does a buyer normally take title to real estate?

    (A) When the deed is delivered and accepted
    (B) When the deed is signed by the grantee
    (C) When the deed is recorded
    (D) When the deed is signed by the grantor

48. If Horace Jennings sold to Katherine Nexon for $100,000, and Nexon assumed Jennings's $24,838.98 mortgage and paid $10,000 as a down payment, what amount does Nexon have to finance?

    (A) $75,161.02
    (B) $65,161.02
    (C) $55,161.02
    (D) $85,161.02

49. The act that requires lenders to inform both buyers and sellers of all fees and charges is the:

    (A) Federal Equal Credit Opportunity Act.
    (B) Truth-in-Lending Act (Regulation Z).
    (C) Real Estate Settlement Procedures Act.
    (D) Real Estate Investment Trust Act.

50. If a landlord breaches the lease and the unit is uninhabitable, what action can the tenant take?

    (A) Suit for possession
    (B) Constructive eviction
    (C) Tenancy at sufferance
    (D) Covenant of quiet possession

51. How can tenancy at sufferance be created?

    (A) By failure to surrender possession
    (B) By payment of rent
    (C) By bringing an unlawful detainer action
    (D) By giving 30 days' written notice

52. When the title passes to a third party upon the death of the life tenant, what is the third party's interest in the property?

    (A) Remainder interest
    (B) Reversionary interest
    (C) Conditional interest
    (D) A redemption interest

53. What is the interest of the grantee when real estate is conveyed only for as long as specified conditions are met?

    (A) Determinable fee
    (B) Restrictive fee
    (C) Base fee
    (D) Precedent fee

54. All of the following are examples of laws affecting the ownership of water EXCEPT:

    (A) riparian rights.
    (B) littoral rights.
    (C) prior appropriation.
    (D) aquatic rights.

55. FHA insurance regulations require that:

    (A) the FHA set the interest rate.
    (B) the buyer and/or seller may pay points.
    (C) the mortgage insurance premium be paid by the seller.
    (D) the closing cost must be paid by the buyer.

56. The United States uses both lien theory and title theory in mortgage law. Under the title theory:

    (A) the mortgagor has title to the property.
    (B) the mortgagee has title to the property.
    (C) the mortgagor and mortgagee jointly hold title.
    (D) a third party holds title in trust.

57. In the foreclosure process, if the sale of a property will not pay the total debt, interest and expenses, the mortgagee may obtain a:

    (A) mortgage lien.
    (B) deed of trust.
    (C) constructive notice.
    (D) deficiency judgment.

58. Brokers who conspire to set commission rates or enter into an agreement to allocate a specific market are subject to which of the following?

    (A) Sherman Act and Clayton Antitrust Law
    (B) The law of agency
    (C) The Blue Sky laws
    (D) The Securities Act of 1933

59. What affect(s) the control and regulation of land use?

    (A) Public and private land use controls
    (B) Zoning ordinances
    (C) Deed restrictions
    (D) all of the above

60. What is the land-use theory used in developing land around main streets, highways and public transportation?

    (A) Multiple-nuclei theory
    (B) Sector theory
    (C) Concentric theory
    (D) Axial theory

REAL ESTATE EXAM MANUAL

61. A property was sold for $5.45 per square foot in 1979. The value of the property has increased by 23%. If sold at the current market value, how much more would the lot cost than in 1979?

   (A) $1,498.75
   (B) $3,447.13
   (C) $1,948.38
   (D) $2,750.00

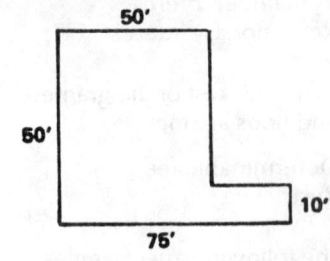

62. Under a percentage lease, the lessee pays $400 per month plus 2.75 percent of gross sales. Last month's gross sales were $198,210.00. How much is the rent?

   (A) $945.08
   (B) $5,850.78
   (C) $5,450.78
   (D) $545.08

63. Which of the following establish(es) a standardized eviction procedure in government-subsidized housing?

   (A) Uniform Residential Landlord and Tenant Act
   (B) Tenant's Eviction Procedures Act
   (C) The Tenant's Relief Act of 1978
   (D) The 1968 Housing Act

64. What type of lease establishes a set rate and requires the lessor to pay taxes, insurance and repairs?

   (A) Net lease
   (B) Percentage lease
   (C) Variable lease
   (D) Gross lease

65. After signing a lease, the lessor obtains which of the following interests in real estate?

   (A) Freehold estate
   (B) Reversionary right
   (C) A leasehold interest
   (D) A remainderman interest

66. If the market value of real estate is $72,000 and the property is assessed at 67% of value, what are the monthly taxes if the tax rate for the area is $6.50 per $100 of assessed value?

   (A) $3,157.38
   (B) $4,857.50
   (C) $261.30
   (D) $48,575.00

67. A $50,000 mortgage on a property represents an 80% loan-to-value ratio. If the real estate was assessed at 82%, the taxes were based on $4 per $100 of assessed value and the taxes were $2,050 annually, what is the market value of the home?

   (A) $62,500
   (B) $51,250
   (C) $41,000
   (D) $50,000

68. State deed stamps are $2.20 per $1,000 of the purchase price. On a sale of $79,000, how much would the seller pay in stamps?

   (A) $173.80
   (B) $1,738.00
   (C) $17.38
   (D) $22.20

BROKER EXAMINATION

69. How many acres are contained in the SE¼ of Section 1, and NE¼ of NE¼ of Section 2, and S½ of the SE¼ of Section 3?

   (A) 160
   (B) 40
   (C) 80
   (D) 280

70. Which of the following is a method of foreclosure that does not require civil action?

   (A) Judicial foreclosure
   (B) Strict foreclosure
   (C) Sheriff's foreclosure
   (D) Nonjudicial foreclosure

71. A conventional loan was closed on July 1 for $57,200 at 13.5% interest amortized over 25 years at $666.75 per month. On August 1, what would be the principal amount of the mortgage?

   (A) $56,533.25
   (B) $57,176.75
   (C) $55,982.20
   (D) $56,556.50

72. In the preceding problem, what would be the interest payment?

   (A) $666.75
   (B) $643.50
   (C) $772.20
   (D) $620.25

73. In the preceding problem, what would be the amount of the payment applied to the principal?

   (A) $42.25
   (B) $643.25
   (C) $643.50
   (D) $23.25

74. If a home sold for $65,900 and the mortgage required a 40% down payment and a 1% origination fee plus $450 in closing costs, how much would the buyer need to close?

   (A) $26,623.60
   (B) $27,205.40
   (C) $27,173.59
   (D) $26,360.00

75. An FHA loan in the amount of $57,500 at 11½% for 30 years was closed on July 15, 1988. The first payment was due on August 1, 1988. What is the amount of the interest adjustment payment the buyer had to make at the closing?

   (A) $6,612.50
   (B) $551.04
   (C) $293.92
   (D) $275.52

76. If a home that originally cost $42,500 is now, three years later, valued at 127% of its original cost, what is its current market value?

   (A) $53,975
   (B) $65,354
   (C) $85,000
   (D) $96,427

77. If a building is 200 feet wide, 300 feet long and five stories high (each story 12 feet in height), how much does the building cost at $.79 per cubic foot?

   (A) $237,000
   (B) $275,982
   (C) $284,800
   (D) $2,844,000

78. If the same building sold for $2.89 per square foot, what is the sale price?

   (A) $867,000
   (B) $86,700
   (C) $8,670,000
   (D) $173,400

79. Who assumes the cost of the abstract or title search?

   (A) The seller
   (B) The purchaser
   (C) The title company
   (D) The mortgage company

80. Who assumes the cost of the title examination?

   (A) The seller
   (B) The purchaser
   (C) The title company
   (D) The mortgage company

SELLER'S COSTS	BUYER'S COSTS
Closing Costs	**Closing Costs**
Broker's commission	Down payment
Loan discount (points)	Credit report
Abstract or title search	Appraisal fee
Attorney's fees	Title examination
Government recording and transfer charges	Title insurance
Appraisal fee	Loan origination fee
Survey	Mortgage registration tax and/or recording fees
Existing loan(s)	Assumption/refinancing fee
Expenses	**Expenses**
Homeowner's insurance	Homeowner's insurance
Tax escrows	Taxes
Mortgage interest adjustment	Interest adjustment
Assessments	Assessments
Rent payment adjustments	Rent payment adjustments
Utilities: heat, water, electricity	Utilities: heat, water, electricity

I. Closing costs—The closing costs (expenses) are expenses incurred by either the buyer or the seller in closing the transaction. Further, the buyer and the seller may incur additional costs in closing the transaction that are basically adjustments of expenses to the closing date. These prorated items represent either expenses incurred but not paid, or refunds of payments paid in advance. These prorations, therefore, are either *accrued expenses* or *prepaid expenses*.

II. Prorations

   A. Accrued expenses (unpaid expenses)—Utilities. These are items owed by the seller but not paid before closing.

   1. Debit to seller
   2. Credit to buyer

	SETTLEMENT STATEMENT			
	Buyer's statement		Seller's statement	
	Debit	Credit	Debit	Credit
Taxes		*	*	

149

REAL ESTATE EXAM MANUAL

B. Prepaid expenses (paid expenses)—Insurance. These are items paid by the seller but not used before closing.
   1. Debit to buyer
   2. Credit to seller

	SETTLEMENT STATEMENT			
	Buyer's statement		Seller's statement	
	Debit	Credit	Debit	Credit
Insurance	*			*

C. Methods of prorating—Prorating can be accomplished using two basic methods. The first method is a calendar year (a 365-day per year basis). The second is a statutory method, or a 360-day year. However, in the Educational Testing Service examination, use the statutory 360-day method for prorating. Under this method, expenses are calculated differently depending on whether they are accrued or prepaid expenses.

   1. Accrued expenses—Accrued expenses can be broken down into an annual, monthly or daily cost. For example, a $360 accrued expense can be separated into a $360 annual expense, $30 monthly expense, or $1 daily expense.
   2. Prepaid expenses—In determining prepaid expenses, it is necessary to calculate the amount of the unused or remaining expenses. Study the following example for the steps involved in this calculation.

• A house was covered by a 3-year fire insurance policy that expires May 13, 1992. The total premium for this policy, $604.80, was paid in full in 1989. The house was sold and the closing date set for July 23, 1990. How much money was credited to the seller (paid by the buyer) at the closing to transfer the unexpired (remaining) term of this insurance policy to the buyer?

   Step 1. Compute the amount the policy cost per year, per month and per day.

   $604.80 ÷ 3 years = $201.60 per year

   $201.60 ÷ 12 months = $16.80 per month

   $16.80 ÷ 30 days = $.56 per day

   Carry all dollars-and-cents calculations with remainders to three decimal places if necessary. Round off to two decimal places only after you complete the steps needed to compute the proration.

   Step 2. Compute the number of days, months and years of insurance coverage that the buyer assumed. Now you will consider the actual number of days in the month of closing.

	years	months	days	
	1992	5	13	May 13, 1992 expiration date
−	1990	7	23	July 23, 1990 closing date

150

If any month or day figure in the expiration date is less than the month or day in the closing date, you must borrow from the column to the left. The *month* you borrow must have the exact number of days as the month of closing. In this example, since 13 days are less than 23 days, borrowing a month means borrowing the 31 days in the month of July. Borrowing a year always means borrowing 12 months.

First, subtract the days.

	years	months	days
		4	44
	1992	5	13
−	1990	7	23
			21

Then, subtract the months.

	years	months	days
		16	
	1991	4	44
	1992	5	13
−	1990	7	23
		9	21

Finally, subtract the years.

	years	months	days
		16	
	1991	4	44
	1992	5	13
−	1990	7	23
	1	9	21	unexpired term

The buyer owed the seller for 1 year, 9 months and 21 days of this policy.

Warning: Calculate the amount of time remaining *very carefully.* If your figures are inaccurate, your entire proration will be wrong.

Step 3. Knowing the rate per year, month and day, and the number of years, months and days of the unexpired term, you can now calculate what the buyer owed.

$201.60 per year × 1 year = $201.60

$16.80 per month × 9 months = $151.20

$.56 per day × 21 days = $11.76

$201.60 + $151.20 + $11.76 = $364.56 insurance proration credited to the seller

The insurance proration of $364.56 was credited to the seller; that is, the buyer paid it.

It is important to be able to distinguish the closing costs to the seller (the seller's expenses in the sale), as well as the costs to the buyer. This will include prorations of both accrued and prepaid items. In completing the worksheet and any subsequent test questions, remember:

- The earnest money deposit is a *credit* to the buyer.
- Closing costs are *debited* to the party incurring the expense.
- Prorated expenses are debited to one party and credited to the other. However, prepaid items are always a *credit to the seller*; accrued items are always a *debit to the seller*.

BROKER EXAMINATION

Instructions: Indicate on the sample closing statement where each of the items should be charged by listing the item number in the appropriate column of the closing statement. Check your answers with the answer key on page 158. The prorated expenses in this statement were accrued and unpaid as of closing. The mortgage, special assessments and existing loans are being assumed by the buyer. The mortgage interest is paid in arrears.

ITEMS:
1. Interest adjustment
2. Assumption/refinancing
3. Mortgage registration tax and/or recording fees
4. Government recording and transfer charges
5. Appraisal fee and credit report (buyer)
6. Mortgage interest adjustment (for reserve account)
7. Broker commission
8. Appraisal fee (seller)
9. Utilities
10. Purchase price
11. Rent payment adjustments
12. Survey
13. Utilities–heat, water, electricity pro rata
14. Deposit
15. Credit report
16. Taxes
17. Title insurance
18. Loan discount (points)
19. Homeowner's insurance (new policy)
20. Use and occupancy permit
21. Assessments
22. Title examination
23. Abstract or title search
24. Attorney's fees (buyer)
25. Loan origination fee
26. Existing loan(s)
27. Tax escrows

| SAMPLE CLOSING STATEMENT ||||
| Buyer || Seller ||
Debit	Credit	Debit	Credit

SETTLEMENT STATEMENT WORKSHEET

Complete the settlement statement worksheet using the following data.

Sale price	$95,900.00
Earnest money deposit	$ 2,000.00
Appraisal report (buyer)	$ 60.00
Title examination (buyer)	$ 50.00
Title insurance (buyer)	$ 114.17
Recording fees (buyer)	$ 12.00
Assumption fee	$ 459.00
Broker's commission	7%
Closing date	September 15

The current mortgage balance is $25,000 at 8% interest, payable in arrears. The buyer will assume the mortgage.

Annual taxes of $1,800, paid in two equal installments; assume the seller has paid the annual taxes.

Then take the 11-question quiz dealing with the Settlement Statement Worksheet and compare your worksheet and quiz answers with the Answer Key.

BROKER EXAMINATION

SETTLEMENT STATEMENT WORKSHEET

Property_____

Seller_____

Buyer_____

Settlement Date_____

	BUYER'S STATEMENT		SELLER'S STATEMENT	
	DEBIT	CREDIT	DEBIT	CREDIT

SETTLEMENT STATEMENT QUIZ

1. On the preceding settlement worksheet, how is the sale price listed?

    I. As a debit to the sellers and a credit to the buyers
    II. As a credit to the sellers and a debit to the buyers

    (A) I only
    (B) II only
    (C) Both I and II
    (D) Neither I nor II

2. How is the earnest money deposit listed?

    (A) As a credit to the buyers and a debit to the sellers
    (B) As a debit to the sellers
    (C) As a credit to the buyers
    (D) As a credit to the sellers

3. How is the amount of the mortgage assumed shown?

    I. As a credit to the buyers
    II. As a debit to the sellers

    (A) I only
    (B) II only
    (C) Both I and II
    (D) Neither I nor II

4. What is the amount of the prorated taxes?

    (A) $900
    (B) $525
    (C) $1,275
    (D) $1,800

5. What is the total of the buyers' debits?

    (A) $97,070.17
    (B) $70,036.84
    (C) $27,000.00
    (D) $97,120.17

6. What is the total credit to the buyers?

    (A) $27,000.00
    (B) $27,083.33
    (C) $70,036.84
    (D) $96,425.00

7. What is the amount of money needed by the buyers to close?

    (A) $70,203.70
    (B) $97,120.17
    (C) $70,036.84
    (D) $96,425.00

8. What is the total debit to the sellers?

    (A) $96,425.00
    (B) $31,796.33
    (C) $64,628.67
    (D) $31,713.00

9. What is the total credit to the sellers?

    (A) $64,628.67
    (B) $31,796.33
    (C) $96,425.00
    (D) $64,628.00

10. What is the amount of cash due to the sellers at the closing?

    (A) $70,203.50
    (B) $64,628.67
    (C) $96,425.00
    (D) $31,796.33

11. What is the interest adjustment paid at the closing?
    I. An $83.33 credit to the buyers
    II. An $83.33 debit to the sellers

    (A) I only
    (B) II only
    (C) Both I and II
    (D) Neither I nor II

REAL ESTATE EXAM MANUAL

ITEMS:	SAMPLE CLOSING STATEMENT			
	Buyer		Seller	
	Debit	Credit	Debit	Credit
1. Interest adjustment		1	1	
2. Assumption/refinancing fee	2			
3. Mortgage registration tax and/or recording fees	3			
4. Government recording and transfer charges			4	
5. Appraisal fee and credit report (buyer)	5			
6. Mortgage interest adjustment (for reserve account)	6			6
7. Broker commission			7	
8. Appraisal fee (seller)			8	
9. Utilities		9	9	
10. Purchase price	10			10
11. Rent payment adjustments		11	11	
12. Survey			12	
13. Utilities—heat, water, electricity pro rata		13	13	
14. Deposit		14		
15. Credit report	15			
16. Taxes		16	16	
17. Title insurance			17	
18. Loan discount (points)			18	
19. Homeowner's insurance (new policy)	19			
20. Use and occupancy permit			20	
21. Assessments		21	21	
22. Title examination	22			
23. Abstract or title search			23	
24. Attorney's fees (buyer)	24			
25. Loan origination fee	25			
26. Existing loan(s)		26	26	
27. Tax escrows	27			27

BROKER EXAMINATION

ANSWER KEY
SETTLEMENT STATEMENT WORKSHEET

Property_____

Seller_____

Buyer_____

Settlement Date_____

	BUYER'S STATEMENT		SELLER'S STATEMENT	
	DEBIT	CREDIT	DEBIT	CREDIT
Sale Price	95,900.00			95,900.00
Deposit		2,000.00		
Mortgage Assumed		25,000.00	25,000.00	
Interest Adjustment		83.33	83.33	
Property Taxes	525.00			525.00
Title Examination	50.00			
Title Insurance	114.17			
Assumption Fee	459.00			
Appraisal Report	60.00			
Recording Fees	12.00			
Broker's Commission			6,713.00	
Subtotal	97,120.17	27,083.33	31,796.33	96,425.00
Due from buyer		70,036.84		
Due to seller			64,628.67	
TOTALS	97,120.17	97,120.17	96,425.00	96,425.00

SETTLEMENT STATEMENT QUIZ ANSWER KEY

Question	Answer	Question	Answer
1.	(B)	7.	(C)
2.	(C)	8.	(B)
3.	(C)	9.	(C)
4.	(B)	10.	(B)
5.	(D)	11.	(C)
6.	(B)		

BROKER EXAMINATION

SOLUTIONS TO BROKER SAMPLE EXAMINATION

The solutions to the Broker Examination contain the question number, the correct answer choice, the type of question and the topic area as well as the page number and outline reference number where the student may refer for information on the material covered in the question. The computations for the math problems have been worked out and may be found immediately following the solutions.

Question	Answer	Type of Question	Topic Area	Outline Reference	Page
1.	(A)	Comprehension, Brokerage	Equitable title	VI. G.	60
2.	(B)	Comprehension, Financing	Purchase money mortgage	II.H.	39
3.	(A)	Comprehension, Laws Relating to Ownership	Lien	IV. A. 1. a.	22
4.	(D)	Comprehension, Laws Relating to Ownership	General lien	IV. A. 1. a. 2.	23
5.	(D)	Comprehension, Brokerage	Title transfer	II.	50
6.	(B)	Comprehension, Transfer of Ownership	Types of deeds	II.	48
7.	(B)	Comprehension, Math	Compute cost and commission	Math Review	77-82
8.	(B)	Comprehension, Financing	Discount points	III. C. 5.	40
9.	(A)	Comprehension, Math	Compute interest adjustment	Math Review	77-82
10.	(A)	Comprehension, Math	Compute the second mortgage	Math Review	77-82
11.	(B)	Definition, Ownership	Habendum clause	Glossary	178
12.	(A)	Comprehension, Transfer of Ownership	Grantor	Glossary	178
13.	(D)	Comprehension, Contract	Elements	VII.	58
14.	(A)	Definition, Transfer of Ownership	Fair Housing	XIII. B. 2.	61
15.	(A)	Definition, Brokerage	Regulation Z	XV.	62
16.	(C)	Definition, Laws Relating to Ownership	Conversion	III. C. 1. g.	22
17.	(B)	Comprehension, Brokerage	Right of first refusal	XI. K.	61
18.	(C)	Comprehension			
19.	(A)	Comprehension, Broker's Examination	Proration-debit/credit	VII.	51
20.	(A)	Comprehension, Broker's Examination	Proration-debit/credit	VII.	51
21.	(C)	Comprehension, Broker's Examination	Proration-debit/credit	VII.	51
22.	(B)	Comprehension, Broker's Examination	Proration-debit/credit	VII.	51
23.	(A)	Comprehension, Broker's Examination	Proration-debit/credit	VII.	51
24.	(A)	Comprehension, Broker's Examination	Proration-debit/credit	VII.	51
25.	(B)	Comprehension, Broker's Examination	Proration-debit/credit	V. C.	50
26.	(B)	Comprehension, Transfer of Ownership	RESPA	V. C.	50

27.	(C)	Comprehension, Transfer of Ownership	RESPA	V. C.	50
28.	(D)	Comprehension, Financing	Contract for deed	II. A. 2.	39
29.	(D)	Comprehension, Transfer of Ownership	Marketable title	IV.	50
30.	(C)	Comprehension, Valuation	Cost approach	I. B.	32
31.	(B)	Comprehension, Financing–not in outline–Lending institutions will look to the stability of buyer's income for loan approval.			
32.	(A)	Comprehension, Valuation	Section	Glossary	186
33.	(C)	Comprehension, Transfer of Ownership	Recording deed	Review local practice; Glossary	185
34.	(B)	Comprehension, Brokerage	Advertising—State statutes generally require all sales people to identify the name and phone number of the brokerage in all advertising.		
35.	(B)	Comprehension, Brokerage	Listing agreement–not in outline–State statutes require that the buyer obtain copies of all written agreements.		
36.	(D)	Comprehension, Brokerage	Ethics–not in outline–REALTOR® Code of Ethics requires obtaining permission to negotiate directly with seller.		
37.	(A)	Comprehension, Brokerage	Ethics—not in outline–REALTOR® Code of Ethics requires that the broker inform another broker that they intend to solicit sales associates.		
38.	(C)	Comprehension, Brokerage	State statute–not in outline–Statute requires the broker to obtain seller's consent to place "for sale" sign on property.		
39.	(A)	Comprehension, Brokerage	Ethics–not in outline–REALTOR® Code of Ethics requires that the dispute be settled through arbitration.		

BROKER EXAMINATION

40.	(D)	Definition, Valuation	Concept of value	II. B.	32
41.	(A)	Definition, Valuation	Cost approach	I. B.	32
42.	(B)	Comprehension, Financing	Yield table–not in outline–Yield tables use interest rate, pay back rate and term of loan in determining yield.		
43.	(B)	Comprehension, Ownership	Timesharing–Each owner has the right to occupy a unit for a specific period of time each year.		
44.	(B)	Comprehension, Valuation	Income approach	I. C.	32
45.	(A)	Comprehension, Valuation	Market data	I. A.	32
46.	(D)	Comprehension, Valuation	Gross rent multiplier	I. C. 2.	32
47.	(A)	Definition, Ownership	Delivery of deed	IV.	50
48.	(B)	Comprehension, Math	Compute new mortgage	Math Review	77-82
49.	(C)	Definition, Transfer of Ownership	RESPA	V. C.	50
50.	(B)	Definition, Laws Relating to Ownership	Constructive eviction	Glossary	171
51.	(A)	Definition, Laws Relating to Ownership	Tenancy at sufferance	III. B. 2. 4.	20
52.	(A)	Definition, Laws Relating to Ownership	Remainder	III. B. 1. 5.	20
53.	(A)	Comprehension, Laws Relating to Ownership	Determinable fee	III. B. 1. b.	20
54.	(D)	Comprehension, Laws Relating to Ownership	Water rights	VI. B.	23
55.	(B)	Comprehension, Financing	F.H.A. mortgage	III. C.	40
56.	(B)	Comprehension, Financing	Title theory	VIII. B.	42
57.	(D)	Comprehension, Financing	Deficiency judgment	V. C.	42
58.	(A)	Comprehension, Brokerage	Antitrust	III. B.	57
59.	(D)	Comprehension	Public and private use	V. & V. B.	24
60.	(D)	Comprehension	Axial theory		
61.	(B)	Comprehension, Math	Compute cost per sq. foot and value	Math Review	77-82
62.	(B)	Comprehension, Math	Compute the rent	Math Review	77-82
63.	(B)	Comprehension, Laws Relating to Ownership	Nonfreehold estates	III. B. 2.	20
64.	(D)	Definition, Laws Relating to Ownership	Gross lease	IV. A. 1.	20
65.	(B)	Definition, Laws Relating to Ownership	Reversionary	III. B. 1. c. 4.	20
66.	(C)	Comprehension, Math	Compute monthly taxes	Math Review	77-82
67.	(A)	Comprehension, Math	Compute market value	Math Review	77-82
68.	(A)	Comprehension, Math	Compute cost of state deed stamps	Math Review	77-82
69.	(D)	Comprehension, Valuation	Section	Glossary	190
70.	(D)	Comprehension, Financing	Nonjudicial foreclosure	V. A. 1.	41

71.	(B)	Comprehension, Math	Compute principal balance	Math Review	77-82
72.	(B)	Comprehension, Math	Compute the interest payment	Math Review	77-82
73.	(D)	Comprehension, Math	Compute the amount of principal	Math Review	77-82
74.	(B)	Comprehension, Math	Compute buyer cost to close	Math Review	77-82
75.	(C)	Comprehension, Math	Compute buyer interest adjustment	Math Review	77-82
76.	(A)	Comprehension, Math	Compute market value	Math Review	77-82
77.	(D)	Comprehension, Math	Compute cost of building	Math Review	77-82
78.	(A)	Comprehension, Math	Compute cost of building	Math Review	77-82
79.	(A)	Comprehension, Broker Examination	Seller costs		149
80.	(B)	Comprehension, Broker Examination	Buyer costs		149

BROKER EXAMINATION

Broker Sample Examination—Math Solutions

7) 137 feet × 50 feet = 6,850 square feet; 6,850 × $4.50 per square foot = $30,825 price of real estate; $30,825 × .0725 (7¼%) commission rate = $2,234.81
8) 10% interest rate + 6 points (6/8) = yield of 10 6/8 %; 4 points = 4/8 %; to retain yield of 10 6/8 interest rate must rise to 10 2/8 % (10 2/8 + 4/8 = 10 6/8); 10 2/8 − 10 = 2/8 (¼)%; therefore interest rate will increase by ¼%.
9) $42,500 mortgage × .0975 (9¾%) interest rate = $4,143.75 annual interest; $4,143.75 ÷ 360 = $11.51 daily interest; $11.51 × 15 days = $172.65 interest adjustment to be paid by buyer.
10) $95,000 price − $15,000 down payment = $80,000 mortgage
48) $100,000 price − $10,000 down payment = $90,000; $90,000 − $24,838.98 assumed mortgage = $65,161.02 new financing
61) Divide property into square and rectangle; 50 × 50 = 2,500 sq. feet area of square; 25 × 10 = 250 sq. feet area of rectangle; 2,500 + 250 = 2,750 sq. feet area of property; 2,750 × $5.45 price per sq. foot = $14,987.50 price in 1979; 14,987.50 × .23 (23%) = $3,447.13 increase in price
62) $198,210 gross sales × .0275 (2¾%) = $5,450.78 percentage rent; $5,450.78 + $400 base rent = $5,850.78 total rent.
66) $72,000 market value × .67 (67%) assessment ratio = $48,240 assessed value; $48,240 ÷ 100 and × $6.50 = $3,135.60 annual taxes; $3,135.60 ÷ 12 = $261.30 monthly taxes
67) $50,000 mortgage ÷ .80 (80%) loan to value ratio = $62,500 market value
68) $79,000 mortgage ÷ $1,000 = 79; 79 × $2.20 = $173.80 cost of stamps
69) 640 acres in section; 160 acres in SE ¼; 40 acres in NE ¼ of NE ¼; 80 acres in S½ of SE ¼; 160 + 40 + 80 = 280 acres
71) $57,200 loan × .135 (13.5%) interest rate = $7,722 annual interest; $7,722 ÷ 12 = $643.50 monthly interest; $666.75 monthly payment − $643.50 interest = $23.25 applied to principal; $57,200 − $23.25 = $57,176.75 loan balance after 1 month.
72) $643.50 See question 71
73) $23.25 See question 71
74) $65,900 price × .40 (40%) down payment = $26,360 down payment; $65,900 − $26,360 = $39,540 amount of mortgage; $39,540 × .01 (1%) = $395.40 origination fee; closing costs = $450; add the three components $26,360 + $395.40 + $450 = $27,205.40
75) $57,500 loan × .115 (11½%) interest rate = $6,612.50 annual interest; $6,612.50 ÷ 360 = $18.37 daily interest; $18.37 × 16 days (July 15–August 1) = $293.92 adjustment
76) $42,500 cost × 1.27 (125%) = $53,975 current value
77) find cubic area of building; 5 stories × 12 feet = 60 feet in height; 200 × 300 × 60 = 3,600,000 cubic feet; 3,600,000 × $.79 per cubic foot = $2,844,000 cost of building.
78) find square footage of building; 200 × 300 = 60,000 sq. feet per floor; 60,000 × 5 floors = 300,000 total square feet; 300,000 × $2.89 per sq. foot = $867,000 sale price

BROKER EXAMINATION
Progress Score

Rating	Percentage	Range	Your Score	
EXCELLENT	96% to 100%	77–80	Broker	80
GOOD	86% to 95%	69–76	Total wrong	–___
FAIR	76% to 85%	61–68	Total right	=___
MARGINAL	70% to 75%	56–60		
NEED IMPROVEMENT	69% or less	55 or less		

Glossary

abandonment. The voluntary and permanent cessation of use or enjoyment with no intention to resume or reclaim one's possession or interest. May pertain to an easement or a property.

abstract of title. A condensed version of the history of title to a particular parcel of real estate, as recorded in the county clerk's records; consists of a summary of the original grant and all subsequent conveyances and encumbrances affecting the property.

abutting. The joining, reaching or touching of adjoining land. Abutting parcels of land have a common boundary.

accelerated depreciation. A method of calculating for tax purposes the depreciation of income property at a faster rate than would be achieved using the straight-line method. Note that any depreciation taken in excess of that which would be claimed using the straight-line rate is subject to **recapture** as ordinary income to the extent of gain resulting from the sale. *(See also STRAIGHT-LINE METHOD.)*

acceleration clause. A provision in a written mortgage, note, bond or conditional sales contract that, in the event of default, the whole amount of principal and interest may be declared to be due and payable at once.

accretion. An increase or addition to land by the deposit of sand or soil washed up naturally from a river, lake or sea.

accrued depreciation. The actual depreciation which has occurred to a property at any given date; the difference between the cost of replacement new (as of the date of appraisal) and the present appraised value.

acknowledgment. A declaration made by a person to a notary public, or other public official authorized to take acknowledgments, that an instrument was executed by him or her as a free and voluntary act.

actual eviction. The result of legal action originated by a lessor, whereby a defaulted tenant is physically ousted from the rented property pursuant to a court order. *(See also EVICTION.)*

actual notice. Express information or fact; that which is known; actual knowledge.

administrator. The party appointed by the county court to settle the estate of a deceased person who died without leaving a will.

ad valorem tax. A tax levied according to value; generally used to refer to real estate tax. Also called the **general tax.**

adverse possession. The right of an occupant of land to acquire title against the real owner, where possession has been actual, continuous, hostile, visible and distinct for the statutory period.

affidavit. A written statement signed and sworn to before a person authorized to administer an oath.

GLOSSARY

agent. One who represents or has the power to act for another person (called the principal). The authorization may be express, implied or apparent. A fiduciary relationship is created under the **law of agency** when a property owner, as the principal, executes a listing agreement or management contract authorizing a licensed real estate broker to be his or her agent.

agreement of sale. A written agreement whereby the purchaser agrees to buy certain real estate and the seller agrees to sell, upon terms and conditions set forth in the agreement.

air lot. A designated airspace over a piece of land. Air lots–like surface property–may be transferred.

air rights. The right to use the open space above a property, generally allowing the surface to be used for another purpose.

alienation. The act of transferring property to another. Alienation may be voluntary, such as by gift or sale, or involuntary, such as through eminent domain or adverse possession.

alienation clause. The clause in a mortgage or deed of trust which states that the balance of the secured debt becomes immediately due and payable at the mortgagee's option if the property is sold by the mortgagor. In effect, this clause prevents the mortgagor from assigning the debt without the mortgagee's approval.

amenities. The tangible and intangible features that increase the value or desirability of real estate.

amortization. The liquidation of a financial burden by installment payments.

amortized loan. A loan in which the principal as well as the interest is payable in monthly or other periodic installments over the term of the loan.

antitrust laws. The laws designed to preserve the free enterprise of the open marketplace by making illegal certain private conspiracies and combinations formed to minimize competition. Violations of antitrust laws in the real estate business generally involve either **price fixing** (brokers conspiring to set fixed compensation rates) or allocation of customers or markets (brokers agreeing to limit their areas of trade or dealing to certain areas or properties).

appraisal. An estimate of the quantity, quality or value of something. The process through which conclusions of property value are obtained; also refers to the report setting forth the process of estimation and conclusion of value.

appraised value. An estimate of a property's present worth.

appreciation. An increase in the worth or value of a property due to economic or related causes which may prove to be either temporary or permanent; opposite of depreciation.

appurtenant. Belonging to; incident to; annexed to. For example, a garage is appurtenant to a house, and the common interest in the common elements of a condominium is appurtenant to each apartment. Appurtenances pass with the land when the property is transferred.

arbitration. A means of settling a controversy between two parties through the medium of an impartial third party whose decision on the controversy (it is agreed) will be final and binding.

assessment. The imposition of a tax, charge or levy, usually according to established rates.

assignment. The transfer in writing of rights or interest in a bond, mortgage, lease or other instrument.

assumed name statute. In most states, a law stating that no person shall conduct a business under any name other than his own individual name, unless such person filed the assumed name he wishes to use with the county clerk in each county where his business is conducted. In the case of brokers and salespeople, statement of such filing should be submitted to the state's real estate commission. An assumed name does not appear on a license but the records of the commission will reflect it.

assumption of mortgage. The transfer of title to property to a grantee wherein he assumes liability for payment of an existing note secured by a mortgage against the property; should the mortgage be foreclosed and the property sold for a lesser amount than that due, the grantee-purchaser who has assumed and agreed to pay the debt secured by the mortgage is personally liable for the deficiency. Before a seller may be relieved of liability under the existing mortgage the lender must accept the transfer of liability for payment of the note.

attachment. The method by which a debtor's property is placed in the custody of the law and held as security pending outcome of a creditor's suit.

attorney-in-fact. The holder of a power of attorney.

attorney's opinion of title. An instrument written and signed by the attorney who examines the title, stating his or her opinion as to whether a seller may convey good title.

automatic extension. A clause in a listing agreement which states that the agreement will continue automatically for a certain period of time after its expiration date. In many states use of this clause is discouraged or prohibited.

balloon payment. The final payment of a mortgage loan that is considerably larger than the required periodic payments because the loan amount was not fully amortized.

bargain and sale deed. A deed that carries with it no warranties against liens or other encumbrances, but that does imply that the grantor has the right to convey title. Note that the grantor may add warranties to the deed at his or her discretion.

base line. One of a set of imaginary lines running east and west and crossing a principal meridian at a definite point, used by surveyors for reference in locating and describing land under the rectangular survey system (or government survey method) of property description.

bench mark. A permanent reference mark or point established for use by surveyors in measuring differences in elevation.

beneficiary. *1.* The person for whom a trust operates, or in whose behalf the income from a trust estate is drawn. *2.* A lender who lends money on real estate and takes back a note and deed of trust from the borrower.

bequest. A provision in a will providing for the distribution of personal property.

bilateral contract. A contract in which each party promises to perform an act in exchange for the other party's promise to perform.

bill of sale. A written instrument given to pass title to personal property.

binder. An agreement that may accompany an earnest money deposit for the purchase of real property as evidence of the purchaser's good faith and intent to complete the transaction.

blanket mortgage. A mortgage covering more than one parcel of real estate, providing for each parcel's partial release from the mortgage lien upon repayment of a definite portion of the debt.

blockbusting. The illegal practice of inducing homeowners to sell their properties by making representations regarding the entry or prospective entry of minority persons into the neighborhood.

Blue Sky laws. The common name for those state and federal laws that regulate the registration and sale of investment securities.

branch office. A secondary place of business apart from the principal or main office from which real estate business is conducted. A branch office generally must be run by a licensed real estate broker working on behalf of the broker operating the principal office.

breach of contract. The failure, without legal excuse, of one of the parties to a contract to perform according to the contract.

broker. One who buys and sells for another for a commission. (*See also* REAL ESTATE BROKER.)

brokerage. The business of buying and selling for another for a commission.

GLOSSARY

broker-salesperson. A person who has passed the broker's licensing examination but is licensed to work only on behalf of a licensed broker.

budget loan. A loan in which the monthly payments made by the borrower cover not only interest and a payment on the principal, but also one-twelfth of such expenses as taxes, insurance, assessments and similar charges.

building code. An ordinance specifying minimum standards of construction of buildings for the protection of public safety and health.

building line. A line fixed at a certain distance from the front and/or sides of a lot beyond which no structure can project; a setback line used to ensure a degree of uniformity in the appearance of buildings and unobstructed light, air and view.

building restrictions. The limitations on the size or type of property improvements established by zoning acts or by deed or lease restrictions. Building restrictions are considered encumbrances, and violations render the title unmarketable.

bundle of legal rights. The theory that land ownership involves ownership of all legal rights to the land—such as possession, control within the law, and enjoyment—rather than ownership of the land itself.

canvassing. The making of telephone calls or visiting from door to door to seek prospective buyers or sellers; in the real estate business, generally associated with acquiring listings in a given area.

capacity of parties. The legal ability of persons to enter into a valid contract. Most persons have full capacity to contract, and are said to be **competent parties.**

capital investment. The initial capital and the long-term expenditures made to establish and maintain a business or investment property.

capitalization. The process of converting into present value (or obtaining the present worth of) a series of anticipated future periodic installments of net income. In real estate appraising, it usually takes the form of discounting. The formula is expressed: $\frac{\text{Income}}{\text{Rate}} = \text{Value}$.

capitalization rate. The rate of return a property will produce on the owner's investment.

cash flow. The net spendable income from an investment, determined by deducting all operating and fixed expenses from the gross income. If expenses exceed income, a negative cash flow is the result.

casualty insurance. A type of insurance policy that protects a property owner or other person from loss or injury sustained as a result of theft, vandalism or similar occurrences.

caveat emptor. A Latin phrase meaning "Let the buyer beware."

certificate of sale. The document generally given to a purchaser at a tax foreclosure sale. A certificate of sale does not convey title; generally it is an instrument certifying that the holder received title to the property after the redemption period had passed and that the holder paid the property taxes for that interim period.

certificate of title. A statement of opinion on the status of the title to a parcel of real property based on an examination of specified public records.

chain of title. The succession of conveyances from some accepted starting point whereby the present holder of real property derives his or her title.

chattel. Personal property.

City Planning Commission. A local governmental organization designed to direct and control the development of land within a municipality.

cloud on title. A claim or encumbrance that may affect title to land.

codicil. An addition to a will that alters, explains, adds to or confirms the will, but does not revoke it.

coinsurance clause. A clause in insurance policies covering real property that requires the policyholder to maintain fire insurance coverage generally equal to at least 80 percent of the property's actual replacement cost.

collateral. Something of value given or pledged to a lender as security for a debt or obligation.

commercial property. A classification of real estate which includes income-producing property such as office buildings, restaurants, shopping centers, hotels and stores.

commingled property. That property of a married couple which is so mixed or commingled that it is difficult to determine whether it is separate or community property. Commingled property becomes community property.

commingling. The illegal act of a real estate broker who mixes the money of other people with that of his or her own—by law, brokers are required to maintain a separate trust account for the funds of other parties held temporarily by the broker.

commission. The payment made to a broker for services rendered, such as in the sale or purchase of real property; usually a percentage of the selling price of the property.

common elements. Those parts of a property that are necessary or convenient to the existence, maintenance and safety of a condominium, or are normally in common use by all of the condominium residents. All condominium owners have an undivided ownership interest in the common elements.

common law. The body of law based on custom, usage and court decisions.

community property. A system of property ownership based on the theory that each spouse has an equal interest in the property acquired by the efforts of either spouse during marriage.

comparables. The properties listed in an appraisal report that are substantially equivalent to the subject property.

competent parties. Those persons who are recognized by law as being able to contract with others; usually those of legal age and sound mind.

composite depreciation. A method of determining the depreciation of a multibuilding property using the average rate at which all the buildings are depreciating.

condemnation. A judicial or administrative proceeding to exercise the power of eminent domain, by which a government agency takes private property for public use and compensates the owner.

condominium. The absolute ownership of an apartment or a unit, generally in a multiunit building, based on a legal description of the airspace which the unit actually occupies, plus an undivided interest in the ownership of the common elements which are owned jointly with the other condominium unit owners. The entire tract of real estate included in a condominium development is called a parcel, or development parcel. One apartment or space in a condominium building or a part of a property intended for independent use and having lawful access to a public way is called a unit. Ownership of one unit also includes a definite undivided interest in the common elements.

consideration. Something of value that induces one to enter into a contract. Consideration may be "valuable" (money or commodity) or "good" (love and affection).

constructive eviction. *1.* Acts done by the landlord which so materially disturb or impair the tenant's enjoyment of the leased premises that the tenant is effectively forced to move out and terminate the lease without liability for any further rent. *2.* A purchaser's inability to obtain clear title.

constructive notice. Notice given to the world by recorded documents. All persons are charged with knowledge of such documents and their contents, whether or not they have actually examined them. Possession of property is also considered constructive notice that the person in possession has an interest in the property.

contract. An agreement entered into by two or more legally competent parties by the terms of which one or more of the parties, for a consideration, undertakes to do or to refrain from doing some legal act or acts. A contract may be either **unilateral,** where only one party is bound to act, or **bilateral,** where all parties to the instrument are legally bound to act as prescribed.

contract for deed. A contract for the sale of real estate wherein the sales price is paid in periodic installments by the purchaser, who is in possession although title is retained by the seller until final payment. Also called an **installment contract.**

contract for exchange of real estate. A contract of sale of real estate in which the consideration is paid wholly or partly in property.

conventional loan. A loan that is not insured or guaranteed by a government or private source.

conveyance. A written instrument that evidences transfer of some interest in real property from one person to another.

cooperative. A residential multiunit building whose title is held by a trust or corporation, which is owned by and operated for the benefit of persons living within the building, who are the beneficial owners of the trust or stockholders of the corporation, each having a proprietary lease.

corporation. An entity or organization created by operation of law whose rights of doing business are essentially the same as those of an individual. The entity has continuous existence until dissolved according to legal procedures.

correction lines. The provisions in the rectangular survey system (government survey method) made to compensate for the curvature of the earth's surface. Every fourth township line (at 24-mile intervals) is used as a correction line on which the intervals between the north and south range lines are remeasured and corrected to a full six miles.

cost approach. The process of estimating the value of a property by adding to the estimated land value the appraiser's estimate of the reproduction or replacement cost of the building, less depreciation.

counseling. The business of providing people with expert advice on a subject, based on the counselor's extensive, expert knowledge of the subject.

counteroffer. A new offer made as a reply to an offer received, having the effect of rejecting the original offer, which cannot be accepted thereafter unless revived by the offeror's repeating it.

cul-de-sac. A dead-end street that widens sufficiently at the end to permit an automobile to make a U-turn.

curtesy. A life estate, usually a fractional interest, given by some states to the surviving husband in real estate owned by his deceased wife. Many states have abolished curtesy.

cycle. A recurring sequence of events that regularly follow one another, generally within a fixed interval of time.

datum. A horizontal plane from which heights and depths are measured.

dba. Doing business as.

debenture. A note or bond given as evidence of debt and issued without security.

debt. Something owed to another; an obligation to pay or return something.

decline balance method. An accounting method of calculating depreciation for tax purposes designed to provide large deductions in the early years of ownership. (*See also ACCELERATED DEPRECIATION.*)

deed. A written instrument that, when executed and delivered, conveys title to or an interest in real estate.

deed of reconveyance. The instrument used to reconvey title to a trustor under a deed of trust once the debt has been satisfied.

deed of trust. An instrument used to create a mortgage lien by which the mortgagor conveys his or her title to a trustee, who holds it as security for the benefit of the note holder (the lender); also called a **trust deed.**

deed restrictions. The clauses in a deed limiting the future uses of the property. Deed restrictions may impose a vast variety of limitations and conditions, such as limiting the density of buildings, dictating the types of structures that can be erected and preventing buildings from being used for specific purposes or from being used at all.

default. The nonperformance of a duty, whether arising under a contract or otherwise; failure to meet an obligation when due.

defeasance. A provision or condition in a deed or in a separate instrument which, being performed, renders the instrument void.

defeasible fee estate. An estate in land in which the holder has fee simple title subject to being divested upon the happening of a specified condition. Two categories: fee simple determinable and fee simple subject to a condition subsequent.

deficiency judgment. A personal judgment levied against the mortgagor when a foreclosure sale does not produce sufficient funds to pay the mortgage debt in full.

delinquent taxes. Those unpaid taxes that are past due.

delivery. The legal act of transferring ownership. Documents such as deeds and mortgages must be delivered and accepted to be valid.

delivery absolute. The handing over of a deed to a third person until the performance of some act or condition by one of the parties.

delivery in escrow. Delivery of a deed to a third person until the performance of some act or condition by one of the parties.

demand. The willingness of a number of people to accept available goods at a given price; often coupled with supply.

density zoning. The zoning ordinances that restrict the average maximum number of houses per acre that may be built within a particular area, generally a subdivision.

depreciation. *1.* In appraisal, a loss of value in property due to all causes, including physical deterioration, functional depreciation and economic obsolescence. *2.* In real estate investment, an expense deduction for tax purposes taken over the period of ownership of income property.

descent. The hereditary succession of an heir to the property of a relative who dies intestate.

determinable fee estate. A defeasible fee estate in which the property automatically reverts to the grantor upon the occurrence of a specified event or condition.

devise. A transfer of real estate by will or last testament. The donor is the devisor and the recipient is the devisee.

diminishing returns. The principle of diminishing returns applies when a given parcel of land reaches its maximum percentage return on investment, and further expenditures for improving the property yield a decreasing return.

discount points. An added loan fee charged by a lender to make the yield on a lower-than-market-value FHA or VA loan competitive with higher-interest conventional loans.

discount rate. The rate of interest a commercial bank must pay when it borrows from its Federal Reserve bank. Consequently, the discount rate is the rate of interest the banking system carries within its own framework. Member banks may take certain promissory notes that they have received from customers and sell them to their district Federal Reserve bank for less than face value. With the funds received, the banks can make further loans. Changes in the discount rate may cause banks and other lenders to re-examine credit policies and conditions.

dispossess. To oust from land by legal process.

dominant tenement. A property that includes in its ownership the appurtenant right to use an easement over another's property for a specific purpose.

dower. The legal right or interest recognized in some states that a wife acquires in the property her husband held or acquired during their marriage. During the lifetime of the husband, the right is only a possibility of an interest; upon his death it can become an interest in land. Many states have abolished dower.

duress. The use of unlawful constraint that forces action or inaction against a person's will.

earnest money deposit. An amount of money deposited by a buyer under the terms of a contract.

easement. A right to use the land of another for a specific purpose, such as for a right-of-way or utilities; an incorporeal interest in land. An easement appurtenant passes with the land when conveyed.

easement by necessity. An easement allowed by law as necessary for the full enjoyment of a parcel of real estate; for example, a right of ingress and egress over a grantor's land.

easement by prescription. An easement acquired by continuous, open, uninterrupted, exclusive and adverse use of the property for the period of time prescribed by state law.

easement in gross. An easement that is not created for the benefit of any land owned by the owner of the easement but which attaches personally to the easement owner. For example, a right to an easement granted by Eleanor Franks to Joe Fish to use a portion of her property for the rest of his life would be an easement in gross.

economic life. The period of time over which an improved property will earn an income adequate to justify its continued existence.

economic obsolescence. The impairment of desirability or useful life arising from factors external to the property such as economic forces or environmental changes which affect supply-demand relationships in the market. Loss in the use and value of a property arising from the factors of economic obsolescence is to be distinguished from loss in value from physical deterioration and functional obsolescence, both of which are inherent in the property. Also referred to as locational obsolescence or environmental obsolescence.

emblements. Those growing crops produced annually through the tenant's own care and labor, and which he or she is entitled to take away after the tenancy is ended. Emblements are regarded as personal property even prior to harvest, so if the landlord terminates the lease, the tenant may still re-enter the land and remove such crops. If the tenant terminates the tenancy voluntarily, however, he or she is not generally entitled to the emblements.

eminent domain. The right of a government or municipal quasi-public body to acquire property for public use through a court action called **condemnation,** in which the court determines that the use is a public use and determines the price or compensation to be paid to the owner.

employee status. One who works as a direct employee of an employer. The employer is obligated to withhold income taxes and social security taxes from the compensation of his or her employees. (*See also INDEPENDENT CONTRACTOR.*)

employment contract. A document evidencing formal employment between employer and employee or between principal and agent. In the real estate business this generally takes the form of a listing agreement or management agreement.

encroachment. A fixture, or structure, such as a wall or fence, which invades a portion of a property belonging to another.

encumbrance. Any lien—such as a mortgage, tax or judgment lien, an easement, a restriction on the use of the land or an outstanding dower right—that may diminish the value of the property.

endorsement. The act of writing one's name, either with or without additional words, on a negotiable instrument, or on a paper attached to it.

equalization. The raising or lowering of assessed values for tax purposes in a particular county or taxing district to make them equal to assessments in other counties or districts.

equitable title. The interest held by a vendee under a contract for deed or an installment contract; the equitable right to obtain absolute ownership to property when legal title is held in another's name.

equity. The interest or value which an owner has in a property over and above any mortgage indebtedness.

erosion. The gradual wearing away of land by water, wind and general weather conditions; the diminishing of property caused by the elements.

escheat. The reversion of property to the state in the event the owner thereof dies without leaving a will and has no heirs to whom the property may pass by lawful descent.

escrow. The closing of a transaction through a third party called an escrow agent, or escrowee, who receives certain funds and documents to be delivered upon the performance of certain conditions in the escrow agreement.

estate for years. An interest for a certain, exact period of time in property leased for a specified consideration.

estate in land. The degree, quantity, nature and extent of interest that a person has in real property.

estate in severalty. An estate owned by one person.

estoppel certificate. A legal instrument executed by a mortgagor showing the amount of the unpaid balance due on a mortgage and stating that the mortgagor has no defenses or offsets against the mortgagee at the time of execution of the certificate. Also called a certificate of no defense.

ethical. Conforming to professional standards of conduct.

et ux. The Latin abbreviation for "et uxor," meaning "and wife."

eviction. A legal process to oust a person from possession of real estate.

evidence of title. A proof of ownership of property, which is commonly a certificate of title, a title insurance policy, an abstract of title with lawyer's opinion or a Torrens registration certificate.

exchange. A transaction in which all or part of the consideration for the purchase of real property is the transfer of like kind property (that is, real estate for real estate).

exclusive agency listing. A listing contract under which the owner appoints a real estate broker as his or her exclusive agent for a designated period of time to sell the property on the owner's stated terms for a commission. However, the owner reserves the right to sell without paying anyone a commission by selling to a prospect who has not been introduced or claimed by the broker.

exclusive-right-to-sell listing. A listing contract under which the owner appoints a real estate broker as his or her exclusive agent for a designated period of time to sell the property on the owner's stated terms and agrees to pay the broker a commission when the property is sold, whether by the broker, the owner or another broker.

executed contract. A contract in which all parties have fulfilled their promises and thus performed the contract.

execution. The signing and delivery of an instrument. Also, a legal order directing an official to enforce a judgment against the property of a debtor.

executor. The male person designated in a will to handle the estate of the deceased. The probate court must approve any sale of property by the executor. The female is called the **executrix**.

executory contract. A contract under which something remains to be done by one or more of the parties.

expenses. The short-term costs that are deducted from an investment property's income, such as minor repairs, regular maintenance and renting costs.

expressed contract. An oral or written contract in which the parties state its terms and express their intentions in words.

Federal Fair Housing Law. The term for the Civil Rights Act of 1968, which prohibits discrimination based on race, color, sex, religion or national origin in the sale and rental of residential property.

Federal Home Loan Bank System (FHLB). A system created by the Federal Home Loan Bank Act of 1932 to provide for a central reserve credit system for savings institutions engaged in home mortgage finance (predominately savings and loans). The system is divided into 12 federal home loan bank districts with a Federal Home Loan Bank (FHLB) in each district. The Federal Home Loan Banks maintain a permanent pool of credit to maintain liquidity of members or to provide means for mortgage lending when local funds are insufficient. Three sources of funds are available for the operation of the FHLB: capital stock, deposits of member institutions and consolidated obligations sold on the market. When member associations need funds they obtain money by borrowing from FHLB. The FHLB Board supervises the system. The board is composed of three members appointed by the President of the United States with the advice and consent of the Senate.

Federal Housing Administration (FHA). A federal administrative body created by the National Housing Act in 1934 to encourage improvement in housing standards and conditions, to provide an adequate home financing system through the insurance of housing mortgages and credit and to exert a stabilizing influence on the mortgage market.

federal income tax. An annual tax based on income, including monies derived from the lease, use or operation of real estate.

Federal National Mortgage Association (FNMA). "Fannie Mae" is the popular name for this federal agency that creates a secondary market for existing mortgages. FNMA does not loan money directly, but rather buys VA, FHA and conventional loans.

Federal Reserve banks. The government controls banks located in each of the 12 Federal Reserve districts, established by the Federal Reserve Act of 1913. The Board of Governors, working closely with the President and the Treasury, controls the Federal Reserve. The Federal Reserve system (through the 12 central banks) supervises and examines members' commercial banks; clears and collects checks drawn on commercial banks; and may influence the cost, supply and availability of money.

fee simple estate. The maximum possible estate or right of ownership of real property continuing forever. Sometimes called a fee or fee simple absolute.

fee simple subject to a condition subsequent. A defeasible fee estate in which the grantor reserves right of reentry to the property when the condition of ownership is violated.

FHA appraisal. An FHA evaluation of a property as security for a loan. Includes study of the physical characteristics of the property and surroundings; the location of the property; the prospective borrower's ability and willingness to repay a loan; and the mortgage amount and monthly payments.

FHA loan. A loan insured by the Federal Housing Administration and made by an approved lender in accordance with the FHA's regulations.

fiduciary relationship. A relationship of trust and confidence, as between trustee and beneficiary, attorney and client and principal and agent.

financing statement. *See UNIFORM COMMERCIAL CODE.*

first mortgage. A mortgage that creates a superior voluntary lien on the property mortgaged relative to other charges or encumbrances against same.

fiscal policy. The government's policy in regard to taxation and spending programs. The balance between these two areas determines the amount of money the government will withdraw or feed into the economy in an attempt to counter economic peaks and slumps.

fixture. An article that was once personal property but has been so affixed to real estate that it has become real property.

forcible entry and detainer. A summary proceeding for restoring to possession of land one who is wrongfully kept out or has been wrongfully deprived of the possession.

foreclosure. A legal procedure whereby property used as security for a debt is sold to satisfy the debt in the event of default in payment of the mortgage note or default of other terms in the mortgage document. The foreclosure procedure brings the rights of all parties to a conclusion and passes the title in the mortgaged property to either the holder of the mortgage or a third party who may purchase the realty at the foreclosure sale, free of all encumbrances affecting the property subsequent to the mortgage.

foreign acknowledgment. An acknowledgment taken outside of the state wherein the land lies.

formal will. A will written by an attorney, with two subscribing witnesses, with necessary language. Such a will may appoint the executor of the estate as independent agent and avoid the necessity of a bond.

franchise. A private contractual agreement to run a business using a designated trade name and operating procedures.

fraud. A misstatement of a material fact made with intent to deceive or made with reckless disregard of the truth, and which actually does deceive.

freehold estate. An estate in land in which ownership is for an indeterminate length of time, in contrast to a leasehold estate.

functional obsolescence. The impairment of functional capacity or efficiency. Functional obsolescence reflects the loss in value brought about by factors that affect the property, such as overcapacity, inadequacy or changes in the art. The inability of a structure to perform adequately the function for which it is currently employed.

future interest. A person's present right to an interest in real property that will not result in possession or enjoyment until some time in the future, such as a reversion or right of reentry.

gap. A defect in the chain of title of a particular parcel of real estate; a missing document or conveyance that raises doubt as to the present ownership of the land.

general contractor. A construction specialist who enters into a formal construction contract with a landowner or master lessee to construct a real estate building or project. The general contractor often contracts with several **subcontractors** specializing in various aspects of the building process to perform individual jobs.

general lien. A lien on all real and personal property owned by a debtor.

general partnership. *See PARTNERSHIP.*

general tax. *See AD VALOREM TAX.*

general warranty deed. A deed that states that the title conveyed therein is good from the sovereignty of the soil to the grantee therein; no one else can claim the property.

GI-guaranteed mortgage. *See VA LOAN.*

government lot. Those fractional sections in the rectangular survey system (government survey method) that are less than one full quarter-section in area.

Government National Mortgage Association (GNMA). "Ginnie Mae," a federal agency and division of HUD that operates special assistance aspects of federally aided housing programs and participates in the secondary market through its mortgage-backed securities pools.

grant. The act of conveying or transferring title to real property.

GLOSSARY

grant deed. A type of deed that includes three basic warranties: *1.* the owner warrants that he or she has the right to convey the property; *2.* the owner warrants that the property is not encumbered other than with those encumbrances listed in the deed; and *3.* the owner promises to convey any after-acquired title to the property. Grant deeds are popular in states that rely heavily on title insurance.

grantee. A person to whom real estate is conveyed; the buyer.

grantor. A person who conveys real estate by deed; the seller.

gross lease. A lease of property under which a landlord pays all property charges regularly incurred through ownership, such as repairs, taxes, insurance and operating expenses. Most residential leases are gross leases.

gross national product. The total value of all the goods and services produced in the U.S. in a year.

gross rent multiplier. A figure used as a multiplier of the gross rental income of a property to produce an estimate of the property's value.

ground lease. A lease of land only, on which the tenant usually owns a building or is required to build his or her own building as specified in the lease. Such leases are usually long-term net leases; a tenant's rights and obligations continue until the lease expires or is terminated through default.

guaranteed sale plan. An agreement between broker and seller that if the seller's real property is not sold before a certain date, the broker will purchase it for a specified price.

guardian. One who guards or cares for another person's rights and property. A guardian has legal custody of the affairs of a minor or a person incapable of taking care of his own interests, called a **ward.**

habendum clause. The deed clause beginning "to have and to hold" that defines or limits the extent of ownership in the estate granted by the deed.

heir. One who might inherit or succeed to an interest in land under the state law of descent when the owner dies without leaving a valid will.

hereditaments. Every kind of inheritable property, including personal, real, corporeal and incorporeal.

highest and best use. That possible use of land that will produce the greatest net income and thereby develop the highest land value.

holdover tenancy. A tenancy whereby a lessee retains possession of leased property after his or her lease has expired and the landlord, by continuing to accept rent from the tenant, agrees to the tenant's continued occupancy as defined by state law.

holographic will. A will that is written, dated and signed in the handwriting of the maker, and that does not need to be notarized or witnessed to be valid.

homeowner's insurance policy. A standardized package insurance policy that covers a residential real estate owner against financial loss from fire, theft, public liability and other common risks.

homeowner's warranty program. An insurance program offered to buyers by some brokerages, warranting the property against certain defects for a specified period of time.

homestead. The land, and the improvements thereon, designated by the owner as his or her homestead and, therefore, protected by state law from forced sale by certain creditors of the owner.

HUD. The Department of Housing and Urban Development; regulates FHA and GNMA.

implied contract. A contract under which the agreement of the parties is demonstrated by their acts and conduct.

implied grant. A method of creating an easement. One party may be using another's property for the benefit of both parties, for example, a sewer on a property.

improvement. *1.* Improvements *on* land—any structure, usually privately owned, erected on a site to enhance the value of the property; for example, buildings, fences and driveways. *2.* Improvements *to* land—usually a publicly owned structure, such as a curb, sidewalk or sewer.

income approach. The process of estimating the value of an income-producing property by capitalization of the annual net income expected to be produced by the property during its remaining useful life.

incorporeal right. A nonpossessory right in real estate; for example, an easement or right-of-way.

increasing returns. When increased expenditures for improvements to a given parcel of land yield an increasing percentage return on investment, the principle of increasing returns applies.

independent contractor. One who is retained to perform a certain act, but who is subject to the control and direction of another only as to the end result and not as to how he or she performs the act. Unlike an employee, an independent contractor pays for all his or her expenses and income and social security taxes and receives no employee benefits. Many real estate salespeople are independent contractors.

industrial property. All land and buildings used or suited for use in the production, storage or distribution of tangible goods.

installment contract. *See CONTRACT FOR DEED.*

installment sale. A method of reporting income received from the sale of real estate when the sales price is paid in two or more installments over two or more years. If the sale meets certain requirements, a taxpayer can postpone reporting such income to future years when his or her other income may be lower.

insurable title. A title to land that a title company will insure.

insurance. The indemnification against loss from a specific hazard or peril through a contract (called a policy) and for a consideration (called a premium).

interest. A charge made by a lender for the use of money.

interim financing. A short-term loan usually made during the construction phase of a building project, often referred to as a construction loan.

intestate. The condition of a property owner who dies without leaving a will. Title to such property will pass to his or her heirs as provided in the state law of descent.

invalid. Having no force or effect.

invalidate. To render null and void.

investment. Money directed toward the purchase, improvement and development of an asset in expectation of income or profits. A good financial investment has the following characteristics: safety, regularity of yield, marketability, acceptable denominations, valuable collateral, acceptable duration, required attention and potential appreciation.

joint tenancy. The ownership of real estate between two or more parties who have been named in one conveyance as joint tenants. Upon the death of a joint tenant, his or her interest passes to the surviving joint tenant or tenants by the right of survivorship.

joint venture. The joining of two or more people to conduct a specific business enterprise. On the one hand, a joint venture is similar to a partnership in that it must be created by agreement between the parties to share in the losses and profits of the venture. On the other hand, it is unlike a partnership in that the venture is for one specific project only, rather than for a continuing business relationship.

judgment. The official decision of a court on the respective rights and claims of the parties to an action or suit. When a judgment is entered and recorded with the county recorder, it usually becomes a general lien on the property of the defendant for a 10-year period.

GLOSSARY

judgment clause. A provision that may be included in notes, leases and contracts by which the debtor, lessee or obligor authorizes any attorney to go into court to confess a judgment against him or her for a default in payment. Also called a **cognovit**.

laches. An equitable doctrine used by courts to bar a legal claim or prevent the assertion of a right because of undue delay, negligence or failure to assert the claim or right.

land. The earth's surface extending downward to the center of the earth and upward infinitely into space.

law of agency. *See AGENT.*

lawyer's opinion of title. *See ATTORNEY'S OPINION OF TITLE.*

lease. A contract between a landlord (the lessor) and a tenant (the lessee) transferring the right to exclusive possession and use of the landlord's real property to the lessee for a specified period of time and for a stated consideration (rent). By state law, leases for longer than a certain period of time (generally one year) must be in writing to be enforceable.

leasehold estate. A tenant's right to occupy real estate during the term of a lease, generally considered to be a personal property interest.

legal description. A description of a specific parcel of real estate sufficient for an independent surveyor to locate and identify it. The most common forms of legal description are: rectangular survey, metes and bounds and subdivision lot and block (plat).

legality of object. An element that must be present in a valid contract. All contracts that have for their object an act that violates the laws of the United States, or the laws of a state to which the parties are subject, are illegal, invalid and not recognized by the courts.

legatee. A person who receives personal or real property under a will.

lessee. The tenant who leases a property.

lessor. One who leases property to a tenant.

leverage. The use of borrowed money to finance the bulk of an investment.

levy. To assess; to seize or collect. To levy a tax is to assess a property and set the rate of taxation. To levy an execution is to seize officially the property of a person to satisfy an obligation.

license. *1.* A privilege or right granted to a person by a state to operate as a real estate broker or salesperson. *2.* The revocable permission for a temporary use of land—a personal right that cannot be sold.

lien. A right given by law to certain creditors to have their debt paid out of the property of a defaulting debtor, usually by means of a court sale.

life estate. An interest in real or personal property that is limited in duration to the lifetime of its owner or some other designated person.

life tenant. A person in possession of a life estate.

liquidity. The ability to sell an asset and convert it into cash at a price close to its true value.

lis pendens. A public notice that a lawsuit affecting title to or possession, use and enjoyment of a parcel of real estate has been filed in either a state or federal court.

listing agreement. A contract between a landowner (as principal) and a licensed real estate broker (as agent) by which the broker is employed as agent to sell real estate on the owner's terms within a given time, for which service the landowner agrees to pay a commission.

listing broker. The broker in a multiple-listing situation from whose office a listing agreement is initiated, as opposed to the **selling broker,** from whose office negotiations leading up to a sale are initiated. The listing broker and the selling broker may, of course, be the same person. (*See also MULTIPLE LISTING.*)

littoral rights. *1.* a landowner's claim to use water in large lakes and oceans adjacent to his or her property. *2.* The ownerships rights to land bordering these bodies of water up to the high-water mark.

lot and block description. A description of real property that identifies a parcel of land by reference to lot and block numbers within a subdivision, as identified on a subdivided plat duly recorded in the county recorder's office.

management agreement. A contract between the owner of income property and a management firm or individual property manager outlining the scope of the manager's authority.

marginal lease. A lease agreement that barely covers the costs of operation for the property.

marginal real estate. That land that barely covers costs of operation.

marketable title. A good or clear salable title reasonably free from risk of litigation over possible defects; also called a merchantable title.

market-data approach. That approach in analysis which is based on the proposition that an informed purchaser would pay no more for a property than the cost to him of acquiring an existing property with the same utility. This approach is applicable when an active market provides sufficient quantities of reliable data that can be verified from authoritative sources. The approach is relatively unreliable in an inactive market or in estimating the value of properties for which no real comparable sales data are available. It is also questionable when sales data cannot be verified with principals to the transaction. Also referred to as the market comparison or direct sales comparison approach.

market price. The actual selling price of a property.

market value. The highest price that a property will bring in a competitive and open market under all conditions requisite to a fair sale. The price at which a buyer would buy and a seller would sell, each acting prudently and knowledgeably, and assuming the price is not affected by undue stimulus.

mechanic's lien. A statutory lien created in favor of contractors, laborers and materialmen who have performed work or furnished materials in erecting or repairing a building.

metes-and-bounds description. A legal description of a parcel of land that begins at a well-marked point and follows the boundaries, using direction and distances around the tract back to the place of beginning.

mill. One-tenth of one cent (.001). Some states use a mill rate to compute real estate taxes; for example, a rate of 52 mills would be 5.2¢ tax for each dollar of assessed valuation of a property.

millage rate. A property tax rate obtained by dividing the total assessed value of all the property in the tax district into the total amount of revenue needed by the taxing district. This millage rate is then applied to the assessed value of each property in the district to determine individual taxes.

misrepresentation. To represent falsely; to give an untrue idea of a property. May be accomplished by omission or concealment of a material fact.

monetary policy. The governmental regulation of the amount of money in circulation through such institutions as the Federal Reserve Board.

money judgment. A court judgment ordering payment of money rather than specific performance of a certain action. (*See also JUDGMENT.*)

money market. Those institutions such as banks, savings and loan associations and life insurance companies, whose function it is to supply money and credit to borrowers.

month-to-month tenancy. A periodic tenancy—the tenant rents for one period at a time. In the absence of a rental agreement (oral or written), a tenancy is generally considered to be month-to-month.

monument. A fixed natural or artificial object used to establish real estate boundaries for a metes-and-bounds description.

mortgage. A conditional transfer or pledge of real estate as security for a loan. Also, the document creating a mortgage lien.

mortgage lien. A lien or charge on a mortgagor's property that secures the underlying debt obligations.

mortgagor. One who, having all or part of title to property, pledges that property as security for a debt; the borrower.

multiple listing. An exclusive listing (generally, an exclusive-right-to-sell) with the additional authority and obligation on the part of the listing broker to distribute the listing to other brokers in the multiple-listing organization.

municipal ordinances. The laws, regulations and codes enacted by the governing body of a municipality.

mutual rescission. The act of putting an end to a contract by mutual agreement of the parties.

NARELLO. The National Association of Real Estate License Law Officials.

negligence. Carelessness and inattentiveness resulting in violation of trust. Failure to do what is required.

net income. The gross income of a property minus operating expenses (not including debt service).

net lease. A lease requiring the tenant to pay not only rent, but also all costs incurred in maintaining the property, including taxes, insurance, utilities and repairs.

net listing. A listing establishing a price, which must be expressly agreed upon, below which the owner will not sell the property and at which price the broker will not receive a commission; the broker receives the excess over and above the net listing price as his commission.

nonconforming use. A use of property that is permitted to continue after a zoning ordinance prohibiting it has been established for the area.

nonhomogeneity. A lack of uniformity; dissimilarity. Since no two parcels of land are exactly alike, real estate is said to be nonhomogeneous.

notarize. To certify or attest to a document, as by a notary.

notary public. A public official authorized to certify and attest to documents, take affidavits, take acknowledgments, administer oaths and other such acts.

note. An instrument of credit given to attest a debt.

notice of abandonment. An instrument filed to release a recorded declaration of homestead.

offer and acceptance. The two components of a valid contract; a "meeting of the minds."

officer's deed. A deed by sheriffs, trustees, guardians and the like.

one hundred-percent-commission plan. A salesperson compensation plan whereby the salesperson pays his or her broker a monthly service charge to cover the costs of office expenses and receives 100 percent of the commissions from the sales that he or she negotiates.

open-end mortgage. A mortgage loan that is expandable by increments up to a maximum dollar amount, all of which is secured by the same original mortgage.

open listing. A listing contract under which the broker's commission is contingent upon the broker's producing a ready, willing and able buyer before the property is sold by the seller or another broker; the principal (owner) reserves the right to list the property with other brokers.

option. The right to purchase property within a definite time at a specified price. No obligation to purchase exists, but the seller is obligated to sell if the option holder exercises right to purchase.

optionee. The party that receives and holds an option.

optionor. The party that grants or gives an option.

ownership. The exclusive right to hold, possess or control and dispose of a tangible or intangible thing. Ownership may be held by a person, corporation or political entity.

package mortgage. A method of financing in which the loan that finances the purchase of a home also finances the purchase of certain items of personal property, such as a washer, dryer, refrigerator, stove and other specified appliances.

participation financing. A mortgage in which the lender participates in the income of the mortgaged venture beyond a fixed return, or receives a yield on the loan in addition to the straight interest rate.

partnership. An association of two or more individuals who carry on a continuing business for profit as co-owners. Under the law, a partnership is regarded as a group of individuals, rather than as a single entity. A general partnership is a typical form of joint venture, in which each general partner shares in the administration, profits and losses of the operation. A limited partnership is a business arrangement whereby the operation is administered by one or more general partners and funded by limited or silent partners who are by law responsible for losses only to the extent of their investment.

party wall. A wall that is located on or at a boundary line between two adjoining parcels for the use of the owners of both properties.

payee. The party that receives payment.

payor. The party that makes payment to another.

percentage lease. A lease commonly used for retail property in which the rental is based on the tenant's gross sales at the premises; often stipulates a base monthly rental plus a percentage of any gross sales above a certain amount.

performance bond. A binding agreement, often accompanied by surety and usually posted by one who is to perform work for another, which assures that a project or undertaking will be completed as per agreement or contract.

periodic estate. An interest in leased property that continues from period to period—week to week, month to month or year to year.

personal property. Those items, called **chattels,** that are not classified as real property; tangible and movable objects.

physical deterioration. A reduction in utility resulting from an impairment of physical condition. For purposes of appraisal analysis, it is most common and convenient to divide physical deterioration into curable and incurable components.

plat. A map of a town, section or subdivision indicating the location and boundaries of individual properties.

plat book. A record of recorded subdivisions of land.

point. A unit of measurement used for various loan charges—one point equals one percent of the amount of the loan. (*See also DISCOUNT POINTS.*)

point of beginning. The starting point of the survey situated in one corner of the parcel in a metes-and-bounds legal description. All metes-and-bounds descriptions must follow the boundaries of the parcel back to the point of beginning.

police power. The government's right to impose laws, statutes and ordinances to protect the public health, safety and welfare, including zoning ordinances and building codes.

power of attorney. A written instrument authorizing a person (the attorney-in-fact) to act on behalf of the maker to the extent indicated in the instrument.

premises. The specific section of a deed which states the names of the parties, recital of consideration, operative words of conveyance, legal property description and appurtenance provisions.

prepayment clause in a mortgage. The statement of the terms upon which the mortgagor may pay the entire or stated amount of the mortgage principal at some time prior to the due date.

prepayment penalty. A charge imposed on a borrower by a lender for early payment of the loan principal to compensate the lender for interest and other charges that would otherwise be lost.

GLOSSARY

prescription. The right or easement to land that is acquired by adverse possession or "squatter's rights." It must be acquired under certain conditions as required by law.

price fixing. *See ANTITRUST LAWS.*

primary mortgage market. *See SECONDARY MORTGAGE MARKET.*

principal. *1.* A sum lent or employed as a fund or investment, as distinguished from its income or profits. *2.* The original amount (as in a loan) of the total due and payable at a certain date. *3.* A main party to a transaction—the person for whom the agent works.

principal meridian. One of 35 north and south survey lines established and defined as part of the rectangular survey system (government survey method).

principle of conformity. The appraisal theory stating that buildings which are similar in design, construction and age to other buildings in the area have a higher value than they would in a neighborhood of dissimilar buildings.

principle of substitutions. The appraisal theory that states that no one will pay more for a property than the cost of buying or building a similar property; or, in the case of investments, the price of a substitute investment.

priority. The order of position or time. The priority of liens is generally determined by the chronological order in which the lien documents are recorded; tax liens, however, have priority even over previously recorded liens.

probate. The formal judicial proceeding to prove or confirm the validity of a will.

procuring cause. The effort that brings about the desired result. Under an open listing, the broker who is the procuring cause of the sale receives the commission.

property management. The operation of the property of another for compensation. Includes marketing of space; advertising and rental activities; collection, recording and remitting of rents; maintenance of the property; tenant relations; hiring of employees; keeping proper accounts; and rendering periodic reports to the owner.

property tax. Those taxes levied by the government against either real or personal property. The right to tax real property in the U.S. rests exclusively with the states, not with the federal government.

proration. The proportionate division or distribution of expenses of property ownership between two or more parties. Closing statement prorations generally include taxes, rents, insurance, interest charges and assessments.

prospectus. A printed advertisement, usually in pamphlet form, presenting a new development, subdivision, business venture or stock issue.

public utility easement. A right granted by a property owner to a public utility company to erect and maintain poles, wires and conduits on, across or under his or her land for telephone, electric power, gas, water or sewer installation.

pur autre vie. A term meaning for the life of another. A life estate pur autre vie is a life estate that is measured by the life of a person other than the grantee.

purchase-money mortgage. A note secured by a mortgage or deed of trust given by a buyer, as mortgagor, to a seller, as mortgagee, as part of the purchase price of the real estate.

qualification. The act of determining the prospect's needs, abilities and urgency to buy and then matching these with available properties.

quitclaim deed. A conveyance by which the grantor transfers whatever interest he or she has in the real estate without warranties or obligations.

range. A strip of land six miles wide, extending north and south and numbered east and west according to its distance from the principal meridians in the rectangular survey system (government survey method) of land description.

ready, willing and able buyer. One who is prepared to buy property on the seller's terms and is ready to take positive steps to consummate the transaction.

real estate. Land; a portion of the earth's surface extending downward to the center of the earth and upward infinitely into space, including all things permanently attached thereto, whether by nature or by man; any and every interest in land.

real estate broker. Any person, partnership, association or corporation who sells (or offers to sell), buys (or offers to buy) or negotiates the purchase, sale or exchange of real estate, or who leases (or offers to lease) or rents (or offers to rent) any real estate or the improvements thereon for others and for a compensation or valuable consideration. A real estate broker may not conduct business without a real estate broker's license.

Real Estate Settlement Procedures Act (RESPA). The federal law ensuring that the buyer and seller in a real estate transaction have knowledge of all settlement costs when the purchase of a one-to-four family residential dwelling is financed by a federally related mortgage loan. Federally related loans include those made by savings and loans; insured by the FHA or VA; administered by HUD; or intended to be sold by the lender to an agency.

reality of consent. An element of all valid contracts. Offer and acceptance in a contract are usually taken to mean that reality of consent is also present. This is not the case if any of the following are present, however: mistake, misrepresentation, fraud, undue influence or duress.

real property. Real property, or real estate as it is often called, consists of land, anything affixed to it as to be regarded as a permanent part of the land, that which is appurtenant to the land and that which is immovable by law.

Realtor®. A registered trademark term reserved for the sole use of active members of local Realtor® boards affiliated with the NATIONAL ASSOCIATION OF Realtors®.

recapture. *See ACCELERATED DEPRECIATION.*

receiver. The court-appointed custodian of property involved in litigation, pending final disposition of the matter before the court.

reconciliation. The final step in the appraisal process, in which the appraiser reconciles the estimates of value received from the market-data, cost and income approaches to arrive at a final estimate of market value for the subject property.

recording. The act of entering or recording documents affecting or conveying interests in real estate in the recorder's office established in each county. Until recorded, a deed or mortgage generally is not effective against subsequent purchases or mortgage liens.

recovery fund. A fund established in some states from real estate license funds to cover claims of aggrieved parties who have suffered monetary damage through the actions of a real estate licensee.

rectangular survey system. A system established in 1785 by the federal government, providing for surveying and describing land by reference to principal meridians and base lines.

redemption period. A period of time established by state law during which a property owner has the right to redeem his or her real estate from a foreclosure or tax sale by paying the sales price, interest and costs. Many states do not have mortgage redemption laws.

redlining. The illegal practice of some institutions of denying loans or restricting their number for certain areas of a community.

release. To relinquish an interest in or claim to a parcel of property.

relocation service. An organization that aids a person in selling a property in one area and buying another property in another area.

remainder. The remnant of an estate that has been conveyed to take effect and be enjoyed after the termination of a prior estate, such as when an owner conveys a life estate to one party and the remainder to another.

rent. A fixed, periodic payment made by a tenant of a property to the owner for possession and use, usually by prior agreement of the parties.

GLOSSARY

rent schedule. A statement of proposed rental rates, determined by the owner or the property manager, or both, based on a building's estimated expenses, market supply and demand and the owner's long-range goals for the property.

replacement cost. The cost of construction at current prices of a building having utility equivalent to the building being appraised but built with modern materials and according to current standards, design and layout. The use of the replacement cost concept presumably eliminates all functional obsolescence, and the only depreciations to be measured are physical deterioration and economic obsolescence.

reproduction cost. The cost of construction at current prices of an exact duplicate or replica using the same materials, construction standards, design, layout, quality of workmanship, embodying all the deficiencies, superadequacies and obsolescences of the subject building.

rescission. The termination of a contract by mutual agreement of the parties.

reservation in a deed. The creation by a deed to property of a new right in favor of the grantor. Usually involves an easement, life estate or a mineral interest.

restriction. A limitation on the use of real property, generally originated by the owner or subdivider in a deed.

reversion. The remnant of an estate that the grantor holds after he or she has granted a life estate to another person–the estate will return or revert to the grantor; also called a reverter.

reversionary right. An owner's right to regain possession of leased property upon termination of the lease agreement.

rezoning. The process involved in changing the existing zoning of a property or area.

right of survivorship. *See JOINT TENANCY.*

riparian rights. An owner's rights in land which borders on or which includes a stream, river, lake or sea. These rights include access to and use of the water.

sale and leaseback. A transaction in which an owner sells his or her improved property and, as part of the same transaction, signs a long-term lease to remain in possession of the premises.

sales contract. A contract containing the complete terms of the agreement between buyer and seller for the sale of a particular parcel or parcels of real estate.

salesperson. A person who performs real estate activities while employed by, or associated with, a licensed real estate broker.

satisfaction. A document acknowledging the payment of a debt.

secondary mortgage market. A market for the purchase and sale of existing mortgages, designed to provide greater liquidity for mortgages; also called the secondary money market.

section. A portion of a township under the rectangular survey system (government survey method). A township is divided into 36 sections numbered 1 to 36. A section is a square with mile-long sides and an area of one square mile, or 640 acres.

self-proving will. A will in which the witnesses give their testimony at the time of signing. This testimony is preserved in a notarized affidavit, to eliminate the problem of finding the witnesses at the maker's death and to assist in the probating procedure.

selling broker. *See LISTING BROKER.*

separate property. The real property owned by a husband or wife prior to their marriage.

servient tenement. The land on which an easement exists in favor of an adjacent property (called a **dominant estate**); also called a **servient estate.**

setback. The amount of space local zoning regulations require between a lot line and a building line.

severalty. The ownership of real property by one person only, also called **sole ownership.**

situs. The personal preference of people for one area over another, not necessarily based on objective facts and knowledge.

sole ownership. *See SEVERALTY.*

GLOSSARY

sovereignty of the soil. The beginning of the record of ownership of land by conveyance from the sovereign or the state.

special assessment. A tax or levy customarily imposed against only those specific parcels of real estate that will benefit from a proposed public improvement, such as a street or sewer.

special warranty deed. A deed in which the grantor warrants or guarantees the title only against defects arising during the period of his or her tenure and ownership of the property and not against defects existing before that time, generally using the language, "by, through, or under the grantor but not otherwise."

specific lien. A lien affecting or attaching only to a certain, specific parcel of land or piece of property.

specific performance suit. A legal action brought in a court of equity in special cases to compel a party to carry out the terms of a contract. The basis for an equity court's jurisdiction in breach of a real estate contract is the fact that land is unique and mere legal damages would not adequately compensate the buyer for the seller's breach.

sponsoring broker. A duly licensed real estate broker who employs a salesperson. Under law, the broker is responsible for the acts of his or her salespeople.

squatter's rights. Those rights acquired through adverse possession. By "squatting" on land for a certain statutory period under prescribed conditions, one may acquire title by limitations. If an easement only is acquired, instead of title to the land itself, one has title by prescription.

statute of frauds. That part of a state law which requires that certain instruments, such as deeds, real estate sales contracts and certain leases, be in writing in order to be legally enforceable.

statute of limitations. That law pertaining to the period of time within which certain actions must be brought to court.

statutory lien. A lien imposed on property by statute, such as a tax lien, in contrast to a voluntary lien which an owner places on his or her own real estate, such as a mortgage lien.

steering. The illegal practice of channeling home seekers to particular areas, either to maintain the homogeneity of an area or to change its character in order to create a speculative situation.

straight-line method. A method of calculating depreciation for tax purposes, computed by dividing the adjusted basis of a property less its estimated salvage value by the estimated number of years of remaining useful life.

subcontractor. *See GENERAL CONTRACTOR.*

subdivision. A tract of land divided by the owner, known as the subdivider, into blocks, building lots and streets according to a recorded subdivision plat, which must comply with local ordinances and regulations.

subletting. The leasing of premises by a lessee to a third party for part of the lessee's remaining term. (*See also ASSIGNMENT.*)

subordination. A relegation to a lesser position, usually in respect to a right or security.

subrogation. The substitution of one creditor for another, with the substituted person succeeding to the legal rights and claims of the original claimant. Subrogation is used by title insurers to acquire rights to sue from the injured party to recover any claims they have paid.

substitution. An appraisal principle that states that the maximum value of a property tends to be set by the cost of purchasing an equally desirable and valuable substitute property, assuming that no costly delay is encountered in making the substitution.

suit for possession. A court suit initiated by a landlord to evict a tenant from leased premises after the tenant has breached one of the terms of the lease or has held possession of the property after the lease's expiration.

suit for specific performance. A legal action brought by either a buyer or a seller to enforce performance of the terms of a contract.

GLOSSARY

suit to quiet title. A legal action intended to establish or settle the title to a particular property, especially when there is a cloud on the title.

summation appraisal. An approach under which value equals estimated land value plus reproduction costs of any improvements, after depreciation has been subtracted.

sum-of-the-years'-digits method. A method of calculating depreciation for tax purposes based on a fraction—the constant sum of all the numbers in the property's useful life is the denominator, and the changing number of remaining useful years is the numerator.

supply. The amount of goods available in the market to be sold at a given price. The term is often coupled with **demand.**

surety bond. An agreement by an insurance or bonding company to be responsible for certain possible defaults, debts or obligations contracted for by an insured party; in essence, a policy insuring one's personal and/or financial integrity. In the real estate business, a surety bond is generally used to insure that a particular project will be completed at a certain date or that a contract will be performed as stated.

survey. The process by which boundaries are measured and land areas are determined; the on-site measurement of lot lines, dimensions and positions of buildings on a lot, including the determination of any existing encroachments or easements.

syndicate. A combination of two or more persons or firms to accomplish a joint venture of mutual interest. Syndicates dissolve when the specific purpose for which they were created has been accomplished.

taxation. The process by which a government or municipal quasi-public body raises monies to fund its operation.

tax deed. An instrument, similar to a certificate of sale, given to a purchaser at a tax sale. (*See also* CERTIFICATE OF SALE.)

taxes. A compulsory contribution required by the government from persons, corporations and other organizations, according to a law, for the general support of the government and for the maintenance of public services.

tax lien. A charge against property created by operation of law. Tax liens and assessments take priority over all other liens.

tax rate. The rate at which real property is taxed in a tax district or county. For example, in a certain county, real property may be taxed at a rate of 56¢ per dollar of assessed valuation.

tax sale. A court-ordered sale of real property to raise money to cover delinquent taxes.

tenancy at sufferance. The tenancy of a lessee who lawfully comes into possession of a landlord's real estate, but who continues to occupy the premises improperly after his or her lease rights have expired.

tenancy at will. An estate that gives the lessee the right to possession until the estate is terminated by either party; the term of this estate is indefinite.

tenancy by the entirety. The joint ownership, recognized in some states, of property acquired by husband and wife during marriage. Upon the death of one spouse, the survivor becomes the owner of the property.

tenancy in common. A form of co-ownership by which each owner holds an undivided interest in real property as if he or she were sole owner. Each individual owner has the right to partition. Unlike a joint tenancy, there is no right of survivorship between tenants in common.

tenant. One who holds or possesses lands or tenements by any kind of right or title.

tenement. Everything that may be occupied under a lease by a tenant.

termination (lease). The cancellation of a lease by action of either party. A lease may be terminated by expiration of term; surrender and acceptance; constructive eviction by lessor; or option when provided in lease for breach of covenants.

termination (listing). The cancellation of a broker-principal employment contract; a listing may be terminated by death or insanity of either party, expiration of listing period, mutual agreement, sufficient written notice or the completion of performance under the agreement.
testate. Having made and left a valid will.
testator. A male will maker.
testatrix. A female will maker.
time is of the essence. A phrase in a contract that requires the performance of a certain act within a stated period of time.
title insurance. That insurance that is designed to indemnify the holder for loss sustained for reason of defects in a title, up to and including the policy limits.
Torrens system. A method of evidencing title by registration with the proper public authority, generally called the registrar. Named for its founder, Sir Robert Torrens.
township. The principal unit of the rectangular survey system (government survey method). A township is a square with six-mile sides and an area of 36 square miles.
township lines. The lines running at six-mile intervals parallel to the base lines in the rectangular survey system (government survey method).
trade fixtures. The articles installed by a tenant under the terms of a lease and removable by the tenant before the lease expires. These remain personal property and are not true fixtures.
trust. A fiduciary arrangement whereby property is conveyed to a person or institution, called a **trustee,** to be held and administered on behalf of another person, called a **beneficiary.**
trust deed. An instrument used to create a mortgage lien by which the mortgagor conveys his or her title to a trustee, who holds it as security for the benefit of the note holder (the lender); also called a **deed of trust.**
trustee. One who as agent for others handles money or holds title to their land.
trustee's deed. A deed executed by a trustee conveying land held in a trust.

undivided interest. *See TENANCY IN COMMON.*
unearned increment. An increase in the value of a property caused by increased population, development and demand for which the owner is not responsible.
Uniform Commercial Code. A codification of commercial law, adopted in most states, that attempts to make uniform all laws relating to commercial transactions, including chattel mortgages and bulk transfers. Security interests in chattels are created by an instrument known as a security agreement. Article 6 of the code regulates bulk transfers—the sale of a business as a whole, including all fixtures, chattels and merchandise.
unilateral contract. A one-sided contract wherein one party makes a promise in order to induce a second party to do something. The second party is not legally bound to perform; however, if the second party does comply, the first party is obligated to keep the promise.
unity of ownership. The four unities which are traditionally needed to create a joint tenancy—unity of title, unity of time, unity of interest and unity of possession.
urban renewal. The acquisition of run-down city areas for purposes of redevelopment.
useful life. In real estate investment, the number of years a property will be useful to the investors.
usury. The practice of charging more than the rate of interest allowed by law.

valid contract. A contract that complies with all the essentials of a contract and is binding and enforceable on all parties to it.
valid deed. An enforceable deed which has a competent grantor and grantee, consideration, conveyance, legal description of land, signature of grantor, acknowledgment, delivery and acceptance.

GLOSSARY

valid lease. An enforceable lease which has the following essential parts: lessor and lessee with contractual capacity; offer and acceptance; legality of object; description of the premises; consideration; signatures; and delivery. Leases for more than one year must also be in writing.

VA loan. A mortgage loan on approved property made to a qualified veteran by an authorized lender and guaranteed by the Veterans Administration to limit possible loss by the lender.

variance. The permission obtained from zoning authorities to build a structure or conduct a use that is expressly prohibited by the current zoning laws; an exception from the zoning ordinances.

vendee. The buyer or purchaser.

vendor. The seller.

venue. A term derived from the Latin word meaning "to come," it refers to the place where an injury is declared to have been done, a fact declared to have happened or a trial brought. An acknowledgment states the county and state where it is taken—its venue.

voidable contract. A contract that seems to be valid on the surface but may be rejected or disaffirmed by one of the parties.

void contract. A contract that has no legal force or effect because it does not meet the essential elements of a contract.

voluntary transfer. *See ALIENATION.*

waiver. The intentional or voluntary relinquishment of a known claim or right.

warranty deed. A deed in which the grantor fully warrants good clear title to the premises. Used in most real estate deed transfers, a warranty deed offers the greatest protection of any deed.

waste. An improper use or an abuse of a property by a possessor who holds less than fee ownership, such as a tenant, life tenant, mortgagor or vendee. Such waste generally impairs the value of the land or the interest of the person holding the title or the reversionary rights.

will. A written document, properly witnessed, providing for the transfer of title to property owned by the deceased, called the **testator**.

wraparound mortgage. A method of refinancing in which the new mortgage is placed in a secondary, or subordinate, position. In essence, it is an additional mortgage in which another lender refinances a borrower by lending an amount over the existing first-mortgage amount without disturbing the existence of the first mortgage.

writ of execution. A court order that authorizes and directs the proper officer of the court (usually the sheriff) to sell the property of a defendant as required by the judgment or decree of the court.

year-to-year tenancy. A periodic tenancy in which rent is collected from year to year.

zoning ordinance. An exercise of police power by a municipality to regulate and control the character and use of property.

About the Authors

Douglas C. Smith is the president of Real Estate Education Company, Edina, Minnesota, and of the Minnesota Real Estate Education Association. He is the former director of development for the Minnesota Housing Finance Agency and the Michigan State Housing Development Authority, and has acted as a consulting editor in the preparation of the second edition of the *Minnesota Supplement* for *Modern Real Estate Practice,* published by Real Estate Education Company. Mr. Smith holds a B.A. from Michigan State University. He is an experienced lecturer and educator on numerous real estate topics and has taught license examination review seminars in Minnesota for the last three years.

John T. Gibbons is a practicing attorney and is a member of the Minnesota and Florida State Bars. Mr. Gibbons graduated summa cum laude from the University of Minnesota and holds a J.D. from Harvard Law School. He has acted as a clerk for the Honorable Philip Neville of the U.S. District Court for Minnesota. Mr. Gibbons has taught the real estate law and mathematics sections of license examination review seminars.

More Real Estate Books That Help You Get Ahead...

Mail the completed form to Real Estate Education Company 520 North Dearborn Street Chicago, Illinois 60610-4975

30-Day Money-Back Guarantee
Please send me the book(s) I have indicated. If I return any book within the 30 day period, I'll receive a refund with no further obligation.
(Books must be returned in unused, salable condition).

Payment must accompany all orders (check one)
☐ Check or money order payable to Longman
☐ Credit card charge, circle one: VISA MasterCard AMEX

Name_____
Address_____
City_____ State_____ Zip_____
Telephone No. (   )
Account No._____ Exp. Date_____
Signature _____
(All charge orders must be signed.)

Qty.	Order Number		Price	Total Amount
		Real Estate Principles/Exam Guides		
___	1. 1510-01	Modern Real Estate Practice, 11th ed	$32.95	___
___	2. 1510-	Supplements for Modern Real Estate Practice are available for many states. Indicate desired state _____	$12.95	___
___	3. 1510-02	Modern Real Estate Practice Study Guide, 11th ed.	$13.95	___
___	4. 1513-01	Real Estate Fundamentals, 3rd ed.	$22.95	___
___	5. 1970-04	Questions & Answers to Help You Pass the Real Estate Exam, 3rd ed. ...	$21.95	___
___	6. 1970-02	Guide to Passing the Real Estate Exam (ACT), 3rd ed.	$21.95	___
___	7. 1970-01	The Real Estate Education Company Real Estate Exam Manual, 5th ed. (ETS)	$21.95	___
___	8. 1970-06	Real Estate Exam Guide (ASI), 2nd ed.	$21.95	___
___	9. 1970-03	How to Prepare for the Texas Real Estate Exam, 4th ed.	$19.95	___
___	10. 1970-07	California Real Estate Exam Guide	$19.95	___
		Advanced Studies/Continuing Education		
___	11. 1556-10	Fundamentals of Real Estate Appraisal, 5th ed.	$38.95	___
___	12. 1557-10	Essentials of Real Estate Finance, 5th ed.	$38.95	___
___	13. 1559-01	Essentials of Real Estate Investment, 3rd ed.	$38.95	___
___	14. 1551-10	Property Management, 3rd ed.	$34.95	___
___	15. 1965-01	Real Estate Brokerage: A Success Guide, 2nd ed.	$35.95	___
___	16. 1560-01	Real Estate Law, 2nd ed.	$38.95	___
___	17. 1512-10	Mastering Real Estate Mathematics, 5th ed.	$25.95	___
___	18. 1961-01	The Language of Real Estate, 3rd ed.	$28.95	___
___	19. 1560-08	Agency Relationships in Real Estate	$25.95	___
		Professional Books		
___	20. 1913-01	List for Success	$18.95	___
___	21. 1913-04	Close for Success	$18.95	___
___	22. 1907-04	Power Real Estate Negotiation	$19.95	___
___	23. 1927-03	Fast Start in Real Estate: A Survival Guide for New Agents	$17.95	___
___	24. 1926-01	Classified Secrets, 2nd ed.	$29.95	___
___	25. 1907-01	Power Real Estate Listing, 2nd ed.	$17.95	___
___	26. 1907-02	Power Real Estate Selling, 2nd ed.	$17.95	___
___	27. 5606-24	The Mortgage Kit	$14.95	___
___	28. 4105-07	How to Profit from Real Estate	$19.95	___
___	29. 4105-06	How to Sell Apartment Buildings	$19.95	___
___	30. 4105-08	Landlord's Handbook	$21.95	___
___	31. 1905-29	A Professional's Guide to Real Estate Finance	$34.95	___
___	32. 1909-01	New Home Sales	$24.95	___
___	33. 1909-03	New Home Marketing	$34.95	___
___	34. 1922-02	Successful Leasing and Selling of Office Property, 3rd ed.	$34.95	___
___	35. 1922-03	Successful Industrial Real Estate Brokerage, 4th ed.	$34.95	___
___	36. 1978-02	The Recruiting Revolution in Real Estate	$34.95	___
___	37. 1922-01	Successful Leasing and Selling of Retail Property, 3rd ed.	$34.95	___

For Fastest Service, Call Our Toll-Free Order Hotline
1-800-621-9621 x650
(in Illinois, 1-800-654-8596 x650)

Total Book Purchase (inc. tax, if applicable)	Shipping and Handling
$ 00.00 – $ 24.99	$ 4.00
$ 25.00 – $ 49.99	$ 5.00
$ 50.00 – $ 99.99	$ 6.00
$100.00 – $249.99	$ 8.00

PRICES SUBJECT TO CHANGE WITHOUT NOTICE.

Book Total ___
Orders shipped to the following states must include applicable sales tax:
AZ, CA, CO, IL, MI, MN, NY, PA, TX, VA and WI.
Add postage and handling ___
(see chart)
TOTAL ___

810077

Real Estate Education Company   520 N. Dearborn Chicago, Illinois 60610-4975

PRACTICAL MONEY-MAKERS FROM REAL ESTATE EDUCATION COMPANY

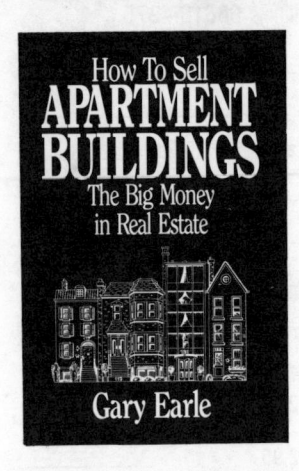

HOW TO SELL APARTMENT BUILDINGS: THE BIG MONEY IN REAL ESTATE,
by Gary Earle

This book provides you with all the details, examples, tables, and illustrations you need to identify the apartment market, understand it and profit. Read this book and you'll discover a practical, remarkably effective sales approach that can help turn your real estate license into a ticket to big commissions.

With *How To Sell Apartment Buildings,* you'll soon reap the rich rewards that go with the territory!

Contents
Sizing Up the Market • Gaining Market Knowledge • How to Price Apartment Buildings • Financing • Tax Aspects of Apartment Ownership • Cataloging Your Territory • Hot Sales Leads from Cold Calls • A Little Letter Can Go a Long Way • Meeting the Seller • Making the Offer • Negotiating the Sale • Closing the Deal • It's All Yours! • Index

6 x 9, hardcover, 200 pages
1988 copyright
Order Number 4105-06

Check box #28 on order form

POWER REAL ESTATE NEGOTIATION,
by William H. Pivar

Negotiating between buyer and seller is the hardest part of any real estate transaction. *Power Real Estate Negotiation* provides hundreds of specific, field-tested tips on negotiating transactions — and how to implement these techniques in direct interpersonal encounters. The unique interactive approach alternates between buyer's and seller's point of view, showing effective strategies and counterplays to each move of the opponent.

Includes:
• Reading the opponent's motivation
• Negotiating price and financing
• Overcoming impasses
• Closing the agreement

Contents
Negotiation Planning • Physical Aspects of Negotiation • General Negotiation Tactics • Negotiating the Price • Negotiating the Financing • Negotiating Other Issues • Impasse • Negotiating Dangers • The Agreement • Index

6 x 9, hardcover, 204 pages
1990 copyright
Order Number 1907-04

Check box #22 on order form

A PROFESSIONAL'S GUIDE TO REAL ESTATE FINANCE: TECHNIQUES FOR THE 1990's,
by Julie Garton-Good

Based on actual real estate practice, this reference provides the real estate professional with immediate answers to the most frequently asked financial questions. When clients call upon you to assist in evaluating financing options, you'll have all the answers in this new comprehensive guide.

Included are complete discussions of mortgage loan types—along with convenient checklists of the major features and pros and cons of each.

A Professional's Guide to Real Estate Finance emphasizes up-to-the-minute information, trend spotting and innovative sales strategies using financing techniques.

Contents
The Mortgage Market • Conventional Fixes-Rate Loans • Adjustable Rate Mortgages • FHA Loans • VA Loans • Special Programs • Buyer Leverage • Index

6 x 9, hardcover, 304 pages
1990 copyright
Order Number 1905-29

Check box #31 on order form

THE LANDLORD'S HANDBOOK: A COMPLETE GUIDE TO MANAGING SMALL RESIDENTIAL PROPERTIES,
by Daniel Goodwin and Richard Rusdorf, CPM

Whether you sell, manage or own small residential income properties, you'll find ideas to save time and headaches and to put money in your pocket. Two Inland Real Estate property management experts share their income-producing secrets.

Over 50 forms and checklists help you establish a smooth, profitable rental operation. Also included are tips on putting "active" self-management techniques to work to maximize tax deductions and profits.

Contents
Self-Management • Resident Relations • Marketing • Applications, Leases & Rental Agreements • Tenant Move-In • Lease Renewals • Tenant Move-Out • Rent Collection • Maintenance • Insurance • Property Taxes • Accounting • Bibliography • Appendix • Index

8-½ x 11, softcover, 236 pages
1989 copyright
Order Number 4105-08

Check box #29 on order form